WILLA CATHER

WILLA CATHER

HER LIFE AND ART

James Woodress

PEGASUS   NEW YORK

Willa Cather is part of a series, Pegasus American Authors, prepared under the General Editorship of Richard M. Ludwig, Princeton University.

Copyright © 1970 by Western Publishing Company, Inc.
All rights reserved. This book, or parts thereof,
may not be reproduced in any form
without permission of the publisher.
Printed in the United States of America.
Library of Congress Catalog Card Number 71-124673

For my mother

JESSIE SMITH WOODRESS

CONTENTS

FOREWORD

WILLA CATHER'S world from the time she went to college in 1890 until she died in New York in 1947 has changed beyond recognition. Today Lincoln, Nebraska, is a lively middle-sized city connected with points east and west by airlines and modern interstate highways. The University of Nebraska is now a multiversity that bears no resemblance to the raw prairie college that Willa Cather attended. Pittsburgh and New York, where she spent her adult years, have undergone the expansion and metamorphoses that have overtaken all of urban America. Yet the land and the places in Nebraska that Willa Cather most characteristically celebrates endure, like her fiction, with a kind of timelessness.

Red Cloud, Nebraska, her home from her tenth until her seventeenth year, has not changed drastically. The town actually is smaller than it was in her day when railroading was more important than it now is. But the Burlington Railroad still runs through the southern outskirts of Red Cloud, and the Republican River, which she wrote about many times, still flows lazily parallel to the railroad tracks under low bluffs and between fringes of cottonwood and willow. The old Cather house at Third and Cedar has been restored and refurnished with original and period pieces, and many other houses and buildings that appear in her fiction survive and are identified for visitors: the Burlington depot, the opera house, the Rosen and Harling houses, Wick Cutter's place, and Dr. Archie's home.

If Red Cloud still is recognizable as the locale of Willa Cather's fiction, the country north and west—the Divide in her novels—is even more eternal and unchanging. The wild red grass is long gone, but the land is sparsely populated, the fields and sky meet on a distant horizon, and a visitor can drive for hours without crossing a paved road or meeting a car. The gaunt, weathered New Virginia Church stands at a lonely crossroad, and not far beyond is the site of the Cather homestead, where Charles and Mary Virginia Cather brought their children from near Winchester, Virginia, and settled in 1883. It requires no mental gymnastics to imagine Jim Burden's first trip across that rolling prairie, as described in *My Ántonia*, or to visualize young Willa Cather herself there.

Willa Cather has been fortunate in the scholars and critics who have chosen to write about her: E. K. Brown, who died in 1951 just before finishing the excellent authorized biography, and Leon Edel, who completed the book in 1953; David Daiches and Edward and Lillian Bloom, who have published very good studies; Mildred Bennett, Virginia Faulkner, and Bernice Slote, who have added a great deal to our knowledge of Willa Cather; Richard Giannone, who wrote an interesting book on music in Willa Cather's fiction; James Schroeter, who put together a very useful collection of reprinted criticism; and a great many writers of critical essays, dissertations, and chapters in books on broader topics.

Alfred Knopf was gazing into a cloudy crystal ball when he wrote on the jacket of Brown's biography: "Here is all the biographical information anyone is likely ever to gather about Willa Cather." Brown was an industrious researcher and had access to Edith Lewis's memoir *Willa Cather Living* (1953), which indeed was written for his use by Willa Cather's old friend and companion of forty years. He did not, however, have the benefit of Mildred Bennett's *The World of Willa Cather* (1951), which is an indispensable mine of information about Red Cloud, the Divide, the Cather family; or Elizabeth Sergeant's *Willa Cather: A Memoir* (1954), which was based on a close friendship during some twenty crucial years. Nor was he able to see more than a fraction of the letters now available in institutional libraries.

During the past half decade a new chapter has been written in

Willa Cather's life by the investigation of her journalistic career in Lincoln and Pittsburgh. The research of Bernice Slote has doubled the number of newspaper columns that Willa Cather was previously known to have written, and has revealed the astonishing vastness of an apprenticeship that Brown only dimly perceived. These youthful prodigies of effort are writings that Willa Cather preferred to leave buried after she became famous. Miss Slote has published the first part of her discoveries in *The Kingdom of Art: Willa Cather's First Principles and Critical Statements, 1893–1896* (1967). Two more volumes, edited by William M. Curtin as *The World and the Parish: Willa Cather's Articles and Reviews, 1893–1902*, are scheduled for publication in 1970.

In addition, the University of Nebraska Press brought out in 1965 a complete edition, with an introduction by Mrs. Bennett, of Willa Cather's stories published between 1892 and 1912—a total of forty-four examples of her apprenticeship, many of them quite good, almost all of them never before reprinted, and some of them originally published under pseudonyms; and Miss Slote in 1962 (revised 1968) edited a new edition of Willa Cather's first book of poems, *April Twilights* (1903), including nine previously uncollected or unidentified poems. Thus the time has arrived for a new biography to gather and to collate the important materials that have become available in the past nineteen years.

In addition to the newly accessible printed materials, there now are perhaps one thousand Willa Cather letters housed in institutional collections from Harvard to the Huntington Library. Although Willa Cather was obsessed with the desire for privacy and destroyed all of her letters she could, most of the friends who survived her seem to have saved her letters. Her will stipulates that none of her correspondence may ever be published, but most of the three dozen libraries that own her letters make them available to scholars and critics, who are free to assimilate the information they contain or to paraphrase their contents. Willa Cather was well aware of the value of letters for biography. She wrote in 1927 that she never could have written *Death Comes for the Archbishop* if she had not had the dozens of letters inserted into William Howlett's *The Life of the Right Reverend Joseph P. Macheboeuf*, which was the chief source for her novel.

Willa Cather's desire for privacy and her efforts to present only her official face complicate the biographer's task. Before Brown's biography appeared, sketches of her life were full of garbled facts, legend, and some outright falsifications. Brown did a pioneering job of straightening out the record, but he worked under the handicap of insufficient source material. His book contains a good many factual errors, though his criticism is fresh and vital, and I have been able to correct some of his errors through access to the large number of letters now available. I also have benefited from the labors of Mildred Bennett, Virginia Faulkner, and Bernice Slote. As more letters find their way into library holdings, and as it becomes possible in a few years, as it surely must, to publish the letters, someone will be able to write the definitive biography of Willa Cather. This book, I hope, will serve until that time comes.

The image of Willa Cather that Brown's biography paints now needs to be modified. Leon Edel in his editor's foreword to Brown's book declares that despite the limitations imposed by restrictions on the use of letters "all future material that will be uncovered about Miss Cather's life will heighten the likeness and the coloring, but will not change the countenance." This, of course, is generally true, and the same thing might be said of many other early biographies; but what now begins to emerge is the unretouched likeness of Willa Cather rather than the official portrait.

The new view of Willa Cather does not diminish her accomplishment in any way. What we now see is an extraordinarily energetic and determined young woman slowly making her way in the world. From college journalism to professional journalism to magazine writing and editing she progressed steadily toward her objective, but the progress was almost painfully slow. The official face she presents to the world in her collected works is the one tenth of the iceberg of her total effort. And when she reached the top, she wanted her apprentice work forgotten. This attitude, of course, is not surprising, but it is the biographer's task to search among the shards to discover the abandoned designs or the crudities later perfected. Now that the University of Nebraska Press has made available her literary beginnings, it becomes possible to trace the patterns more fully than before. The themes and subjects that she treated so luminously in her mature work all begin in her earliest apprenticeship. She was a romantic and a primitive from the beginning, but it was not until she was forty that she could effectively utilize her own experience to weave the myths of the American past into the magical fabric of her mature novels. There is much trial and error in her apprentice work, but the outlines were all present by the time she was twenty.

Although Willa Cather wrote an old friend in 1945 that she never had been very ambitious, the truth was just the opposite. Her entire career down to the publication of *O Pioneers!*, her first important book, shows a very ambitious young woman from the provinces, determined to make good. She did what she had to do to make a living and was not above writing potboilers and doing hack work. Yet she had all the while a single-minded dedication to the pursuit of her art. During the years of struggle, moreover, her attachment to family, old friends, and home remained very strong, and she returned to Lincoln and Red Cloud frequently to renew her sources. Her feeling for Nebraska, however, was ambivalent until she had been away for perhaps fifteen years; then the pioneer period of her childhood became the epic material of her romances and led her to still deeper excursions into the past. She went through a period in the twenties when she was alienated from American life, somewhat like the writers of the "lost generation," and in the Thirties she became obsessed with privacy and secrecy and largely withdrew from social intercourse. She retained her friendships, however, and lived a normal though restricted life.

Her old age is not sad, like the blackness of Mark Twain's final pessimism. She achieved most of the things she wanted in life and knew that her career was a success. Although she hated much of the world that swirled around outside her self-imposed isolation, she did not become embittered and did not have to write, as Howells in his old age did to James, that she had become a dead cult with "her statues cut down and the grass growing over them." Her literary reputation flourished, and that was what really mattered.

There never has been any loss of interest in Willa Cather. Although she sometimes thought otherwise, the critics almost always have treated her well—from H. L. Mencken's delighted discovery of her first novels to the latest bibliography published by the Modern Language Association. It is a lean year for Willa Cather scholarship when the annual MLA bibliography does not list half a dozen items about her. And people have gone on reading her, despite the roadblocks that she placed by testamentary restrictions against anthologizing, reprinting, and dramatizing her works. A writer of lesser stature might well have consigned herself to oblivion by forbidding, as Willa Cather did, the reprinting of her works in inexpensive text and paperback editions.

I know of no other American writer of this century who is more likely to go on being read than Willa Cather. The statement that she makes in her preface to Sarah Orne Jewett's stories is prophetic: "If I were asked to name three American books which have the possibility of a long, long life, I would say at once: *The Scarlet Letter*, *Huckleberry Finn*, and *The Country of the Pointed Firs*. I can think of no others that confront time and change so serenely." And the last of the three, she adds, fairly shines with "the reflection of its long, joyous future." Of the best of Willa Cather, one could say the same.

ACKNOWLEDGMENTS

IN THE WRITING of this book I have incurred many obligations, and I wish to thank the following individuals: Bernice Slote of the University of Nebraska for answering innumerable questions, supplying me with documents, directing me to sources I might have missed, and reading my manuscript; Virginia Faulkner of the University of Nebraska Press for answering many queries and for lending me the manuscript of Curtin's *The World and the Parish;* Mildred R. Bennett of the Willa Cather Pioneer Memorial at Red Cloud for putting at my disposal manuscript materials in her custody and for answering queries; Mr. and Mrs. Cecil Yorke of Capitola, California, for letting me read the letters written to the Seibels; Mary Weddle for lending me copies of letters written to Mrs. George P. Cather and owned by her father. George C. Ray of Lincoln; Harry Finestone of San Fernando Valley State College for lending me materials he collected in his own work on Willa Cather; Allan Nevins for making available letters he received from Willa Cather; Duane J. Reed of the Nebraska State Historical Society for courtesies during and after I visited Lincoln; Rowe E. Portis, Jr., of the University of Virginia Library for showing me about the Barrett Collection; Carolyn E. Jakeman of the Houghton Library for making available letters owned by Harvard; Samuel Bogorod and Susan Alnick of the University of Vermont for research assistance; John Broderick of the Library of Congress for searching the Manuscript Division for Willa Cather letters.

In addition I am indebted to the following libraries that made letters in their possession available to me either as photocopies or when I visited their collections: Allegheny College, Amherst College, Boston Public Library, Brown University, Bryn Mawr College, Buffalo and Erie County Public Library, University of California at Berkeley, Chicago Historical Society, Colby College, Columbia University, Dartmouth College, Harvard University, Holy Cross College, Henry E. Huntington Library and Art Gallery, Middlebury College, University of Nebraska, Nebraska State Historical Society, Newark Public Library, Newberry Library, University of North Carolina, University of Notre Dame, University of Pennsylvania, Pennsylvania State University, Phillips Exeter Academy, Princeton University, University of Southern California, University of Vermont, University of Virginia, Wellesley College, Wisconsin State Historical Society.

Quotations from the works of Willa Cather are protected by copyright and have been reprinted by permission of the publisher, Alfred A. Knopf, Inc; from *Willa Cather Living*, by Edith Lewis, copyright 1953 by Edith Lewis, reprinted by permission of Alfred A. Knopf, Inc.; from *Willa Cather, a Critical Biography*, by E. K. Brown, copyright 1953 by Margaret Brown, reprinted by permission of Alfred A. Knopf, Inc.

For permission to quote various passages from Willa Cather's first four novels I wish to thank Houghton Mifflin. For permission to quote from *April Twilights (1903)*, *The Kingdom of Art*, *The World and the Parish*, and *Willa Cather's Collected Short Fiction* I wish to thank the University of Nebraska Press.

My final debts are to the Research Committee of the University of California at Davis for grants that speeded the preparation of this book, to Marjorie Donovan for research assistance, to JoAnn Cedarleaf for many secretarial services, to Norna Wilkin for typing, to Jan Dooley for indexing, and to Roberta Woodress for companionship, research assistance, good advice, and patient forebearance.

Davis, California   J.W.

WILLA CATHER

CHAPTER 1

Virginia and Nebraska: 1873–1890

I

IN 1873 THE SOUTH was slowly convalescing from the wracking agonies of the Civil War. Although Virginia escaped much of the punishment inflicted on the Confederacy during the Reconstruction period and was readmitted to the Union by 1870, the state had lost thousands of its young men and had been a battleground during much of the conflict. The Shenandoah Valley in particular, as a strategic highway connecting North and South, had been stubbornly fought over throughout the war. Winchester, the county seat of Frederick County, changed hands many times. "Stonewall" Jackson humiliated the federal troops in the valley in 1862, and General Sheridan finally defeated Confederate General Early there in March 1865, a few weeks before the war ended at Appomattox Courthouse. Although the valley was predominantly southern in its sympathies and, unlike West Virginia, did not split away from the Confederacy, many pro-northerners lived there, and the sectional split that divided father and son, brother and brother, was nowhere more evident. Prominent among the Union supporters in the valley was William Cather, grandfather of Willa Cather.

The Cathers had come to Virginia in colonial times. Originally from Wales, they may have taken the family name from a mountain with the Welsh name Cadair Idris, near where the family originated. According to family tradition an ancestor had fought

19

for Charles I, and after the Restoration twin Cather brothers had been rewarded by Charles II with a land grant in North Ireland. The first of the Cathers in America, however, was Jasper, who fought in the Revolution, settled in the Shenandoah Valley, and died in 1812. One of his sons was James, whose eight children included William, the Union sympathizer just mentioned. William, who gave up his inherited Calvinism to become a Baptist, was a strong personality and a man of considerable physical power. In his photograph he looks like an Old Testament prophet—high, bald crown, luxuriant beard, and the eyes of a zealot. Some of his vigor and independence certainly was passed on to his grand-daughter. He appears memorably in *My Ántonia* as Jim Burden's grandfather, a man of impressive dignity, an awesome figure to the boy from Virginia, who had come to live with his grandparents in Nebraska.

In 1846 William Cather married Emily Anne Caroline Smith, whose father kept a popular tavern on the Northwest Turnpike, and five years later he settled on a farm, which he named Willow Shade, near the present town of Gore, then called Back Creek Valley. By 1863 he had increased his landholdings to more than three hundred acres and built an imposing brick house. The farms in that area were not particularly fertile, and the farmers used few slaves. William, like most of his neighbors, owned no slaves, did not believe in slavery, and ran his farm with the aid of hired labor and his sons, George and Charles. The two boys, however, had to cross to West Virginia during part of the war to escape conscription. As the only member of his family to remain loyal to the North, William was ostracized by his relatives during the war, but he did not waver in his allegiance. The family split was especially painful, for William's father, James, had served in the legislature when it voted secession. After the war William became a U.S. marshal and prospered while most of his neighbors were bankrupt. He was the only man in the community rich enough to hire a Baptist minister to conduct a school at Willow Shade, and he later sent both his son Charles and future daughter-in-law Mary Virginia Boak to study in Baltimore.

Caroline Smith, Willa Cather's paternal grandmother, was the equal of her husband in energy and resolution. In *My Ántonia* she appears as a "spare, tall woman, a little stooped . . . quick-footed and energetic in all her movements." Her voice was high and rather shrill and had a sort of anxious note in it, because she always was eager that "everything should go with due order and decorum." Her laugh also was high and a bit too strident, "but there was a lively intelligence in it." At the age of fifty-five she was still a strong woman of unusual endurance, and after moving to Nebraska she found herself obliged to raise three orphaned grandchildren.

Willa Cather knew only one of her maternal grandparents. This was Grandmother Boak, the prototype of Rachel Blake in *Sapphira and the Slave Girl* (1940). Born Rachel Seibert, she had married William Boak, who was three times a member of the Virginia House of Delegates; but he had died in Washington while serving as an official of the Interior Department. Married at fourteen and widowed at thirty-eight, Rachel Boak returned to Back Creek Valley near William Cather's farm at Willow Shade with her five children, among whom was Mary Virginia, the future wife of Charles Cather. Mrs. Boak's father, Jacob Seibert, the model for the miller, Henry Colbert, in *Sapphira*, gave her a house in the village, and it was there that Willa Cather was born on December 7, 1873.

Rachel Boak was a remarkable woman who left an indelible impression on her granddaughter. Not only does she appear in *Sapphira*, but she also appears as the grandmother in the story "Old Mrs. Harris." In the former she goes about the village and country befriending the poor and miserable and healing the sick, a "stalwart woman in a sunbonnet, wearing a heavy shawl over her freshly ironed calico dress." Her head had a determined look, and her grave dark eyes were set back under a broad forehead. "The Back Creek people had grown used to seeing her come and go along the roads and mountain paths, on her way to some house where misfortune had preceded her."

Some thirty years later, in her seventies, she was living with her daughter and son-in-law in Red Cloud, Nebraska. As "Old Mrs. Harris," she was an old lady with deep-set brown eyes that looked at one directly and seemed to "ask nothing and hope for nothing." There was a kind of "nobility about her head," as there is about an old lion's, and "an absence of self-consciousness, vanity, preoccupation—something absolute." Her gray hair was parted in the middle, wound in two little horns over her ears, and done in a flat knot behind. Her mouth was large, composed, resigned. It was Rachel Boak who took charge of Willa Cather's early education and read to her often from her favorite books, which included the Bible, *Pilgrim's Progress*, and *Peter Parley's Universal History.*

Charles Fectigue Cather, father of Willa, was born in 1848 and married Mary Virginia Boak on December 5, 1872. He was an engaging young man, tall, fair-haired, gentle, easygoing, lacking completely the indomitable will and evangelical zeal of his Calvinist-turned-Baptist father. His older brother, George, inherited the parental drive and force. Charles was handsome in a boyish southern way and never hurt anybody's feelings. Willa Cather loved him dearly and was always much closer to him than to her mother. Charles had studied law for two years in Baltimore, and though he never practiced, he often was called on to help his neighbors untangle their affairs; when he gave up farming in Nebraska for a real-estate office in Red Cloud, his legal training was useful. He too appears in a fictional portrait in "Old Mrs. Harris," as Mr. Templeton. There he is "too delicate to collect his just debts," and "his boyish, eager-to-please manner, his fair complexion and blue eyes and young face, made him seem very soft to some of the hard old money-grubbers on Main Street."

Mary Virginia Boak was a person to be reckoned with. A handsome woman but unfortunately also domineering, she provided the energy and the sparks that drove her household and more than made up for Charles Cather's easy manner. She ruled her family tyrannically, exacted a strict adherence to domestic discipline, and punished disobedience with a rawhide whip. Yet she also had the good sense to give her children a measure of freedom to develop their own personalities, and she herself had a great capacity for enjoying life and for caring about things—whether the coffee was hot, whether a neighbor's child was ill, whether the weather was right for a picnic. She also was the one who healed the breach in the Cather family after the war by personally delivering invitations to a party to all the estranged members of the clan. None of them could resist the determined southern belle whose three brothers had fought for the Confederacy. As Victoria Templeton in "Old Mrs. Harris" she is seen from her mother's point of view: "Victoria had a good heart, but she was terribly proud and could not bear the least criticism." Willa Cather inherited her mother's temperament, and the two personalities often clashed. Although the daughter scrupulously performed her filial obligations toward her mother, it was her father whom she really loved. While they lived in Virginia, Mrs. Cather bore Willa, Roscoe, Douglass, and Jessica. The last of her seven children, James, Elsie, and John, were born in Nebraska.

At the time Willa Cather was born, Charles Cather and his bride had been living with Mrs. Boak in Back Creek Valley, thirteen miles west of Winchester. They named their first-born Wilella, after the father's youngest sister, who had died of diphtheria in childhood, but they always called her Willie.* The following year when William Cather went to Nebraska to visit his older son, George, who already had migrated westward, the Charles Cathers moved into the farm at Willow Shade. There Willa Cather spent her next eight years; there her first memories were recorded. It was a stable, well-ordered world despite the lingering effects of the Civil War. The land had been settled for nearly a century and a half. Generations of Cathers already filled the graveyards in the valley.

Willow Shade was a beautiful house to remember. Its three-story sturdy brick façade, pierced by large, evenly spaced single windows, was fronted by a portico with fluted columns, and behind the main structure was a solid two-story brick wing. Each room in the house had a fireplace for heating, six great willows shaded the spacious lawn, and a rather formal box hedge extended from the

---

*The name Willa is her own invention and appears written thus in her hand, altered from the original, in the family Bible. Her parents also did not give her a middle name, though in her childhood she called herself Willa Love Cather for the doctor who had delivered her. After going to Pittsburgh, she adopted her grandmother's maiden name, spelling it Sibert. She then pretended that she had been named for her uncle William Sibert Boak, who had died serving in the Confederate army during the war. She dropped the middle name from her by-line in the 1920's but continued to use it in the monogram for her stationery, and it appears finally in her will.

portico towards a full-running creek spanned by a rustic bridge. Beyond that was the turnpike. Although the farm was rocky and not suited for raising crops, Charles Cather fattened sheep for the Baltimore market. Apparently he made an adequate living, but many Virginians from the Shenandoah Valley left for the West during the seventies, drawn by the reports of fabulously rich soil in the new states west of the Mississippi. The household at Willow Shade was a busy place with preserving, butter-making, quilting, weaving, spinning, and candle-making constantly going on. There were house servants, both black and white, and a steady flow of visitors—sometimes relatives who stayed a day or a month, often the tin-peddler or Uncle Billy Parks, the broom-maker. There was no sense of isolation, as Willow Shade was on the main road from Winchester to Romney. Visitors came from Winchester and sometimes from Washington. In addition to the growing Cather family the establishment was augmented by Mrs. Boak, who came to live with her daughter, and Margie Anderson, nurse and housemaid, who also accompanied the family to Nebraska.

Many of the people in Willa Cather's life who touched her deeply appear sooner or later in her fiction. Margie Anderson and her mother, Mary Ann, belong in this group. Margie is the Mandy in "Old Mrs. Harris," Mahailey in *One of Ours,* and "Poor Marty" in a poem published in the *Atlantic Monthly* in 1931. Margie was a pathetic creature, not very bright, not very efficient, but a patient, devoted soul beloved by all the Cathers. She always liked to talk about old times in Virginia when Willa Cather came home from New York in later years, and Charles Cather, who always took the Winchester paper, kept her up on the news from home. She died in 1928 and is buried in the Cather family lot in Red Cloud:

> *Little had she here to leave,*
> *Naught to will and none to grieve.*
> *Hire nor wages did she draw*
> *But her keep and bed of straw.*

Her mother was one of Willa Cather's favorite people and appears in *Sapphira* as Mrs. Ringer, the woman who was born interested. She knew all the gossip and lived for the stories of other people's lives. When Willa Cather visited her great aunt Sidney Gore in 1896, she also visited Mrs. Anderson, who lived alone on the wooded Hollow Road leading from the village to Timber Ridge. The double-S road up to Mrs. Anderson's house, Willa Cather wrote in 1943, was the most beautiful piece of country road that she had ever found anywhere in the world. Mrs. Anderson in 1896 had not changed. She was still full of local history, as she was in the seventies when Willa Cather watched her coming down the road. The family usually sent her word when the child was shut up in the house with a cold, and she always came.

Her stories of the local people were no more stimulating, however, than the tales from *Peter Parley's Universal History* read aloud by Grandma Boak. Willa Cather's parents used to tell her that when she was a child, she could be kept quiet for a long time by being put in an imaginary chariot made by placing one straight chair upside down on another. There she would sit silently reliving Peter Parley and riding her chariot while beside her ran an invisible slave repeating frequently, "Cato, thou art but man!"

The most memorable event of Willa Cather's childhood, however, occurred when she was five. This was the return of Nancy Till, the scene that provides the epilogue for *Sapphira.* On a clear, windy March day in 1879 Willa Cather was in bed with a cold in her mother's bedroom on the third floor of Willow Shade. She had been put there so that she could watch the turnpike and see the stage when it first appeared. Nancy was coming home from Montreal, where she had lived for twenty-five years following the midnight flight in which Rachel Boak had taken her across the Potomac and delivered her to agents of the Underground Railroad. Suddenly her mother hurried into the room, wrapped her in a blanket, and carried her to the window as the stage stopped before the house and a woman in a black coat and turban descended. Then she was put back in bed. Old Till, the housekeeper and mother of Nancy, stayed in the room with the child so that the recognition scene could be enacted in her presence. There was talking on the stairs, and a minute later the door opened:

Till had already risen; when the stranger followed my mother into the room, she took a few uncertain steps forward. She fell meekly

25

into the arms of a tall, gold-skinned woman, who drew the little old darky to her breast and held her there, bending her face down over the head scantily covered with grey wool. Neither spoke a word. There was something Scriptural in that meeting, like the pictures in our old Bible.

Sixty-four years later Willa Cather still could remember the scene as though it just had happened. She wrote in 1943 that Nancy's dress in the novel is described in more detail than she could remember about a friend she had seen the week before. It all happened just as she told it, and it was the most exciting event of her life up to that time. Nancy already had become a legend, and Mrs. Cather often had sung her daughter to sleep with:

> *Down by de cane-brake, close by de mill,*
> *Dar lived a yaller gal, her name was Nancy Till.*

The departure of the Charles Cather family from Virginia took place in the spring of 1883. When his four-story sheep barn burned down, Charles Cather decided to sell out and join his father, brother, and other Virginians in Nebraska. His brother, George, had married a New England girl and left the South for good the year Willa was born. His parents, William and Caroline, had made a trip to Nebraska in the winter of 1874–1875 and returned there to live two years later. The family split over the Civil War may have had something to do with these moves, but the strongest motivation was climate. One of William Cather's daughters had tuberculosis and died two weeks after they reached the new country. Another daughter who went with them, a widow whose husband had died of the same disease, later fell victim herself. A third daughter had died of tuberculosis in Virginia, and all four of William Cather's brothers also had succumbed. It is small wonder the climate of the Shenandoah Valley was generally regarded as unhealthy. That plus the general westering spirit of Americans and the reports of topsoil twelve feet deep were enough to send an army of Virginia farmers to homestead on the prairies of the Middle West.

Charles Cather auctioned off his farm and all his equipment in February for six thousand dollars, and by April the family had reached Nebraska. It was a formidable expedition: parents, four children ranging from nine to infancy, Margie Anderson and her brother Enoch, Mrs. Cather's mother Rachel Boak, and two cousins. Most of their furniture also went into the auction, and the few things they took with them, like dishes, were packed in Confederate paper money. Even Old Vic, the favorite sheepdog for whom Charles Cather used to make leather shoes to protect his feet from the rocks, was given to a neighbor. Willa Cather remembered poignantly Old Vic on the day of their departure. Just as the family was about to board the train at Back Creek, the old dog broke loose and came running across the fields dragging his chain. It was more than a child could bear.

Although the story of Nancy Till teased Willa Cather's mind for nearly six decades before she used it in *Sapphira and the Slave Girl,* she did make use of Virginia memories in her earliest writing. A number of her apprentice stories fall into this category, including "The Elopement of Allen Poole" (1893), one of the first stories she wrote; "Night at Greenway Court" (1896); "The Sentimentality of William Tavener" (1900); and "The Namesake" (1907). These stories are interesting chiefly as apprentice work and biography, but they do show that she drew on the total range of her experience from the very start of her literary career. The first, "The Elopement of Allen Poole," is an amateurish tale of a moonshiner who is shot by the revenuers and dies in the arms of his girl on the night of their planned elopement; yet the evocation of place is good. Because Willa Cather's best writing is retrospective, it seems clear that she needed the distance of years between her experience and its fictional use. The memories in this story, which derive from her ninth year, had sufficient time to be thoroughly assimilated. Allen throws himself down in the woods beside a laurel bush:

It was the kind of summer morning to encourage idleness. Behind him were the sleepy pine woods, the slatey ground beneath them strewn red with slippery needles. Around him the laurels were just blushing into bloom. Here and there rose tall chestnut trees with the red sumach growing under them. Down in the valley lay the fields of wheat and corn, and among them the creek wound between its willow-grown banks. Across it was the old, black, creaking foot-bridge which had neither props nor piles, but was swung from the arms of a great sycamore tree. The reapers were at work in the wheat fields; the mowers swinging their cradles and the binders following close behind. Along the fences companies of bare-footed children were picking berries. On the bridge a lank youth sat patiently fishing in the stream where no fish had been caught for years. Allen watched them all until a passing cloud made the valley dark, then his eyes wandered to where the Blue Ridge lay against the sky, faint and hazy as the mountains of Beulah Land.

The next two stories making early use of the Virginia material are less interesting. "The Sentimentality of William Tavener" unites East and West, as the setting is Nebraska but the story is mostly a reminiscence of Virginia. It probably came from Willa Cather's parents or grandparents, who remembered the circus they once had attended, unbeknownst to each other, long before she was born. "A Night at Greenway Court" is historical melodrama laid in the eighteenth-century manor house of Lord Fairfax, and it probably owes more to the young author's fascination with Anthony Hope Hawkins than to her memories of Virginia.

"The Namesake," which makes the last use of Virginia material until *Sapphira*, has intrinsic interest that goes beyond its incidental use of early memories. This story conjures up the image of Willa Cather's uncle who was killed in the Civil War. The locale of the story is Paris, and the artist who tells the tale places the action near Pittsburgh; but the uncle who inspired the narrator's bronze figure, *The Color Sergeant*, is William Sibert Boak, the uncle whose name Willa Cather adopted for her own middle name. She also wrote a poem called "The Namesake," dedicated to "W. S. B. of the Thirty-Third Virginia," which ends with the lines:

> *And I'll be winner at the game*
> *Enough for two who bore the name.*

This story, written before Willa Cather had come very close to winning at the game, makes clear the powerful pull of family and old memories that figure so largely in her most memorable work. The artist narrator, Lyon Hartwell, although the son of American parents, was born and raised abroad. He is somehow able to cap-

28

ture the spirit of America better in his sculptures than any of his co-artists then working in Paris who have had genuine American upbringing. Hartwell explains to his friends the inspiration for his statue, which is the figure of a young soldier running and clutching the folds of a flag, the staff of which has been shot away. Hartwell had gone to Pennsylvania to take care of an invalid aunt living in his grandfather's old home on the banks of the Ohio River. During his two years in Pennsylvania he had one day found in the attic an old trunk containing his uncle's clothes, exercise books, letters home from the army, first books, and even some toys. Inside the cover of a dog-eared *Aeneid* was inscribed "Lyon Hartwell, January, 1862," the year before he had gone off to war at the age of fifteen. Inside the back cover was a crude drawing of the federal flag, and under it in a boyish hand were two lines of "The Star-Spangled Banner." "It was a stiff, wooden sketch, not unlike a detail from some Egyptian inscription," Hartwell narrates, "but, the moment I saw it, wind and color seemed to touch it."

This experience established contact between the sculptor and the uncle for whom he had been named. The experience of that night, he relates, almost rent him to pieces. "It was the same feeling that artists know when we, rarely, achieve truth in our work; the feeling of union with some great force, of purpose and security, of being glad that we have lived":

For the first time I felt the pull of race and blood and kindred, and felt beating within me things that had not begun with me. It was as if the earth under my feet had grasped and rooted me, and were pouring its essence into me. I sat there until the dawn of morning, and all night long my life seemed to be pouring out of me and running into the ground.

At this point in Willa Cather's career the pull of family experience was powerful, but the tug of Virginia was weak. She denied her uncle his allegiance to the Confederacy in the story, for by that time she had not lived at Willow Shade for twenty-four years.

II

The State of Nebraska, which Willa Cather first saw in April 1883, at the age of nine, is part of the great plain that stretches west of the Missouri River, gradually rising until it reaches the Rocky Mountains. It is a rolling alluvial plain that grows gradually more sandy toward the West until it breaks into the white sand hills of western Nebraska and Kansas and eastern Colorado. It is watered by slow-flowing, muddy rivers that run full in the spring, often cutting into farmland along their banks, but that lie low and shrunken by midsummer. The climate gives variety to this plateau, for it has short, bitter winters, flower-laden springs, long, hot summers, and triumphant autumns that last until Christmas. Autumn in Nebraska, as Willa Cather found, was "a season of perpetual sunlight, blazing blue skies, and frosty nights . . . the season of beauty and sentiment, as spring is in the Old World."

The earliest settlements in Nebraska were along the Missouri River—Bellevue, Omaha, Brownville, Nebraska City—as the river was the natural pathway into the region. But before 1860 civilization did no more than nibble at the eastern edge of the state along the river bluffs. The whole of the great plain to the west was still a sunny wilderness, where the tall red grass and the buffalo and the Indian hunters were undisturbed. Frémont, Kit Carson, the Mormons, crossed the state in the early days, and the gold-seekers followed by the thousands after 1849. When the first telegraph line was strung across the Missouri at Brownville, the initial message flashed over the wire was "Westward the course of empire takes its way."

The Overland Stage, as Mark Twain describes it memorably in *Roughing It,* jolted regularly across the prairie in the sixties, following the meandering course of the Platte River and the Oregon Trail. There was also much freight traffic over the plains in that decade. Huge trains of wagons pulled by multiple spans of oxen toiled over the six-hundred-mile trail to the Colorado mining camps at the rate of ten to twenty miles a day through an endless sea of grass. The buffalo trails still ran north and south—deep, dusty paths the bison wore when, single file, they came north in spring for the summer grass and went south again in the fall. Along the trails were the buffalo wallows, where rain water collected and the first settlers found water for their homesteads. The wagon drivers could recognize these water holes from a distance by their clouds of golden coreopsis growing out of the water. The grass was full of quail and prairie chickens, and ducks swam on the lagoons.

When the railroad came in 1869, a new era began. First the Union Pacific crossed the state to connect with the Central Pacific and form the first transcontinental railroad. And in the same year the Burlington started pushing westward across the southern edge of Nebraska towards Denver. Settlers began to pour in to plow the virgin soil, but at first the cultivated fields and broken land seemed mere scratches in the grassy sea that never stopped until it broke against the foothills of the Rockies. By 1883, when the Cather family got off the Burlington at Red Cloud, only the eastern part of the state was well populated. The Virginia settlement in Webster County was set down on what was mainly still raw, untamed prairie. The Cathers traveled by farm wagon from the Burlington depot at Red Cloud to their new home some sixteen miles northwest over rutted tracks that scarcely made a blemish on the wild land.

The effect of this translation from Willow Shade to the Nebraska flatlands was traumatic for nine-year-old Willa Cather. "I shall never forget my introduction to it," she told an interviewer in 1913:

We drove out from Red Cloud to my grandfather's homestead one day in April. I was sitting on the hay in the bottom of a Studebaker wagon, holding on to the side of the wagon box to steady myself—the roads were mostly faint trails over the bunch grass in those days. The land was open range and there was almost no fencing. As we drove further and further out into the country, I felt a good deal as if we had come to the end of everything—it was a kind of erasure of personality. . . . I had heard my father say you had to show grit in a new country, and I would have got on pretty well during that ride if it had not been for the larks. Every now and then one flew up and sang a few splendid notes and dropped down into the grass again. That reminded me of something—I don't know what, but my one purpose in life just then was not to cry, and every time they did it, I thought I would go under.

31

She did not go under, and in her adult years she wore her allegiance to Nebraska like a badge. For the first week, however, she "had that kind of contraction of the stomach which comes from homesickness." She did not like the canned food they had to eat and made a pact with herself that she would not eat much until she could get back to Virginia and get some fresh mutton. The land seemed to her as bare as a piece of sheet iron, or as she put it another time, as "naked as the back of your hand." She told another interviewer in 1921: "I was little and homesick and lonely and my mother was homesick and nobody paid any attention to us. So the country and I had it out together." By the end of the first autumn the shaggy grass country had gripped her with a passion that she never was able to shake. "It has been the happiness and the curse of my life."

The first interview cited above was given three years before she began writing *My Ántonia,* but the impact of the prairie is the same on young Jim Burden as it was on young Willa Cather. To heighten the dramatic effect, she places the time of arrival at night, and as Jim peers over the edge of the wagon, he sees nothing but land, "not a country at all but the material out of which countries are made. . . . I had the feeling that the world was left behind, that we had got over the edge of it, and were outside man's jurisdiction." Never before had he looked up at the sky without seeing the familiar mountain ridge against it, but this view was the complete dome of heaven. It is interesting to note that the hills of home always drew Willa Cather despite her affection for and attraction to the prairie. When she discovered Jaffrey, New Hampshire, while she was writing *My Ántonia,* she immediately fell in love with that place. She returned there year after year for a month or more, and when she began to think about death, she did not want to be buried on the flatlands in the family plot at Red Cloud with her parents. She asked to be buried on a hillside at Jaffrey where one could look up and see a "familiar mountain ridge" against the sky.

The real beginning of Willa Cather's life of the imagination was in the next eighteen months. During this period she lived on her grandfather's homestead on the Divide, those high plains between the Republican and the Little Blue rivers. Her grandparents went back to Virginia for a visit, leaving the Charles Cathers in charge of the farm. Uncle George's farm was several miles across the prairie, and there were a good many Virginians scattered about, enough so that they already had a post office called Catherton, but the people who really interested her were the foreigners. Added to the shock of the new country was the shock of meeting people who did not speak English and who possessed an alien culture.

"We had very few American neighbors," she recalled; "they were mostly Swedes and Danes, Norwegians and Bohemians. I liked them from the first and they made up for what I missed in the country. I particularly liked the old women; they understood my homesickness and were kind to me. . . . these old women on the farms were the first people who ever gave me the real feeling of an older world across the sea." Most of them did not speak much English, but they managed to tell her a great many stories, and since she was only a child they felt free to talk to her. The effect of these contacts was almost electric: "I have never found any intellectual excitement any more intense than I used to feel when I spent a morning with one of these old women at her baking or butter making. I used to ride home in the most unreasonable state of excitement; I always felt . . . as if I had actually got inside another person's skin."

The last phrase is important, for Willa Cather's creative imagination required total absorption in her fictional creations. The phrase occurs more than once in her letters and interviews, and when she had finished writing novels that created strong central characters like Ántonia Shimerda, Thea Kronborg in *The Song of the Lark*, Father Latour in *Death Comes for the Archbishop*, she always felt a sense of loss. The images she was photographing on the brain during these eighteen months provided her first important literary material. A friend once had told her that great minds like Balzac or Shakespeare got thousands and thousands more distinct mental impressions every day of their lives than most men in a lifetime. Her mind worked the same way. Once the image was recorded on her brain, it never left her. But it was not available for immediate use. Her ability to remember mannerisms, turns of phrase, idioms, and all sorts of verbal nuances was like her ability to record visual images. Taking notes on her material, she told an interviewer,

33

would kill the material. It was the memory that was important, and that is what went with the vocation. "When I sit down to write, turns of phrase I've forgotten for years come back like white ink before fire."

One of the first stories she heard on the Divide was the account of the suicide of Francis Sadilek, the Bohemian farmer who smashed his fiddle and then shot himself. One recognizes this tale as an early episode in *My Ántonia*, the death of Papa Shimerda; but it also provided the material for Willa Cather's first published story, "Peter," which was written during her freshman year in college. She rewrote it once and republished it twice more before using it finally in her novel. Other tales she heard during her tenth and eleventh years also went into *My Ántonia*, "The Bohemian Girl," *O Pioneers!*, and additional early stories.

Jim Burden's impressions during his first months on the Divide are Willa Cather's impressions: "All the years that have passed have not dimmed my memory of that first glorious autumn. The new country lay open before me: there were no fences . . . and I could choose my own way over the grass uplands, trusting the pony to get me home again." As Jim did, she rode along the sunflower-bordered wagon tracks to visit their nearest neighbors, the German Lambrechts, whose children were her first playmates. These German settlers, who lived in a sod house, are reminiscent of the German neighbors of Alexandra Bergson in *O Pioneers!* Lydia Lambrecht became a lifelong friend, as did Annie Sadilek, the prototype of *My Ántonia*, though Willa Cather may not have met Annie until after moving to town. Jim Burden remembers: "Sometimes I went south to visit our German neighbours and to admire their catalpa grove, or to see the big elm tree that grew up out of a deep crack in the earth and had a hawk's nest in its branches. Trees were so rare in that country . . . that we used to feel anxious about them, and visit them as if they were persons." There were other times that he rode to visit a huge prairie-dog town, but he had to be on guard against the rattlesnakes that preyed on the prairie dogs. Rattlesnakes were always a menace, and one of the first things Willa Cather noticed after arriving at Catherton was the steel-tipped cane her grandmother carried to kill snakes with when she worked in the garden. One of the memorable episodes of *My Ántonia* is the scene in which Jim Burden kills a huge rattler before the fascinated gaze of Ántonia.

Jim Burden's impressions, however, like Willa Cather's memories, are recorded years after the fact. By then the ugliness of the western prairie had been filtered out of the picture, leaving only a retouched mythic landscape. When she suggests that she and the country had it out together by the end of the first autumn, she is foreshortening considerably. There is ample evidence, especially in her early stories, to show that the glow that lights the country in *O Pioneers!* and *My Ántonia* was a good while in coming. Soon after her first collection of stories was published, *The Troll Garden* (1905), she wrote Witter Bynner to explain the bleak tone of her western tales. She guessed then that her early experiences had clung to her, for she had been pretty much depressed as a child by all the ugliness around her. The contrast with the beautiful Shenandoah Valley she had left was shattering. One simply could not imagine anything so bleak and desolate as a Nebraska ranch in the 1880's, and she remembered coming as close to dying of homesickness as any healthy child could. About eighteen miles from their farm there was one miserable little sluggish stream, which in the spring was about ten feet wide and in the late summer no more than a series of black mudholes. Along its banks grew a few cottonwoods and dwarf elms. She and her little brothers would do almost anything to get to that creek. The country, moreover, was so treeless than when they went to town for supplies, they could hardly wait to reach a halfway point where a row of Lombardy poplars had been planted as a windbreak. And their first Christmas was never to be forgotten. She and her brothers were taken to a Christmas celebration at the Norwegian church. The Christmas tree was a naked little box elder wrapped in green tissue paper cut in fringes to simulate pine needles. In *My Ántonia* the Burdens' hired man, Jake, brings home a real Christmas tree, a five-foot cedar, on which they hang gingerbread animals, strings of popcorn, and brilliantly colored paper figures.

III

In September 1884 Charles Cather again held a public auction, sold his livestock and farm equipment, and moved his family into town. Why they left Catherton after only eighteen months is not entirely clear, but it was said publicly that the growing family needed to be closer to medical attention and to schools. Willa was going on eleven, and the three-month term of the newly organized rural school at Catherton did not offer much of an education. It is also likely that Mrs. Cather, who had been ill on the homestead, never adjusted to the prairie life. There is no evidence that she was unwilling to accompany her husband to Nebraska, but her background and temperament made her more of a town woman than a pioneer's wife. Charles, too, was not the pioneer type and no doubt felt a lot more comfortable in town. At any rate, he opened an office in Red Cloud, where he made farm loans, wrote title abstracts, and sold insurance.

Red Cloud was then a town of 2,500 persons, a division point on the Burlington Railroad, and a busy place. Eight passenger trains a day went through the town, going and coming between Kansas City and Denver. Because the dining car had not yet been invented, many of the trains stopped in Red Cloud and the passengers got off for meals. The Burlington tracks were laid a mile south of town along the Republican River, and the hotel and roundhouse that the railroad built were connected to the town by horsecar. The town, which had been founded before the railroad came, did not grow towards the depot but remained where it was. It consisted of one main business street running north and south with several blocks of stores and offices, and at its widest point from east to west there were perhaps ten blocks of houses. The State Bank Building, made of native brick, had been built the year before the Cathers moved into town, and it dominated the business section; the opera house, which was to be one of the centers of Willa Cather's interest, would be erected over a hardware store just to the north in the following year.

The town of Red Cloud had existed for fourteen years. Its history began in 1870 when Silas Garber, a former captain in the Union army, and his two brothers traveled up the Republican River Valley on horseback and staked their claims on the present site of the town. They built a stockade and began to plow and plant. Although the stockade was to protect them from Indian attacks, the settlement never was molested. They were, however, beyond the line of the established communities, and Indian hunting parties passed through the region in search of buffalo, deer, and elk, which still were plentiful. With what seems in retrospect unusual whimsy for a group of pioneers they named their new settlement for a renegade Sioux chief. The town prospered, and in 1873 Garber went on to greater things, becoming governor of the state; but he came back to Red Cloud and built a spacious house, where he lived until his death. He is an important character in the dramatis personae of Willa Cather's life, for he is the Captain Forrester of *A Lost Lady.*

There perhaps is no small town in America that has been described more often in fiction than Red Cloud. It is the Sweetwater of *A Lost Lady,* the Frankfort of *One of Ours,* the Haverford of *Lucy Gayheart,* the Moonstone of *The Song of the Lark,* the Hanover of *O Pioneers!,* and the Black Hawk of *My Ántonia.* In addition it is the locale of the stories in *Obscure Destinies,* of "The Best Years," and of a good many stories of her apprentice period. Sometimes the town is placed in Colorado, as it is in *The Song of the Lark,* but the topography of the community always tallies with that of Red Cloud.

The house that the Cather family moved into also has been used often in Willa Cather's fiction. It still stands, a story-and-a-half frame building, on the southwest corner of Third and Cedar streets just a block away from the business district. Although the house was a bit more cramped than their former three-story brick home at Willow Shade, housing was scarce and the Cathers had to take what they could get. Yet the house has considerable charm, and it stands today, carefully restored, in the center of an ample, well-shaded corner lot. Downstairs, besides sitting room, dining room, and kitchen, there were bedrooms for the parents and small children. Grandma Boak's room, described in "Old Mrs. Harris," had to serve as a passageway between dining room and kitchen. Up a narrow stairway from the kitchen one climbed to the large unfinished attic, and there all the older children lived in a kind of dormitory. In "The Best Years" this loft is the private world of the children, "where there were no older people poking about to spoil things." The attic ran the whole length of the house, and its charm for the children was that it was unlined: "No plaster, no beaver-board lining; just the roof shingles, supported by long, unplaned, splintery rafters that sloped from the sharp roof-peak down to the floor." Up the center of this attic passed two brick chimneys "going up in neat little stair-steps from the plank floor to the shingle roof—and out of it to the stars!"

When Willa Cather grew too old to share the dormitory with her brothers, an ell-shaped gable wing of the main attic was partitioned off to give her a private room. This is the room that Thea Kronborg occupies in *The Song of the Lark* when she begins to make her own money by giving music lessons. This room, also unplastered, was "snugly lined with soft pine. The ceiling was so low that a grown person could reach it with the palm of the hand, and it sloped down on either side. There was only one window, but it was a double one and went to the floor." Willa worked in Cook's drugstore to earn the wallpaper, given to her in lieu of wages, that she put on the walls of this room. This paper, brown roses on a yellowish background, still lines the walls, though it is faded by time and weather stains. In this room she kept her books and could escape from the rest of the family.

Willa Cather's serious schooling began when the family moved into Red Cloud. The first year she was put in Gertrude Scherer's class, but the next year she drew Evangeline King, the principal of the school. "Miss King," she reminisced in 1909, "was the first person whom I cared a great deal for outside of my own family. I had been in her class only a few weeks when I wanted more than anything else in the world to please her." Willa Cather looked back on that year as one of the happiest she ever spent, and when she came to write "The Best Years," published posthumously, she drew an affectionate portrait of Miss King as Evangeline Knightly. As Willa went on to high school, Miss King always helped and advised her and even tried to teach her algebra. "But not even Miss King—who could do almost anything—could do that." Miss King later became school superintendent of Webster County and after that joined the faculty of Kearney State Teachers College. Two other teachers who also left their mark on Willa

Cather were Mr. and Mrs. A. K. Goudy. Mrs. Goudy, principal of the high school, became a particular friend and correspondent for forty years. When Willa Cather went to the University of Nebraska, the Goudys moved to Lincoln, and he became state superintendent of schools. When she visited Italy for the first time in 1908, she wrote Mrs. Goudy that she had seen in the Naples museum the wonderful head of Caesar that had illustrated the high-school text of Caesar's commentaries she had read under Mr. Goudy.

Willa Cather's extracurricular reading during her adolescent years was perhaps even more important than her formal education. Red Cloud may have been a raw little prairie town, but it contained a fair share of cultivated people. Among them were Mr. and Mrs. Charles Wiener, who lived just around the corner. Mrs. Wiener was an educated Frenchwoman, her husband a Red Cloud merchant. They both spoke French and German, and when they discovered their neighbor's child had an insatiable desire to read, they introduced her to French and German literature in translation. They had a large library and gave her the run of it. The relationship between the Wieners and Willa Cather appears rather accurately drawn in "Old Mrs. Harris," which might have been subtitled "Portrait of the Artist as a Teen-ager." As Vickie Templeton sits in the Rosens' library one hot summer afternoon, Mrs. Rosen observes her:

She wasn't pretty, yet Mrs. Rosen found her attractive. She liked her sturdy build, and the steady vitality that glowed in her rosy skin and dark blue eyes—even gave a springy quality to her curly reddish-brown hair, which she still wore in a single braid down her back. Mrs. Rosen liked to have Vickie about because she was never listless or dreamy or apathetic. A half-smile nearly always played about her lips and eyes, and it was there because she was pleased with something, not because she wanted to be agreeable. Even a half-smile made her cheeks dimple. She had what her mother called 'a happy disposition.'

Vickie, for her part, loved the Rosens' cool, darkened library, where she could slip in and read or take a sofa pillow and lie on the floor looking up at the pictures and feeling a happy, pleasant excitement from the heat and glare outside and the deep shadow

39

and quiet within. There was no other house the least like the Rosens': " . . . it was the nearest thing to an art gallery and a museum that the Templetons had ever seen. All the rooms were carpeted alike. . . . The deep chairs were upholstered in dark blue velvet. The walls were hung with engravings. . . . There were a number of water-colour sketches, made in Italy by Mr. Rosen himself when he was a boy." And there was the library: it had a complete set of the Waverley novels in German, "thick, dumpy little volumes bound in tooled leather . . . many French books, and some of the German classics done in English such as Coleridge's translation of Schiller's *Wallenstein*." Willa Cather was lucky in having the Wieners next door, and apparently they realized her extraordinary talent and encouraged her, as the Rosens do Vickie Templeton, to go to college.

The Wieners' library, however, was not the only source for the books that young Willa Cather devoured. She read constantly and indiscriminately, good books, trashy books, whatever came her way. The evidence in her early writing is that she had ranged widely in her reading—so widely that no brief summary can do justice to her huge, eclectic consumption of literary material. Like Vickie Templeton, she had not been taught to respect masterpieces, but cared about a book only because it took hold of her. Her family owned a good many books, many of which have been preserved, and one can assume that she read everything in this collection. Among the Cather books were complete editions of the standard nineteenth-century classics: Dickens, Scott, Thackeray, Poe, Hawthorne, Ruskin, Emerson, Carlyle. There also were volumes of Shakespeare and Bunyan, anthologies of poetry, the works of Thomas Campbell and Thomas Moore, some translations of Latin and Greek classics, religious books, books on the Civil War, bound volumes of the *Century*, and ladies' magazines; and although now lost, there once were copies of Ben Jonson's plays and Byron's poems. Finally, there were popular romances, such as the novels of Ouida, which Mrs. Cather liked. Fairly recent novels, such as *Anna Karenina*, one of Willa's favorites, probably came from the drugstore, perhaps when she worked for Dr. Cook and took her pay in merchandise.

She also had her own library during her high-school years, and some of these volumes survive, all carefully labeled "Private Library" and numbered. The earliest dated volume in this group is a battered copy of the *Iliad* in Pope's translation with the year 1888 inside the cover and the number seventy. Other titles of the same period are Jacob Abbott's *Histories of Cyrus the Great and Alexander the Great,* George Eliot's *The Spanish Gypsy,* Carlyle's *Sartor Resartus,* Alexander Winchell's *Sketches of Creation,* a paperback edition of *Antony and Cleopatra,* and *Pilgrim's Progress.* The last, a book that she first encountered when Grandma Boak read it to her, was one of her great favorites. She told Edith Lewis that she had read it eight times during one of her first winters in Nebraska. Another book that once must have been in her private library is *Huckleberry Finn,* which came out the year she moved to Red Cloud. In the thirties she reread that book for what she thought was the twentieth time.

She certainly was drawing on her own memories of childhood reading when she wrote a book column in Pittsburgh in 1897. Then she recommended "that dear old book" *The Count of Monte Cristo* and another favorite, Dinah Mulock's *John Halifax, Gentleman.* She also included, with *Pilgrim's Progress,* a second book "essential to a child's library," *The Swiss Family Robinson.* "Any child who has not read these has missed a part of his or her childhood." And she added to the list the works of Howard Pyle, especially *Otto of the Silver Hand,* from which a child can get a "very fair idea of what that phrase 'the Middle Ages' meant." Pyle remained one of her heroes, and even before she met him later as a co-worker on *McClure's Magazine,* she sent him a copy of *The Troll Garden* inscribed as follows: "Will Mr. Howard Pyle accept through me the love of seven big and little children to whom he taught the beauty of language and of line, and to whom, in a desert place, he sent the precious message of Romance."

People as well as books contributed to the growth of Willa Cather's mind during her adolescence. Her fondness for visiting the immigrant farm wives on the Divide already has been noted, and she sought out interesting adults wherever she could find them. Dr. McKeeby, the family physician, was a particular friend. He pulled her through a childhood sickness that may have been polio and doctored the entire family for many years. Willa's earliest

41

ambition was to become a doctor, and in pursuit of this ambition she often went on calls with Dr. McKeeby. Later she put him into *The Song of the Lark* as Dr. Archie, the sponsor of Thea Kronborg's artistic career. Willa also made calls with Dr. Damerell, another Red Cloud physician, and on one occasion she administered chloroform while the doctor amputated a boy's leg.

Her interest in adults is well demonstrated in the story "Two Friends," one of the tales in *Obscure Destinies.* Here the narrator is a young girl who hangs about the general store and bank to hear Mr. Dillon and Mr. Trueman hold their nightly conversations. "I liked to listen to those two because theirs was the only 'conversation' one could hear about the streets. The older men talked of nothing but politics and their business, and the very young men's talk was entirely what they called 'josh'; very personal, supposed to be funny, and really not funny at all. It was scarcely speech, but noises, snorts, giggles, yawns, sneezed with a few abbreviated words and slang expressions which stood for a hundred things." Mr. Dillon, the banker, and Mr. Trueman, the cattleman, however, talked about everything—crops and the farmers they dealt with, trips they had taken, and plays they had seen. Their talk was a window into the larger world. "I found many pretexts for lingering near them [as they sat talking on the sidewalk in front of Dillon's store], and they never seemed to mind my hanging about." In the story the two friends finally split over the issue of Bryan and free silver, an event that could not have happened in actuality until after Willa Cather had left Nebraska. In real life, however, they were Mr. Richardson and Mr. Miner, the latter a neighbor of the Cathers' and owner of the general store where Willa did indeed hang about a great deal.

Another of the girl's adult friends, an educated Englishman named William Ducker, was perhaps the most influential of all her "friends of childhood." Ducker, who moved to Red Cloud in 1885, clerked in a store owned by his brother. He generally was regarded by his family as a failure, but he did not seem to mind. His passion was Latin and Greek literature, and soon after he arrived, Willa Cather began to read the classics with him. She already had learned Latin and probably began learning Greek at this time. Under his tutelage she read Virgil, Ovid, the *Iliad,* and the *Odes* of Anacreon, and after she went to the university, where she continued her Latin and Greek, she read with him during the summers. They also had long talks together about good and evil, life and death, and all the big questions. Ducker understood and valued his pupil, and left an indelible memory. Willa Cather's books are studded with classical references and allusions, and his death was probably her first great loss. He died in 1893 when she was home from college for the summer vacation. One afternoon she was walking home with him from his store when he said: "It is just as though the light were going out, Willie." A few minutes after she left him, one of his children came running to call her back. She returned to find him dead on the couch of his living room with a copy of the *Iliad* open on the floor beside him.

Another neighbor whose extracurricular influence on Willa Cather was strong and lasting was Mrs. Julia Miner, whose husband was Mr. Dillon of "Two Friends." Mrs. Miner had been born in Oslo (then Christiana), the daughter of the oboe soloist in Ole Bull's Royal Norwegian Orchestra. As a child she had gone to rehearsals and concerts and studied music, and when the vicissitudes of life made her the wife of a Nebraska merchant, she installed a new Chickering piano in her Red Cloud parlor. The Miners lived just a block away on Third Avenue and Seward Street, and three of their daughters, Carrie, Irene, and Mary, became Willa Cather's lifelong friends. When Mrs. Miner played for the children, she gave Willa her first experience of serious music. Willa had an innate love of music, and Mrs. Miner's stories of her musical Norwegian childhood and her competent playing of the standard works stimulated what was to be an absorbing, lifetime interest.

The importance of Mrs. Miner in Willa Cather's life is readily observable in *My Ántonia,* where she appears as Jim Burden's neighbor Mrs. Harling: "Mrs. Harling was short and square and sturdy-looking, like her house. . . . Her face was rosy and solid, with bright, twinkling eyes and a stubborn little chin. She was quick to anger, quick to laughter, and jolly from the depths of her soul." Jim liked to cross the street to their house because it always was a gay, noisy place, except when Mr. Harling was home. Someone was always at the piano. Frances played when she came home

43

from her job in her father's store at noon. Sally played after she got home from school, and even Nina, the youngest, played "The Swedish Wedding March." Jim recalls: "Mrs. Harling had studied the piano under a good teacher, and somehow she managed to practise every day. I soon learned that were I sent over on an errand and found Mrs. Harling at the piano, I must sit down and wait quietly until she turned to me." He remembered her vividly as she played—a short square person planted firmly on the stool, her little fat hands moving quickly and neatly over the keys while her eyes were fixed on the music with intelligent concentration. Mrs. Miner died while *My Ántonia* was being written, and when Willa Cather wrote Carrie Miner Sherwood a letter of condolence, she said she had tried hard to recall certain tricks of voice and gesture in creating Mrs. Harling. Her character, she said, was a clear little snapshot of Mrs. Miner as she first remembered her, and she added that there had been a little of Mrs. Miner in almost every mother she ever had done.

Willa Cather had no formal music education, however, and little desire to study music. For her music was a great emotional release, not an intellectual exercise. She developed a great love for opera and classical music and a tremendous interest in performing artists, but she drove Professor Schindelmeisser mad when he tried to give her piano lessons. The professor was a derelict musician and alcoholic, who wandered into town and made his living by teaching the piano. Mrs. Miner recognized him as a first-rate musician and engaged him to teach her children. Willa Cather's mother also hired him, but Willa spent most of her lesson time asking her teacher about life in the old country and his musical adventures. When he told Mrs. Cather that she was wasting her money giving her daughter lessons, she told him to keep coming, as Willa was getting a lot out of listening to him play and talking to him. Professor Wunsch in *The Song of the Lark,* who gives Thea Kronborg her first music lessons, is Schindelmeisser's fictional counterpart. Although Thea grows up to become a Wagnerian soprano, there is a good deal of the youthful aspiring Willa Cather in that character, and Professor Wunsch, who "came from God knows where," talks to Thea after her music lessons, just as Schindelmeisser did to his pupil.

Willa Cather's adult friends certainly knew that she was a remarkable girl, but the average Red Cloud resident probably thought of her as that "show-off" Cather youngster. She was not disposed to conceal her talents during her Red Cloud years, and she must have been rather conspicuous in that small community. Half a century later she would go to any lengths to avoid society, but as an adolescent Willa Cather was gregarious and fond of people. She was conspicuous not only because of her natural superiority but also because she developed a wide streak of nonconformity. The long hair that Vickie Templeton wears was not the memory of Willa's high-school classmates. By the time she was fifteen she had cut her hair shorter than most boys and was signing her name "William Cather, Jr." or "Wm. Cather, M.D." She expressed vast contempt for skirts and dresses, and wrote in a friend's album that slicing toads was her hobby and that amputating limbs was perfect happiness. Such a child must have taken some knocks from the local busybodies.

There is no evidence, however, that she was not popular with her contemporaries, and one natural outlet for her energy and intelligence was amateur theatricals. During her first year in Red Cloud the *Argus* reported on May 14, 1885, that the Sunday-school concert at the Baptist church had featured Miss Willie Cather, who "electrified the audience with elocutionary powers." And the following month there was a similar item. The performance no doubt was her rendition of "Hiawatha," which she was in the habit of reciting in a costume complete with bow and arrow. By the time she was thirteen she was making up and staging her own plays in the upstairs attic and in the Miners' parlor. When she was fourteen, she and the Miner girls put on a play in the new opera house for the benefit of the victims of the blizzard of '88. They presented *Beauty and the Beast*, with Margie Miner as the beauty, Mary Miner as the beast, and Willie Cather, dressed in suit, hat, and waxed mustache, as the merchant-father. The Red Cloud *Chief* was much impressed with her performance. It was characteristic that Willa should have taken a male role, for it is perfectly clear that she would have much preferred to be born a boy, and later she again dressed as a man—the old alchemist in black velvet knee pants—when she represented Cook's drugstore in the Merchants' Carnival.

The opera house, which provided a stage for *Beauty and the Beast,* was perhaps the one place in town that held the most attraction for her. There she was introduced to the world of the theater, and though the quality of the road-shows that visited Red Cloud must have been low, the memory of plays and light operas there was golden. She wrote in 1929 that "half a dozen times during each winter . . . a traveling stock company settled down at the local hotel and thrilled and entertained us for a week." It was a wonderful week for the children. The excitement began when the advance man posted the bills on the lumberyard fence and the windows of the drug and grocery stores. Willa and her friends used to stand for hours studying every word on the posters and trying to decide whether they could get their parents to let them go every other night or just on opening and closing nights. No child ever got to go every night unless his father owned stock in the opera house. If the company arrived at night, she continued, "my chums and I always walked a good half mile to the depot . . . to see that train come in. . . . We found it delightful to watch a theatrical company alight, pace the platform while their baggage was being sorted, and then drive off—the men in the hotel bus, the women in the 'hack.' If by any chance one of the show ladies carried a little dog with a blanket on, that simply doubled our pleasure." Then the children invented pretexts to visit the hotel to see the actors lounging about.

One particular production that she recalled was Frank Lindon's performance in *The Count of Monte Cristo*: "When old Frank Lindon in a frilled shirt and a velvet coat blazing with diamonds, stood in the drawing room of Mme. Danglars' and revealed his identity to Mme. de Morcery, his faithless Mercedes, when she cowered and made excuses, and he took out a jeweled snuff box with a much powdered hand, raised his eyebrows, permitted his lip to curl, and said softly and bitterly, 'a fidelity of six months!' then we children were not in the opera house in Red Cloud; we were in Mme. Danglars' salon in Paris." Those were the good old days. "It did us good to weep at 'East Lynne,' even if the actress was fairly bad and the play absurd. Children have about a hundred years of unlived life wound up in them, and they want to be living some of it."

When the opera house was dark, Willa Cather and her friends

46

lived in a rich world of their own imagination. During Willa's fourteenth year Dr. McKeeby became mayor and Mr. Cather an alderman. Willa organized her own town and city government in the Cather yard and was elected mayor. The town consisted of packing boxes from Miner Brothers' Store, arranged along the south fence under cottonwood and wild plum trees. The memory of this playtime turns up in an early story published in 1898, "The Way of the World," in which an all-boy town reminiscent of "Sandy Point" is invaded and destroyed by a girl. The story no doubt owes something to *Tom Sawyer,* but it anticipates interestingly the child's world of Crane's *Whilomville Stories* and Tarkington's *Penrod.*

The area around Red Cloud also provided ample opportunity for childhood adventures. There were picnics in the fine cottonwood grove adjacent to Governor Garber's house a short distance out of town, or there were visits to Uncle George's farm in Catherton. But the most exciting place of all was the river and in particular one spot in the river known as Far Island. "Far Island is an oval sand bar, half a mile in length and perhaps a hundred yards wide, which lies about two miles up from Empire City in a turbid little Nebraska river." Such is the opening sentence of a story, "The Treasure of Far Island," published in 1902. The children, especially Willa and her brothers Roscoe and Douglass, loved that island, and there they played Long John Silver and Jim Hawkins, for *Treasure Island,* one of their favorite books, appeared in 1883. They camped on the island and built their fires on the dazzling white, ripple-marked sandy beach. The center of the island was thick with thousands of yellow-green willows and cottonwood seedlings, brilliantly green even in the hottest summer weather. The island was no-man's land, but every summer a new chief claimed it, and Willa Cather's memory also kept a tight hold on it. The island appears not only in "The Treasure of Far Island," but also in one of her most successful early stories, "The Enchanted Bluff" (1909). In the latter the boys of the town camp on the island during the last night of summer vacation. They are about to scatter for good, and the male narrator soon will leave to begin teaching school. As they lie on the sand looking up at the stars, they plan someday to climb the Enchanted Bluff somewhere down in New

47

Mexico. The narrator of the tale wakes early the next morning, and as he looks at the other sleeping boys he thinks of their aspirations. "It was still dark, but the sky was blue with the last wonderful azure of night. The stars glistened like crystal globes and trembled as if they shone through a depth of clear water. Even as I watched, they began to pale and the sky brightened. Day came suddenly, almost instantaneously. I turned for another look at the blue night, and it was gone." So were youth and the young days on Far Island. In her first book, *April Twilights,* the dedicatory poem, which is addressed to her brothers Roscoe and Douglass, speaks

> *Of the three who lay and planned at moonrise,*
> *On an island in a western river.*
> *Of the conquest of the world together.*

Those golden days ended for Willa Cather in June 1890, when she graduated from high school and prepared to enter the university at Lincoln. Her childhood over, though she was only sixteen and a half, the bright Medusa was drawing her from the anonymity of the prairie town to a larger world of striving and achievement. Her parting message to Red Cloud, which both attracted and repelled her, was her graduation oration, "Superstition *versus* Investigation." She was one of three graduates that year, the second class to graduate from Red Cloud High School, and followed John Tulleys, who discoursed on "Self-Advertising" (he was very much in favor), and Alex Bentley, who asserted that "New Times Demand New Measures and New Men." The Red Cloud *Chief* predicted bright futures for both the boys, and while it complimented Willa Cather on her knowledge of history and the classics, it was silent about her prospects.

"Superstition *versus* Investigation" was a spirited attack, though it avoided personalities, on the local people who had objected to "Wm. Cather, M.D." 's experiments in vivisection:

Scientific investigation is the hope of our age, as it must precede all progress; and yet upon every hand we hear the objections to its pursuit. The boy who spends his time among the stones and flowers is a trifler, and if he tries with bungling attempt to pierce the mystery of animal life he is cruel. Of course if he becomes a great anatomist or a brilliant naturalist, his cruelties are forgotten or forgiven him; the world is very cautious, but it is generally safe to admire a man who has succeeded. We do not withhold from a few great scientists the right of the hospital, the post-mortem or experimenting with animal life, but we are prone to think the right of experimenting with life too sacred a thing to be placed in hands of inexperienced persons. Nevertheless, if we bar our novices from advancement, whence shall come our experts?

The oration began by invoking the spirit of Bacon and inductive science, and it went on to take testimony from Harvey and Newton. The performance is precocious and contrasts sharply with the blatant hucksterism and the bloodless pap of the other speakers. There was a certain amount of Gopher Prairie in Red Cloud, as Willa Cather recognized in early stories like "The Sculptor's Funeral." In later years, however, she tended to emphasize the home-town presence of people like the Wieners and Will Ducker.

CHAPTER 2

The Lincoln Years: 1890–1896

I

LINCOLN, the capital of Nebraska, was a small part of the world when Willa Cather descended from the Burlington accommodation in September 1890, but it was twelve times the size of Red Cloud and by comparison a metropolis. Its thirty thousand inhabitants were sprawled over several square miles of flat, open prairie in the typical midwestern pattern of city planning: perfectly rectangular blocks laid out by theodolite and surveyor's chains in a north-south, east-west grid. Lettered streets ran one way, and numbered the other. The capitol building was at the center of town, and a mile to the north at the top of Eleventh Street stood the chief building of the university. The city still had a raw look about it, but there were five major hotels, five private schools, a public library, and plenty of saloons and churches. Lincoln would not have seemed beautiful to Henry James, but it was old enough to have well-developed trees, and to Willa Cather it *was* attractive. As her first stop on the road from Red Cloud to New York, it was sufficiently grand and challenging.

Life in Lincoln was not primitive. The settlers from the East had not been in contact with the wild land long enough to be influenced by the frontier. They brought their eastern culture with them, and while they were digging up the buffalo grass to build houses and streets, they were unpacking their Limoges china, Landseer lithographs, and Ticknor and Fields books. Lincoln was an instant city: It had been empty prairie in 1867 when Nebraska became a state, and it was a thriving town twenty years later. It quickly became a railroad center, as it was on the direct route between Chicago and Denver, and by the end of the century nineteen different rail routes led into it. This fact is important because it made Lincoln a convenient stop for first-rate traveling theatrical companies on their way to Denver and San Francisco. When Willa Cather became dramatic critic for the *Nebraska State Journal*, she was able to review plays and musical events worth criticizing.

Lincoln at this time had two thriving theaters, the Lansing and the Funke, both large and well appointed. Together they could accommodate three thousand spectators, and when both were open sometimes one hundred traveling companies passed through Lincoln in one year. Often there were five or six plays a week, and one could see Julia Marlowe, Helena Modjeska, Margaret Mather, Richard Mansfield, Joseph Jefferson, and many others. Orchestras and touring opera companies also paid their periodic respects to the Nebraska capital. Bohemian farmers like Papa Shimerda may have been blowing their brains out in Webster County, but in Lancaster County there were people in top hats and tails eating oysters and sipping French champagne at their after-theater parties.

The University of Nebraska was about the same age as Lincoln. Its four buildings were laid out on four city blocks, neatly planted in grass and new trees surrounded by a high iron fence. The largest building was University Hall, an ornate red-brick structure with mansard roof and a square bell-tower. The library was housed in two crowded rooms on the second floor, and although a new library was begun in 1893, it was not finished during Willa Cather's undergraduate days. The student population was small (between three and four hundred students), but the university already had attracted a number of prominent scholars to its faculty and had begun giving graduate work in some disciplines. Willa Cather was trying for dramatic contrast, rather than accurate description, when she described the university through her narrator Jim Burden in *My Ántonia:* "Our instructors were oddly assorted; wandering pioneer school-teachers, stranded ministers of the Gospel, a few enthusiastic young men just out of graduate schools." Yet she is reporting accurately when Jim adds: "There was an atmosphere of endeavour, of expectancy and bright hopefulness about the young college that had lifted its head from the prairie only a few years before."

A rather impressive number of people of future distinction were there in Willa Cather's time. There was Roscoe Pound, later dean of Harvard Law School, and his sister Louise, afterwards a distinguished scholar and teacher; Dorothy Canfield, later Dorothy Canfield Fisher, Pulitzer Prize winning novelist; Alvin Johnson, who was to become head of the New School for Social Research; William Westermann, a future classicist and ancient historian of eminence; and Lieutenant John J. Pershing, then instructor in math and military science and afterwards commander-in-chief of the American Expeditionary Forces in the First World War.

The girl who left Red Cloud to begin the next great adventure must have been like Thea Kronborg in *The Song of the Lark*. It was herself and her own adventure that mattered. "If youth did not matter so much to itself, it would never have the heart to go on. Thea was surprised that she did not feel a deeper sense of loss at leaving her old life behind her." It seemed, on the contrary, as she looked at the cornfields flashing past the train window, "that she had left very little. Everything that was essential seemed to be right there in the car with her." Willa Cather had the same self-sufficiency, the same resolute determination to confront her destiny. She did not yet know what her destiny was, but there was no hanging back. Getting to college had not been easy, and the money problem that plagues Vickie Templeton also harried Willa Cather. Charles Cather was land poor, and his growing family, which now numbered six children, kept him perpetually hard pressed; but when he saw his daughter's great eagerness to get an education, he borrowed the money she needed.

The expense actually was modest, and the three hundred dollars that Mr. Rosen lends Vickie Templeton probably was enough to see a careful student through two years of college. One could get room and board for fifteen dollars a month, and the university fees consisted of a ten-dollar registration fee and a ten-dollar chemistry breakage fee. Books and incidental expenses would have been proportionately cheap. Once she got to Lincoln, Willa Cather did not have to skimp. She boarded at the best eating-place in town and was able to go to Omaha to the theater on occasion. She did have to tend her own stove in her rooming house, something she never had done before, but her later memories of her poverty-stricken college days seem a good bit exaggerated. At least they do not apply to her first two years. By the time depression hit Nebraska in 1893 she was a junior, working for the *Journal,* and largely self-supporting.

She roomed at the home of "Aunt Kate" Hastings, a friend of the family, and if Jim Burden's room at the university in *My Ántonia* is a literal description of her own quarters, she got two rooms for the price of one. Her bedroom, originally a linen closet, was unheated and just big enough for a cot, and her other room she fixed up as her study. "I worked at a commodious green-topped table placed directly in front of the west window which looked out over the prairie," Jim recalls. In the corner at her right she put her books on shelves she made and painted herself, and on the blank wall to the left she tacked up a large newly purchased map of Rome. Rome was the one place in all the world, she had written in a friend's album in 1888, that she most wanted to visit. Over the bookcase she hung a photograph of the Tragic Theater at Pompeii.

It is not surprising that Willa Cather's young alter ego should be Jim Burden, for she was still going through her phase of trying her best not to be a girl. She continued to wear her hair short during her first couple of years at the university and wore starched shirts instead of more frilly feminine shirtwaists. She continued to play male roles in dramatic productions and persisted in signing her name William Cather. This last went on, Louise Pound remembered, until her friends made her stop it. William Westermann recalled her first appearance in the elementary Greek course that he was enrolled in. While the students were sitting in the classroom waiting for the instructor to arrive, the door opened and a head appeared with short hair and straw hat. A masculine voice inquired if this were the beginning Greek class, and when someone said it was, the body attached to the head and hat opened the door wider and came in. The masculine head and voice were attached to a girl's body and skirts. The entire class laughed, but Willa Cather, apparently unperturbed, took her seat and joined the waiting students.

She was not yet a member of the freshman class, however. Despite the fact that the university was small, new and served a state full of the unassimilated foreign-born, its standards were high, and rather than admit those not sufficiently prepared, the university operated a two-year preparatory school in conjunction with its baccalaureate and graduate offerings. Red Cloud High School graduates did not meet all the admission requirements, and Willa Cather was put in the "second prep." This meant that she had to take an additional year of preparation before she could enter the university. Thus she had five years of education in Lincoln before her graduation in June 1895.

She threw herself into her work with characteristic energy and enthusiasm. There was nothing in her personality of the easygoing way of her southern family. While her parents liked to sit about in leisurely discussion, never in any rush to face daily problems, she attacked her assignments with a great deal of vigorous concentration. Professor Wunsch's feeling about Thea Kronborg certainly applies to Willa Cather: "It was his pupil's power of application, her rugged will, that interested him." Viola Roseboro', later her colleague on *McClure's Magazine,* told Edith Lewis: "If Willa Cather had been a scrubwoman, she would have scrubbed much harder than other scrub-women." No grades survive among the records of the University of Nebraska, but Miss Lewis reports that Willa Cather once stood first in her Latin class of fifty-three and used to get up at five o'clock to study. There is no doubt that faculty and classmates alike thought she was a brilliant student and predicted great things for her.

Willa Cather went to Lincoln planning to study science, but she soon switched to the humanities. In the summer of 1890 she wrote Mrs. Goudy that she was chiefly interested in astronomy, botany, and chemistry. The following summer back in Red Cloud she still was doing science in her spare time. She then wrote one of her new Lincoln friends, Mariel Gere, that· she was dividing her time among reading French history and George Eliot, taking endless rides on the prairie, and dissecting frogs to study their circulatory systems. When she matriculated as a freshman in 1891, she took both chemistry and math, but math proved to be a subject she could never learn, and she did not work off an incomplete in that course until just before she graduated. Her inability to do math may have deflected her from a scientific career even before her undergraduate literary triumphs revealed her real vocation. In retrospect one can see that she was a born writer, but until she had been in Lincoln more than a year she did not know it.

Perhaps the decisive event in changing her course occurred in March 1891, after her English teacher, Professor Ebenezer Hunt, assigned a theme on "The Personal Characteristics of Thomas Carlyle." Carlyle was one of the authors she already had read and pondered, and she rose to the assignment like a hungry trout after a mosquito. Professor Hunt must have been astonished when he read the theme. Any English teacher who has corrected the witless humor and the semiliterate prose of generations of students dreams of such a moment. The performance was a tour de force, and when Professor Hunt returned the papers he wrote on the board one of her rhetorical flights:

Like the lone survivor of some extinct species, the last of the mammoths, tortured and harassed beyond all endurance by the smaller, though perhaps more perfectly organized offspring of the world's maturer years, this great Titan, son of her passionate youth, a youth of volcanoes, and earthquakes, and great, unsystematized forces, rushed off into the desert to suffer alone.

On a Sunday morning soon afterwards Willa Cather opened the *Journal* and found her essay in print. Without her knowledge Professor Hunt had given the essay to the *Journal,* and somehow the undergraduate literary magazine, the *Hesperian,* also got a copy. Both had published it on the same day. Thirty-six years later the author remembered: "Up to that time I had planned to specialize in science; I thought I would like to study medicine. But what youthful vanity can be unaffected by the sight of itself in print! It has a kind of hypnotic effect. I still remember that essay, and it was a splendid example of the kind of writing I most dislike; very florid and full of high-flown figures of speech." She further recalled that it did not deal at all with the personal characteristics of Carlyle but poured out the fervent feelings she had had on reading *The French Revolution* and *Sartor Resartus.* Yet she had to admit that the essay was honest: "Florid as it was, it didn't over color the pleasure and delightful bitterness that Carlyle can arouse in a very young person. It makes one feel so grown up to be bitter!"

The mouth-filling period that Professor Hunt picked out to write on the board is perhaps the most baroque sentence in the entire essay. Although the whole composition is highly charged with the author's emotional response to Carlyle, there are many short, pithy sentences, plenty of vigorous declarative sentences. What is most interesting about the essay, however, is not the rhetoric but the image of young Willa Cather projected against the figure of Thomas Carlyle. Shot through the essay are sentences more revealing of the author than of the subject. The personal characteristics are those of Willa Cather, and most of them are characteristics that endured a lifetime.

Consider some of her observations: "He was a recluse, not that he had any aversion for men, but that he loved his books and loved Nature better." "His love and sympathy for humanity were boundless, and he understood great minds and earnest souls as no other man ever has. In this lay his power as a biographer and as a historian." "Carlyle posed but poorly as a political economist." "He went far out into one of the more desolate spots of Scotland, and made his home there. There among the wild heaths . . . he did his best work. He drew his strength from those wild landscapes." "Like Scott, he lived much in the open air." "The wife of an artist, if he continues to be an artist, must always be a secondary consideration with him." "He never strove to please a pampered public." "Nothing has so degraded modern literature as the desperate efforts of modern writers to captivate the public." "He was proud to the extreme, but his love was predominant over his pride." " . . . for his brother's sake he wrote for money. It seemed to him like selling his own soul. He wrote article after article for reviews, and cut up his great thoughts to fit the pages of a magazine. No wonder he hated it; it was like hacking his own flesh, bit by bit, to feed those he loved."

These quotations read like program notes for the life of Willa Cather: things she would be and do, things she was, things she would avoid. Written when she was seventeen, they show that her life-patterns were drawn early. Finally, there is the most important statement of all, one that posits a lifelong conviction and a lifelong action. It comes immediately after her declaration that an artist's wife (and she meant husband too) must play second fiddle to his career: "Art of every kind is an exacting master, more so even than Jehovah. He says only, 'Thou shalt have no other gods before me.' Art, science, and letters cry, 'Thou shalt have no other gods at all.' They accept only human sacrifices."

If publication of the Carlyle essay did not turn Willa Cather toward a writing career, she must have made her decision during the eight months that followed. The next November the *Journal* printed another essay, this time a long, two-part discussion, "Shakespeare and Hamlet." Again the essay is as much about the author and her dreams as it is about Shakespeare and his character. It ends with an inquiry into the nature of art and an analysis of what it takes to be an artist. Shakespeare as the supreme practitioner provides the springboard into this discussion. It is as though she had hitched her wagon to his star. The great secret of Shakespeare's power was the supreme love, rather than supreme intellect. Some writers are mere men of letters, presidents of literary clubs and editors of magazines, but the real writers are those who have suffered the agonies of creation, "the agony of the Doric women who bore the sons of the gods." And what must an artist do to be saved? The answer she casts in the form of Christ's answer to the rich young man. The mere man of letters, like the rich young man, will turn sorrowfully away. He will not give up the world to follow art. This essay, written in the fall of 1891, suggests that already Willa Cather's religion was to be art and that she was prepared to follow wherever it led her. On various occasions in the future she was to write of art in religious terms and nowhere more strikingly than in her comments on Shakespeare. After seeing Richard Mansfield in a great performance on Shakespeare's birthday in 1894, she wrote, " . . . one felt that he was worthy to act on that night . . . on which three hundred and thirty years ago . . . God a second time turned his face in love toward man."

By the time the Shakespeare essay appeared in print, she had plunged into a busy life of campus literary extracurricular activities. In October and November the first issues appeared of a new literary magazine, the *Lasso,* which carried on its masthead the names of Willa Cather and Louise Pound as associate editors. The *Lasso* was published only for one year, but editing it led to other enterprises, the chief of which was a position on the staff of another student literary magazine, the *Hesperian*, in her sophomore year. She was first an associate editor of the magazine and then managing editor during her junior year. Before her career as a campus journalist ended, she had served as literary editor of the 1894 *Sombrero*, the yearbook published by her class of '95.

During the two years that Willa Cather worked on the *Hesperian*, she began to write fiction. Her first tale was "Peter," the suicide story, which apparently she wrote during her freshman year. Her English teacher, Herbert Bates, was so impressed with it that he sent it off to a Boston magazine, *The Mahogany Tree*, which published it in May. She then reprinted the story in the *Hesperian* in November 1892. It is the tale of an old Bohemian musician who has emigrated to the Nebraska prairie with his wife and children. Because he is old and hardly able to play his beloved violin any longer, his practical farmer son wants to sell the instrument. The old man, defeated by the prairie and unable to part with his fiddle, cannot bear to go on living.

He took Antone's shotgun down from its peg, and loaded it by the moonlight which streamed in through the door. He sat down on the dirt floor, and leaned back against the dirt wall. He heard the wolves howling in the distance, and the night wind screaming as it swept over the snow. Near him he heard the regular breathing of the horses in the dark. He put his crucifix above his heart, and folding his hands said brokenly all the Latin he had ever known, *"Pater noster, qui in coelum est."* . . . He held his fiddle under his chin a moment, where it had lain so often, then put it across his knee and broke it through the middle. He pulled off his old boot, held the gun between his knees with the muzzle against his forehead, and pressed the trigger with his toe.

This is a piece of narrative that any college freshman could be proud of. She liked it well enough to rewrite it and republish it for a third time in Pittsburgh eight years later. This time she dropped the *thee*'s and *thou*'s that she had used to suggest the familiar *you* of the Czech language, sharpened the conflict between the artist father and his practical son, and expanded the beginning. The bulk of the tale remained the same, however, until she worked it

into a far more intricate design in the magical prose of *My Ántonia.*

The story not only is interesting as her first published piece of
narrative, but it also is significant thematically. The tale ends with
this paragraph:

In the morning Antone found him stiff, frozen fast in a pool of
blood. They could not straighten him out enough to fit a coffin, so
they buried him in a pine box. Before the funeral Antone carried
to town the fiddlebow which Peter had forgotten to break. Antone
was very thrifty, and a better man than his father had been.

Here at the start of her career is the hardheaded businessman
farmer, a preview of Nat Wheeler in *One of Ours* and Ivy Peters
in *A Lost Lady.* The story even foreshadows the conflict between
spirit and body that looms so large in *The Professor's House.* The
rewriting of the story in 1900, which built up the confrontation
between father and son, makes clear that Willa Cather even then
was consciously working what was to become one of her major
themes.

Before she reprinted "Peter" in November, she already had
used her second story, "Lou, the Prophet," in the *Hesperian* in
October. This tale, which is just as precocious as the first one, also
makes use of Nebraska material; and it too is a somber concoction
of death and despair in the wild land of the Divide. Lou is a
homesick young Dane who has been trying to scratch a living
from the reluctant prairie for seven years. He is rewarded for his
herculean efforts by drought and crop failure, and becomes at the
end a crazy religious fanatic who disappears when the police
come to get him.

His bill of fare never changed the year round; bread, coffee, beans
and sorghum molasses, sometimes a little salt pork. After breakfast
he worked until dinner time, ate, and then worked again. He
always went to bed soon after the sunset, for he was always tired,
and it saved oil. Sometimes, on Sundays, he would go over home
after he had done his washing and house cleaning, and sometimes
he hunted. His life was as sane and as uneventful as the life of his
plow horses, and it was as hard and thankless.

It is quite clear that the alchemy of time and distance has not yet mellowed Willa Cather's memory of Nebraska farm life. Yet one constantly comes up against a paradox in dealing with her feelings about the land. Her early stories of Nebraska life are all grim, even though her letters of the time suggest that the Divide attracted her and aroused feelings of love and nostalgia from the very beginning. During her first summer back from Lincoln she took endless rides over the prairie, and the spectacle of the harvest was a thing she always loved. Another summer when she was back in Red Cloud, she wrote the Gere sisters that she wanted them to come down from Lincoln to see the country while it was looking like a garden—green and beautiful beyond words, with cornfields like forests everywhere. The tone and content of "Lou, the Prophet" strike one much like the stories that Hamlin Garland was writing about this time. His bleak tales of farm life in the midwest, published as *Main-Travelled Roads,* had appeared just the year before this story. Perhaps Willa Cather thought the proper tone for a story of midwestern farm life was that of Garland or of E.W. Howe's *The Story of a Country Town.* Her complete lack of interest later in Garland, Howells, Dreiser, or any of the midwestern realists might well have been reaction against what she regarded as her own false start. She certainly wanted to forget her early stories and bitterly resented anyone's wanting to republish them.

Three more early stories appeared in the *Hesperian* during 1892 and 1893, but two of them, "A Tale of the White Pyramid" and "A Son of the Celestial," can be dismissed as experiments that led nowhere. The third, however, is even grimmer and more terrifying than "Peter" and "Lou, the Prophet." It is a grisly tale of man's inhumanity to man, in which a poor, simple-minded Russian farm worker is victimized by the society he has not asked to be part of. The character, Serge Povolitchky, is the bastard child of a Russian immigrant girl and a railroad contractor. As a farm worker on the ranch of a man with the good English name of Davis, Serge befriends a mongrel dog, the first thing in his life he ever has had a chance to love. The farmer in a fit of anger one day kills the dog, and Serge instantly reacts by splitting the farmer's head with an ax. In jail, Serge is too stupid to make barrel hoops and is punished by solitary confinement, tortured, and killed. "The Clemency of the Court" is the ironic title of this pathetic tale.

During her years as an undergraduate Willa Cather followed the curriculum of the "philosophical" program. This plan called for Latin, modern languages, and science, though electives were possible. Since she also was interested in Greek, she took courses in Greek poetry and drama that normally were taken by students following the "classical" program. After her first year, in which she took chemistry and math, she took no more science—only languages and literature, with the exception of one course in philosophy. By the time she graduated, she had taken eighteen semester courses of English, including two years of Shakespeare, and a good bit of Greek, Latin, French, and German. For the first two years of this curriculum she worked hard, but by her third year she was getting most of her education outside the classroom. She remembered that she did very little studying in her final years and passed her examinations largely on inspiration.

By the time she became a junior, she was no longer a docile student, and her impatience with the quality and nature of her instruction grew. Before she graduated, she quoted approvingly in her newspaper column a remark Beerbohm Tree had made in an address at Harvard. While he thought that a university education was of inestimable importance to chemists, engineers, tradesmen, and bookkeepers, Tree doubted its beneficial effect on artists. She had no sympathy with precise scholarship and said as early as her Shakespeare essay that the emotional plane of life is "infinitely higher than the intellectual." This level was not reached by "mastering the pages of a Latin grammar." Her own criticism is highly emotional and impressionistic, and she had no time for literary analysis or parsing sentences. In French, for example, she had read widely—perhaps more widely than her instructor—and had an excellent knowledge of literature, but she had to be threatened with failing her course before she could be made to learn the grammar.

The head of the English department, Lucius Sherman, became her special bête noire, for he specialized in a kind of extremely detailed literary analysis. He made exhaustive studies of sounds as expressions of emotions, and devised elaborate diagrams for the analysis of words. His *Elements of Literature* was about the dullest book Willa Cather ever had encountered, and she lost no occasion to satirize his methods of analysis. His *Analytics of Literature,* which often involved word counting of sentence lengths and word types in order to formulate universal laws of literary composition, she thought was absolutely arid pedantry. The scientific analysts, she wrote in the Shakespeare essay, never find life in what they analyze; " . . . they never feel the hot blood riot in the pulses, nor hear the great heartbeat. That is the one great joy which belongs exclusively to those of us who are unlearned, unlettered."

Professor Bates, however, was a vastly different sort, and he gave Willa Cather the kind of stimulation and encouragement that she needed. He had been trained at Harvard under Barrett Wendell and was a strong encourager of creative writing. He published poetry himself and became a good friend. He is responsible for at least part of the personality of Gaston Cleric in *My Ántonia:*

I have sometimes thought that his bursts of imaginative talk were fatal to his poetic gift. He squandered too much in the heat of personal communication. How often I have seen him draw his dark brows together, fix his eyes upon some object on the wall or a figure in the carpet, and then flash into the lamplight the very image that was in his brain. He could bring the drama of antique life before one out of the shadows—white figures against blue backgrounds.

It was his talk that she valued, as well as his knowledge. In the novel Jim Burden recalls vivid memories of the evenings he spent with Cleric, who could recite Dante, canto after canto, and sometimes stayed far into the night talking about Latin and English poetry and Italy.

Willa Cather was always highly selective in her friends. She chose the people she wanted and ignored the rest, but she never quite managed to be as independent as she liked to seem. Some of her classmates thought her very aloof and unsocial and remembered that she scared the boys away because of her mannish attire and unfeminine manner. After she went to Pittsburgh and was caught up there in a very active social life, she wrote back to Mariel Gere that there had been many times in Lincoln when she was lonely because she had not had very many friends. In college she was constantly trying to prove herself and had no time for the social amenities. Yet she did take part in dramatics, debating, and literary-society activities and eventually got over trying to be a man. Mrs. Gere persuaded her to let her hair grow, and in her graduation picture she looks quite like a typical belle of the era.

If her circle of friends seemed small, it was select, and those in it valued her and were devoted to her. In retrospect her friends seem to be the people most interesting and worth knowing, just as they had been in Red Cloud. Among them were the Pounds, the Westermanns, the Canfields, the Geres, Will Owen Jones, and Dr. Julius Tyndale. The Pounds, however, were early casualties, for she satirized Roscoe in her column in the *Hesperian* and alienated the entire family, a break that was not healed, if it ever was, for many years. The Westermanns, a cultivated German family that owned the *Evening News,* gave her the contact with European culture that she had had in Red Cloud in the Wieners' home. They lived in a big house on S Street, adjacent to the campus, the former residence of the chancellor, and Willa Cather went there often. The Erlichs in *One of Ours* were drawn from the Wester-manns, whose house is described in the novel: "They had not walked more than two blocks from the Armory when Julius [Er-lich] turned in at a rambling wooden house with an unfenced, terraced lawn. He led Claude [Wheeler] around to the wing, and through a glass door into a big room that was all windows on three sides, above the wainscoting. The room was full of boys and young men, seated on long divans or perched on the arms of easy-chairs, and they were all talking at once." There were in fact six Wester-mann boys, whose mother seemed to Claude "very young to be the head of such a family." Willa Cather became especially fond of Mrs. Westermann.

The Canfields were very important people at the university, as James Canfield was then chancellor. Dorothy, who was six years Willa Cather's junior, was still a schoolgirl during these years, but a precocious one, and she and Willa began a friendship that lasted a lifetime. They even collaborated on a football story that ap-peared in the *Sombrero,* a tale of no importance except that it was written by two girls who grew up to be Pulitzer Prize winning novelists. There was a good bit of hero-worship in the relationship between Dorothy and Willa, and this continued after Willa went to work in Pittsburgh and James Canfield moved his family to Columbus to become chancellor of Ohio State University.

The Geres, Will Owen Jones, and Dr. Tyndale were friends of Willa Cather's career in journalism. Charles Gere was editor and publisher of the *Journal* and her employer for the last three years she was in Lincoln. His daughters, Mariel, Ellen, and Frances, all were close friends. On the *Journal*'s sixtieth anniversary Willa Cather wrote a graceful reminiscence of Mr. Gere, whose patience with her early writing seemed to her monumental. "I was paid one dollar a column, which was certainly quite all my high-stepping rhetoric was worth. Those out-pourings were pretty dreadful, but . . . he let me step as high as I wished. It was rather hard on his readers, perhaps, but it was good for me, because it enabled me to riot in fine writing until I got to hate it, and began slowly to recover." She added that sometimes there would be a twinkle in his eye that made her distrustful of her rhetorical magnificence, but he never corrected her. Will Owen Jones was the young managing editor of the *Journal,* who also taught journalism at the university. Although she had met him before she was a junior, she took a course from him that year. Dr. Tyndale, an uncle of the Westermann boys, who had come to Lincoln to practice medicine in 1893, wrote drama criticism as a hobby. He had come from the East, knew quite a bit about the theater, and wrote cocky, humorous reviews. About the time Willa Cather began writing drama criticism, the *Courier* complained that the theater-reviewing in Lincoln, except for the columns of Dr. Tyndale in the *News,* was "a dreary waste of undiluted mediocrity." Willa Cather's friendship with this fifty-year-old single doctor, who was a rather gay blade, caused a lot of talk among the self-appointed guardians of public morals. But he was an important friend, the one who arranged for her to spend a week in Chicago seeing opera during the spring of her senior year, and there is a bit of him in the character of Dr. Englehardt in one of her late stories, "Double Birthday."

II

In the fall of 1893 Willa Cather's career moved into a new phase. The rapid industrial development of Nebraska, which had begun in the latter eighties, was arrested by a succession of crop failures and a depression that spread over the entire country. Charles Cather, who owned a large amount of heavily mortgaged land in Webster County, was hard pressed to meet his obligations, and the farmers to whom he had loaned money were equally unable to keep up mortgage payments. Roscoe Cather, who was only sixteen, began teaching country school to help out at home, and Willa had to begin making her own living. When the chance came to make a dollar a column writing for the *Journal,* she diverted her abundant energies from college work to filling the pages of the newspaper. During the next two and one half years her output was prodigious—more than three hundred separate pieces (columns and reviews), many of them running to essay length. For all practical purposes she went professional during the first semester of her junior year. She was a long way from becoming a novelist, but the distance she already had traveled from Red Cloud High School in three years was remarkable.

Her first column, "One Way of Putting It" appeared in the *Journal* on November 5, 1893, and during that fall her hand may be seen in some of the drama reviews. She still was managing editor of the *Hesperian,* and until she got out a special Charter Day issue in February 1894, she could not do much reviewing for the paper. Her first signed drama review appeared in December, but from the second semester on she was the *Journal's* regular drama critic and Sunday columnist. Her column, later given the permanent name of "The Passing Show," was a regular feature until 1900, long after she had moved to Pittsburgh. It began with unexceptional human interest material: a visit to a prison chapel, an account of a Salvation Army tent meeting, impressions of a political rally. There are several sketches that are embryonic stories, several Theophrastean "characters," and one interesting vignette of a businessman with a manuscript novel in his desk that foreshadows the narrative device of *My Ántonia.* Later her column concerned itself with the arts: books, literature, music, and theatrical matters not dealt with in her reviews.

As drama critic she quickly made a name for herself. Her reviews were bright, lively, hard-hitting, and she was the chief reason the Des Moines *Record* said in June 1895: "The best theatrical critics of the west are said to be connected with the Lincoln, Neb., press." Gustave Frohman, who visited the city a little before, declared: "Lincoln papers are noted for their honesty and candor in dramatic matters . . . and poor companies begin to tremble long before they get here." Will Owen Jones in 1921 recalled that she wrote dramatic criticism of "such biting frankness that she became famous among actors from coast to coast. . . . Many an actor of national reputation wondered on coming to Lincoln what would appear the next morning from the pen of that meatax young girl of whom all of them had heard."

This memory is not much of an exaggeration, for Willa Cather did not pull her punches. She expected writers, singers, actors, to give their all to their art, and she had meant it when she had written that the god of art accepts only human sacrifices. During her first year of full-time reviewing she wrote that an artist's "only safe course is to cling close to the skirts of his art, forsaking all others." When Mlle. Celeste appeared in *The Count of Monte Cristo* in Lincoln in January 1894, she wrote: "Mademoiselle Celeste is a dream of beauty. There are few handsomer women to be found in either the higher or lower walks of the profession, but her acting is weak, insipid and pointless. She is innocent of all art or even of a clever imitation of it, and her voice was a continual and painful surprise." During the following drama season she wrote of Miss Effie Ellsler in *Doris:* "Miss Ellsler is a well meaning little woman with an impossible little nose, an irritating placidity of manner and a shrill domestic little stage shriek that is suggestive of mice. She delivered the most histrionic lines with correct elocution and unalterable calm, just as though she were ordering clam chowder and baked whitefish." On the other hand she praised good performances when she saw them: Alexander Salvini in *The Three Guardsmen*, Richard Mansfield in Clyde Fitch's *Beau Brummell*, Nat Goodwin in *A Gilded Fool.* She kept a box score so that she could refute the complainers who thought she never liked anything, and in November 1894 she reported that so far that season she had praised fourteen companies and damned fifteen.

The following February she was saluted in the *Nebraskan*, a student paper that rivaled the *Hesperian*:

> *This is for 'Billy' of journalist fame,*
> *Who writes her roasts in words of flame*
> *And gives it to everyone just the same.*

The lines were accompanied by a sketch of a smoking pen.

Her reviews, however, were not chiefly concerned with value judgments. She was interested in the whole world of art and ranged widely in her notices. Her work showed a maturity and poise not to be expected in so young a critic, and her knowledge of drama and literature, continental and classic as well as English, was extensive. Thus her reviews were informed and informative and demonstrated a competence that lent authority to the value judgments. She inclined to be impressionistic and to make frequent use of biographical anecdotes; she was interested in her own responses and very confident of her ability to evaluate. Some of her notions of the reviewer she summarized a year after she had begun reviewing: "A critic's first instincts are the best because they are the truest. . . . He must take his impression as he gets it and rush it upon paper. . . . That is the great object . . . to have the flare of the footlights and the echo of the orchestra in it . . . to reproduce to some extent the atmosphere of the play." This she did well, and when she stuck to plays she was convincing. On occasion her brashness got her into trouble, as when she reviewed a Mendelssohn concert that she found tiresome, monotonous, and disappointing, and concluded that "the day is past when he was called a great artist."

Her skill as a newspaper writer matured so rapidly that she was invited to help teach a course in journalism during the summer of 1894. For the annual Nebraska Chautauqua Assembly in July Will Jones organized a class in practical journalism with Willa Cather as one of his instructors. The assembly took place just west of Crete, where the Chautauqua grounds occupied 109 acres along the Big Blue River. Thousands of people came every year to participate in these sessions of popular culture and entertainment. Willa Cather, already a well-known journalist in Lincoln, also was engaged to report the events for the *Evening News*. She covered the eleven-day sessions in nine well-written, informative, lighthearted reports. One of the visiting experts on French, Dutch, and German painting, with stereopticon views, was the sculptor Loredo Taft of the Chicago Art Institute. She reported his talks enthusiastically, and thirty-six years later wrote him a fan letter in appreciation of his fountain that she enjoyed every time she passed through Chicago.

Another significant event that summer was a visit with her brother Roscoe and Mariel Gere to the decaying river community of Brownville, about the only town in Nebraska that had a past. Forty years before, the town had been founded on the Missouri River, the first settlement in the Nebraska Territory; but the river silted up, the Union Pacific was routed through Omaha, and the founding fathers built a brand-new town for the state capital. When Willa Cather visited Brownville, the main street was lined with empty brick buildings and gaping cellar holes where the buildings had fallen down, and the pavement and gutters were overgrown with grass. This trip to Brownville resulted in her first long feature article, which the *Journal* published in August; an early story of her apprentice period, "A Resurrection"; and a second feature article written later in Pittsburgh, "The Hottest Day I Ever Spent." Her first account of Brownville emphasized the decay and blasted hopes of its pioneers; the reworking created Japanese and Swedish companions to accompany the narrator into the fiery inferno of a record-breaking Nebraska heat wave.

Her last year at the university was a steady grind of newspaper work and little extracurricular student activity. Carrying a full course load and reviewing all the theatrical events for the *Journal* really was two jobs. She spent the day in classes, then went to the theater at night. After the show she had to go to the *Journal* office to write her review, and frequently she did not get home until two in the morning. When she went back to Red Cloud after graduation, she wrote Mrs. Goudy that she was dead tired, body and brain. It may have been on one of these late nights at the *Journal* office that she met Stephen Crane, who had come to Nebraska for the Bacheller Syndicate to report drought conditions. After two summers of burning winds and withered crops parts of the state were a disaster area, and by the winter of 1894–1895 death and famine ravaged the land. Crane arrived early in February and stayed two weeks writing his report. The blizzard that takes place in "The Blue Hotel" occurred while he was there.

More than five years later when Willa Cather wrote about her meeting with Crane, she placed it in the late spring when a hot wind was blowing up from Kansas. The rest of her account seems equally untrustworthy, either as Cather autobiography or as Crane biography. Since she wrote the article under a pseudonym and published it immediately after Crane died, it may not have been intended to be true. At any rate, she never revived the account—even when she put together a group of literary encounters in *Not Under Forty* (1936). In the article she creates a callow college boy who wants to know about writing. Crane appears as a prototypal romantic writer, thin to emaciation, gaunt and unshaven, and talks about life and literature. He curses his trade, tells his interviewer he will be fortunate if he does not become a writer, and goes about tense, brooding, preoccupied. There is not a word about his reportorial assignment in Nebraska to cover the economic and social consequences of the drought. "He had the precocity of those doomed to die in youth," Willa Cather concludes, and one imagines that if she had written an imaginary interview with another doomed young genius whom she admired—John Keats—the tone of the essay might have been similar.

The most interesting detail in the article, whether or not it came from Crane, is pure Willa Cather: "After he got a notion for a story, months passed before he could get any sort of personal contact with it, or feel any potency to handle it. 'The detail of a thing has to filter through my blood, and then it comes out like a native product, but it takes forever.'" This remark, she added, "rather took a hold of me," and well it might have, for it was precisely the sort of creative process that she would employ. There is no suggestion in this essay of 1900 that she had reviewed *War Is Kind* and *On Active Service* the year before and found the former an insult to the public and the latter "coarse and dull and charmless." Later she did write a good essay on Crane when she introduced *Wounds in the Rain* in the Knopf edition of his works in 1926.

Her account of William Jennings Bryan, also written at the same time, sounds more authentic. She met Bryan on a streetcar in Lincoln when she was a "second prep" and he was stumping the first congressional district in his first campaign for public office. He had just made a speech and was carrying an ugly floral tribute. A talkative old lady sitting near him inquired sympathetically:

"Is it for a funeral?"

Mr. Bryan looked quizzically at his encumbrance and replied politely:

"Well, I hope not, madam."

After this encounter Willa Cather saw him occasionally, for he was always at home to students in his library in the evenings. She must have been in his library a number of times, for she describes it in detail. It fascinated her because it was so different—except for the classics—from any library she would have collected: lives of American statesmen, marked and annotated schoolboy fashion; works on political economy, mostly by quacks; much poetry of a didactic or declamatory nature; little fiction more recent than Thackeray. Bryan urged everyone to read *Les Misérables*, advice she agreed with, but he was interested in Hugo the practical politician and orator, not Hugo the novelist. When he was in good form, his conversation, she remembered, was "absolutely overwhelming in its richness and novelty and power, in the force and aptness of his illustrations." She also heard him speak in Nebraska, but probably was not present, though her essay says she was, when he delivered his "Cross of Gold" speech and stampeded the Democratic convention in Chicago in July 1896.

For Willa Cather, Bryan synthesized "the entire middle West; all its newness and vigor, its magnitude and monotony, its richness and lack of variety, its inflammability and volubility, its strength and its crudeness, its high seriousness and self-confidence, its egotism and its nobility." He never made a Democrat out of her and never even succeeded in interesting her in the political process. The campaign of 1896, however, did provide her with some fictional material for "Two Friends," but Bryan is the only political figure she ever wrote an essay about. Like Carlyle, whom she characterized as a bad political economist, she was equally inept and completely indifferent to politics. It was only the kingdom of art that she cared for.

Willa Cather's college career ended when she graduated in June 1895. She wanted a literary career, but she had to make a living. The problem of the artist in a hostile, materialistic world was very much on her mind when she took part in a literary-society program in the chapel during commencement week. Her anxieties and preoccupations are clearly revealed in the paper she read on Poe, who symbolized for her unrewarded and unappreciated genius. After summarizing Poe's great accomplishment and flinging derogatory comments at Longfellow's popularity and the littleness of Poe's New York associates like Rufus Griswold and N. P. Willis, she addressed herself to the real problem.

I have wondered so often how he did it. How he kept his purpose always clean and his taste always perfect. How it was that hard labor never wearied nor jaded him, never limited his imagination, that the jarring clamor about him never drowned the fine harmonies of his fancy. His discrimination remained always delicate, and from the constant strain of toil his fancy always rose strong and unfettered.

This was the real question for an aspiring writer who had to hack out a living in journalism. Could one serve the gods of art and mammon without being corrupted? She intended to try, but she knew it would not be easy. It is for this reason, no doubt, that she always made a clear distinction between her journalism and her art.

The year following her graduation was a time of frustration but not of idleness. The conventional picture of Willa Cather languishing in Red Cloud is not correct, though she did not have a real job and was doubtless eager to move on to a larger field of action. But she was neither a Hawthorne dying of boredom in Salem nor a Leopardi yearning to escape from Recanati. At the beginning of August the *Courier,* a weekly paper devoted to news of the arts and society, announced that "Miss Willa Cather who for the past two years has been the dramatic critic and theatrical writer for the *Journal,* will become a member of the *Courier* staff. Miss Cather's reputation extends beyond Nebraska. She is thoroughly original and always entertaining." Subsequently her name began appearing on the masthead as associate editor and remained there until

71

the end of November. Her column, "The Passing Show," moved from the *Journal* to the *Courier*, but she continued to review plays for the *Journal*. Then in December the *Journal* announced that beginning on the fifteenth her column would appear regularly in its Sunday issue. It appeared there until she left for Pittsburgh the next summer, but even after she left Nebraska, she continued to send back columns to both the *Journal* and the *Courier* during most of the time she was working on newspapers and magazines in Pittsburgh.

The picture of Willa Cather that emerges from this year is one of continuous journalistic activity. She lived in Lincoln during the fall and made a couple of trips back to Red Cloud, and she lived in Red Cloud after the first of January but was back in Lincoln for substantial periods in January, February, March, and June, and may have been there for brief visits in April and May. Whenever she was in town, she reviewed plays. Red Cloud was less than 150 miles away, easily accessible by rail, and her newspaper employers could supply passes whenever she needed them. There is no doubt that she was a star and a valuable property for whatever newspaper employed her. The *Nebraska Editor* described her in the fall of 1895 as a "young woman with a genius for literary expression," whose work on the *Courier* had made it one of the brightest papers in the state. "If there is a woman in Nebraska newspaper work who is destined to win a reputation for herself, that woman is Willa Cather." That others recognized her competence is shown by the invitation she received to deliver a short paper at a meeting of the Nebraska State Press Association in January on the topic "How to Make a Newspaper Interesting." This was a subject she knew something about, as her column was the liveliest thing in town; and when the Beatrice *Weekly Express* covered the meeting of the press association, it spoke of Miss Cather as "a young woman who is rapidly achieving a western reputation, and who will soon have a national reputation." What seems surprising in retrospect is that the *Journal*, which advertised her column as one of its valued features, did not have the wit to make her an associate editor and thereby insure her full-time services.

During her stay at home early in the year she realized that she did not want to live in Red Cloud, even if she could have made her living there as a fiction writer. In 1905 she could write that Red Cloud was the only place she wanted to live and that soon she hoped to get back for a year, but in January 1896 she dated a letter from there as "Siberia," partly from the bitterness of the weather and partly from a sense of exile. She had just been to a dance of the elite and bon ton of Red Cloud with her brother Douglass as escort. The boys were rowdy, seats were planks laid on chairs, and the sandwiches were served from a bushel basket. The next month she was back in Lincoln attending the fancy dress Patriarchs' Ball and masquerading as Folly. In March she was again at home writing Mariel Gere, asking for news of Lincoln and complaining of boredom. It was Lent in Red Cloud, and the mad festivities of the provinces had ceased. She was acting as nurse-maid while her parents were off in Hastings, and was having a busy time of it. Jack, four years old, had swallowed two pennies, and Jim had cut his lip. She had read *Alice in Wonderland* to Jim sixteen times and was sick of it.

At this juncture she tried to get a teaching job at the university. Her friend Herbert Bates had resigned at the end of the fall semester, and there was a vacancy. She wrote Charles Gere on March fourteenth, asking for his help in getting her an instructor-ship, but she might have known that her feud with Lucius Sher-man, the chairman of the English department, would have scuttled her chances. Bates recommended her without qualifica-tion, but there are few instances on record of resigning faculty members choosing their successors. She continued her columns for the *Journal*, but they were not enough.

The bright spot of this period was her first appearance in the pages of a nationally circulated magazine. The January number of the *Overland Monthly* had carried "On the Divide," a grim story reminiscent of those she previously had published in the *Hes-perian*. The story opens: "Near Rattlesnake Creek, on the side of a little draw, stood Canute's shanty. North, east, south, stretched the level Nebraska plain of long rust-red grass that undulated con-stantly in the wind." It was still many years before she was to change the "rust-red grass" to grass "the colour of wine-stains." She still was writing more in the *Main-Travelled Roads* manner than in the evocative fashion suggestive of myth and Homer's wine-dark sea. Yet the tale begins to have subtleties not present in the first stories of her apprenticeship. Canute is a huge, hulking, lonely Norwegian farmer who drinks himself into insensibility every night to forget his awful loneliness. But he has a soul, and his agonies of the spirit are carved crudely on the wide windowsills of his shanty. His clumsy carvings were "a veritable dance of death by one who had felt its sting." The plot of the story, however, is not so interesting as the description of Canute and his surroundings, and it deals with Canute's cave-man courtship of Lena Yansen. Lena, it should be noted, is the first of several characters by that name who culminate in Lena Lingard of *My Ántonia*. The story is much below Willa Cather's mature work; it is what she would have called one of the unsound apples that a grower, careful of his reputation, leaves on the ground. One is not surprised that the tale appealed to the *Overland Monthly*, which was about to begin printing Jack London. Canute Canuteson and Wolf Larsen have a good bit in common.

Willa Cather's great break came sometime late in the spring, when she was offered a job on a magazine in Pittsburgh. Axtell, Orr, and Company, publishers of the *Home Monthly*, needed an editor, and Willa Cather jumped at the chance. How a Pittsburgh publisher happened to hire a girl just out of the University of Nebraska to edit his magazine perhaps never will be known. There are a few clues, but no facts. George Gerwig, a Lincoln insurance man with an M.A. in English, had moved to Allegheny, Pennsylvania (now part of Pittsburgh), in 1892. He had written drama criticism for the *Journal* before Willa Cather and was one of her early friends. He visited Lincoln in late March 1896, when she was unsuccessfully trying to get a teaching position. It is a reasonable guess that he knew of the opening and recommended her for the job. Edith Lewis remembers that Charles Axtell, one of the publishers, was a friend of Charles Gere, who certainly would have supported her for the position if he had been asked. Regardless of how she got the job, she was ready to move on to greater things and left Red Cloud for Pittsburgh shortly before June twenty-sixth to begin the next phase of her career.

CHAPTER 3

Pittsburgh: 1896–1906

I

THE GIRL who left Nebraska in June 1896 to seek her fortune in the East was just twenty-two, a sturdily built young woman about five feet, three inches tall, with a clear, rosy, dimpled complexion, reddish-brown hair, and gray-blue eyes that looked at one straight. She wanted to leave home but was apprehensive about what lay ahead. She stopped briefly in Chicago, visited the Doré exhibit at the Art Institute, and continued on to Pittsburgh. As the train rolled across Indiana and the land began to be hilly, as she crossed clear streams and passed groves of trees planted by nature rather than man, her excitement mounted. The conductor, noticing her gleeful absorption in the landscape, wanted to know if she were getting back home.

In Pittsburgh she was met by her new boss, Charles Axtell, whom she at first rebuffed because he did not look like the publisher of a magazine. When he took her home to stay with his family until she found a place to live, she was charmed by the hilly residential streets and the ivy-covered homes that contrasted sharply with the still-tentative appearance of man-made structures in Nebraska. As soon as she entered the Axtells' house, however, she found herself in the bosom of rock-ribbed, conservative Presbyterian Pittsburgh. The grim hair-cloth furniture of the parlor was under the surveillance of a single picture, the crayon portrait of grandpa, the sternest Presbyterian of them all. Fortunately grandpa was not home, for she feared, she wrote Mariel Gere, that the auger-eyed ancestor would have penetrated her thin disguise, as the old sage did Lamia's, and would have denounced her as the devotee of French fiction and the consort of musicians and strolling players.

75

The conservative, Calvinist tone of the Pittsburghers, half of whom were Presbyterian, bothered her no little at first. Her early letters from Pittsburgh and columns sent back to the *Journal* are full of impatient astonishment and irony. The Axtells were very nice to her, but their personalities were as chilly as a wine cellar, the result of believing in infant damnation, she guessed. Their social life all centered on the church, and whenever they gave a party they invited their Sunday-school classes. To avoid getting involved in Presbyterianism, she told the Axtells that she had been raised a Baptist, but unfortunately the Baptist minister lived next door and they called him over ten minutes later. When she told her hosts how many hours of course work she had carried at the University of Nebraska, they wanted to know how she possibly could have done so much while writing for the newspapers and keeping up her church work. Later in her correspondence with the *Journal* she reported satirically on the rumpus raised in Pittsburgh when Anna Held sang "O, Won't You Come and Play with Me" at a supper party given at the Duquesne Club by Henry Clay Frick, a prominent Presbyterian; and she made merry over the efforts of the Pittsburgh clergy to suppress Frederick Archer's free Sunday organ recitals at Carnegie Hall.

Willa Cather, however, was no bohemian, and when her jibes at the church influence in Pittsburgh brought suggestions from Mariel Gere that she was going bohemian, she replied indignantly. She could surprise friends and pain enemies by living conventionally, and she intended to do it. She presently moved into a boardinghouse in the east end of the city, and by the middle of July was putting in long hours mastering her new job. But her job was only a means to an end, which was to become a writer. There is no god but one god, and art is his revealer, she wrote Mariel Gere. That was her creed and she was going to follow it to a hotter place than Pittsburgh, if need be. She did not then think that she ever would accomplish very much herself as a creator, but she could worship art and get as much good out of that as most people did out of their religions.

The *Home Monthly* was not much of a magazine. It had been established two years before as the *Ladies' Journal,* an obvious imitation of C.H.K. Curtis's Philadelphia gold mine, the *Ladies' Home Journal.* Willa Cather joined the staff when Axtell, Orr, and

Company bought the magazine and changed its name to the *Home Monthly*. It aimed at the half million firesides within a hundred miles of Pittsburgh, so an editorial in the August issue proclaimed, and its pages would be "pure and clean in tone." Willa Cather went into the venture with her eyes open, for it offered her a toehold in the larger world; but she reported that the magazine was going to be mostly home and fireside stuff about babies and mince pies. The financial outlook, however, was good, and she could stand writing about the care of children's teeth for a while.

Although she was supposed to be assistant editor to Mr. Axtell, her boss took his family off for a vacation soon after she arrived, and she had to put out the August issue, the first under the magazine's new name, all by herself. She also wrote half of the first number because there was an insufficient backlog of manuscripts, and she had to supervise the press work because the printing foreman was inexperienced with magazine publishing. Her experience as managing editor of the *Hesperian* came in handy, and she actually spent half of one night in the composing room helping make up the page forms. In addition to writing half of the first issue and helping the printer, she had to read and buy manuscripts for future issues and handle the correspondence. Fortunately she had a stenographer who knew how to spell (she always was a poor speller), but she was so busy during the first month that her chief recreation was racing the electric cars on her bicycle as she pedaled to and from the office. But she liked the challenge of the job, even though it was a grind, and she enjoyed being in charge of something and of use in the world. And even in the first month it brought her some of the opportunities she most had wanted, meetings with several New York drama critics and a forty-six-minute talk with Rudyard Kipling, one of the contemporary writers she admired most.

After a month in Pittsburgh her social life underwent a great transformation. Her Lincoln classmates who had regarded her as antisocial and "stuck-up" would have been astonished at the change. She was too. She wrote Mariel Gere in a rather amazed tone about all the picnics, boat rides, and excursions she had been invited to and added that she already belonged to the "swell" women's club of the city. When she wrote on August tenth, she had been on a picnic with the Press Club up to Erie the previous week, on an excursion to Rock Point up in the mountains on Sunday, and most recently on a steam-launch party thirty miles up the river and back, complete with catered dinner and Negro musicians strumming on banjos in the moonlight.

Her social debut in Pittsburgh was an extraordinary event. Mrs. Gerwig had taken her to a high tea given for the federated women's clubs of the city. The exercises of the day were devoted to Carlyle, and when Willa Cather, newcomer to the city, was called on politely to say something about Carlyle, she got up and rattled off the Carlyle essay that she had written as a "second prep." She gave it, she reported, with the fire and fervor of the tragic muse, and as she soared, it all came back to her. The assembled clubwomen were stunned. They fell all over her afterwards, and she wrote Mariel Gere that women had been calling on her ever since until she was almost distracted. Thus launched, she kept busy with women's activities during her early Pittsburgh years, though she did not let those affairs keep her from writing. It is ironic to compare her club activities in this period with the frequent disparaging comments she made, both in this period and later, about the futility of women's clubs and the efforts of their members to acquire quick and painless culture.

The city of Pittsburgh that Willa Cather was to live in for the next ten years was then as now the metropolis of western Pennsylvania. Built where the Allegheny and Monongahela rivers join to form the Ohio, the city always had occupied a strategic position, from colonial times when the French built Fort Duquesne there to the era of rapid industrial growth after the Civil War. Close to sources of coal and possessing excellent water and rail communications, it became a major manufacturing center by the end of the century. When Willa Cather arrived, it was already the great steel-producing center and a city of about 300,000 people. Across the river was the independent city of Allegheny, where she later would be a high-school English teacher. The business of Pittsburgh was business, and the city was dominated by its great men, like Frick, Carnegie, Mellon, and Westinghouse. A fair representative of the Pittsburgh business community, as seen by Willa Cather, is a character named Marshall McKann in her story "A

Gold Slipper." McKann, a coal baron, describes himself as "a hard-headed business man." He is dragged to a concert by his culture-conscious wife, but he has no interest or knowledge whatsoever of art or music and regards artists as "fluffy-ruffles people."

Yet the wealth amassed in Pittsburgh by the Mellons and the Carnegies already was being used to make the city a center of culture. As the robber barons disgorged their riches and Carnegie practiced what he was preaching in "The Gospel of Wealth," Pittsburgh, like other cities, began acquiring concert halls and libraries. The Carnegie Library and Music Hall, which also contained an art gallery, had opened just a year before Willa Cather arrived, and the Pittsburgh Symphony was established a few months previous to her coming. For Willa Cather these were cultural resources much vaster than she had known in Lincoln, and she took immediate advantage of them. Her feeling was certainly like that of the title character in "Paul's Case," whose spirits were released by the first strains of the symphony orchestra when he ushered at Carnegie Hall: "He felt a sudden zest of life; the lights danced before his eyes and the concert hall blazed into unimaginable splendour." Pittsburgh also was more splendidly endowed with theaters than Lincoln had been, and she was able to see more plays, even though the quality of the performances probably was no better. She did not wait long after beginning her work on the *Home Monthly* before obtaining a job as part-time drama critic for the Pittsburgh *Leader* and involving herself in the theatrical life of the city.

Willa Cather had prepared herself well for the Pittsburgh years. She arrived in Pennsylvania with a well-stocked mind, an extraordinary acquaintance with books classical and modern, and a lively literary style. Though not yet master of her creative imagination, her progress during this period was steady and unrelenting. At the age of twenty-two her literary idols were Stevenson, Kipling, Dumas *père*, Thackeray as author of *Henry Esmond*, Flaubert as historical romancer in *Salammbô*, Daudet, and Victor Hugo. Her poets, besides the godlike Shakespeare, were Byron, Keats, Browning, de Musset, and other French romantics. Two years before, she had added to her literary enthusiasms Du Maurier's *Trilby* and Anthony Hope Hawkins's *The Prisoner of Zenda*. She never lost her taste for romance, and demanded a passionate response to life in the books she admitted to her list of favorites. Later she was to demand that fictional life have splendor, an attitude closely linked to her early passion for romance.

At the same time, however, she differentiated sharply between what she regarded as romance that was true and pulp fiction for chambermaids. There was a world of difference between *The Count of Monte Cristo, Treasure Island,* and *Les Misérables* and the cheap productions of Marie Corelli or Ouida, and she never could heap enough scorn on the latter. She demanded fidelity to nature in her literature, though what she meant by this was anything but the definition subsumed in the term "realism," particularly as it was used in the nineties.

In fact, the term "realism" at this juncture provoked a kind of instinctive negative reaction. Her disparagement of William Dean Howells, the high priest of realism in the nineties, illustrates well her critical position. His name appears frequently in her writings, never very favorably, though sometimes she grudgingly admits his importance and limited abilities. *The Rise of Silas Lapham* she thought a very dull novel, and while Howells could create real people, his characters were always "very common little men in sack coats." She must have been thinking of Howells when she wrote that the fault of most American writers is one of magnitude: "They are not large enough; they travel in small orbits; they play on muted strings. They sing neither of the combats of Atridae nor the labors of Cadmus, but of the tea-table and the Odyssey of the Rialto." Yet the literary tastes of Howells and Willa Cather were really not irreconcilable, and they shared many literary enthusiasms in common. They could agree on the greatness of Jane Austen, George Eliot, Tolstoy, Turgenev, Henry James, Flaubert, Frank Norris, and a good many others, and they both deplored the vogue of historical romance in the nineties that produced books like *When Knighthood Was in Flower.* Howells was simply one of her blind spots, and she never overcame what seems to have been simple prejudice and a clash in temperament.

A good insight into Willa Cather's mind at the time she went to Pittsburgh may be seen in her last long article written in Lincoln. This is an essay on Ruskin, in which she goes beyond her early worship of Carlyle. She does not renounce her allegiance to Carlyle's shaggy, untamed yea-saying, but she bends her knee to Ruskin for his style and love of beauty. He is, she wrote, the author of "some twelve or fifteen volumes of the most perfect prose of our generation." Outstripping his master Carlyle, he has "taken the wild and stirring strains of the peasant philosopher and set them to delicious harmony" and over the "rugged wisdom of the sage he has diffused the effulgent glory of a poet." He is perhaps "the last of the great worshippers of beauty, perhaps the last man for many years to come who will ever kneel at the altar of Artemis, who will ever hear the oracle of Apollo." He is, finally, perhaps "the last head on which the failing light of the Renaissance has lingered." His creed is, to express it roughly, that "beauty alone is truth and truth is only beauty; that art is supreme; that it is the highest, the only expression of whatever divinity there may be in man."

There is an interesting elegiac note in this essay, especially when she quotes Ruskin's denunciation of nineteenth-century technology: " . . . there is not a quiet valley left in England which you have not filled with bellowing fire; there is no particle of English earth into which you have not trampled coal dust." Willa Cather in Pittsburgh saw the bellowing fires of the Homestead steel plant and the trampled coal dust everywhere in the grimy, commercial city that she once referred to as "the city of dreadful dirt." This interest in Ruskin, this love of good historical romance, this harking back to a nobler, better past, all exist early in her career and become the significant notes and the great strengths of her later fiction.

Her busy social life and extracurricular drama reviewing did not keep her from writing fiction during her early months in Pittsburgh. Seven of her stories appeared in the *Home Monthly* during the year that she worked on the magazine, and another came out in the next issue after she had returned to Red Cloud for the summer. In addition to writing stories and editing the magazine, she also was filling it with editorials and nonfiction features, and sending her column back to Lincoln for the *Journal.* One can only marvel at the vast energy she expended during this year.

Some of the stories she wrote are obviously trivial efforts designed to fill space, and need not detain us. Two of them are fairy tales, "The Princess Baladina—Her Adventure" and "The Strategy of the Were-Wolf Dog," the sort of thing that Willa Cather previously had invented to entertain her younger brothers and sisters. Another is the Brownville story, "A Resurrection," and a fourth is the "Prodigies," a tale of exploited child-singers that reflects for the first time her growing absorption in the world of music and opera. "Nanette: An Aside" is her first treatment of an opera singer, and "The Burglar's Christmas" is a feeble version of the prodigal-son story laid in Chicago.

Two of these stories, however, "The Count of Crow's Nest" and "Tommy, the Unsentimental," are significant in Willa Cather's development as a fiction writer. The former is a two-part serial, the longest story she yet had done. She showed it to a member of the *Cosmopolitan* staff, who wanted to buy it for his magazine and offered one hundred dollars; but she had to say no because she needed it for her own magazine. This offer, nonetheless, raised the glittering prospect of being able to sell her stories to New York magazines, and this indeed was strong encouragement. The story, which is laid in a Chicago boardinghouse, makes use of her experiences as a music and drama critic and shows an advance in her command of narrative technique. The tale is told from the point of view of a minor character, one of the inmates of the boardinghouse, who becomes the friend and confidant of an impoverished old European, Count de Koch. The Count, who is spending his old age exiled to darkest Chicago, possesses letters the publication of which would blast the reputations of some very important people. The plot concerns the struggle for possession of the letters by the Count's no-good daughter, a third-rate singer. One suspects that Willa Cather already was studying Henry James's technique, for the point of view adopted is Jamesian and the story reminds one slightly of *The Aspern Papers.*

The second story, "Tommy, the Unsentimental," is a Nebraska story that has in it elements of autobiography. It concerns Tommy, whose real name is Theodosia, tomboy daughter of a widower banker in Southdown (Red Cloud). Tommy assists her father and minds the bank when he is away on business. She is an unusual girl, like Willa Cather, whose head is screwed on tight. Her best friends are her father's business friends, and she knows almost no women. There are, in fact, few women in Southdown who are in any sense "interesting, or interested in anything but babies and salads." She plays whist and billiards with men and makes their cocktails for them, "not scorning to take one herself occasionally." The plot concerns Tommy's twenty-five-mile dash by bicycle to stop a run on a bank managed by her boy friend, the ineffectual Jay Ellington Harper. She accomplishes her mission and at the same time unsentimentally turns the young man over to her city friend Jessica, a girl who *is* interested in babies and salads.

The story is well told, perhaps the best story Willa Cather had written up to that time, and it stands in interesting contrast to the sentimental pabulum that she found in the *Home Monthly*'s inventory when she arrived to edit the magazine. But if Tommy is unsentimental in social relations, she is nostalgic in her feelings about Nebraska. During the story she goes off to school in the East for a year, and when she returns to the Divide, she reports: "It's all very fine down East there, and the hills are green, but one gets mighty homesick for this sky, the old intense blue of it. . . . And this wind . . . I couldn't sleep in that lifeless stillness down there." This is the first time in Willa Cather's fiction that her prairie homeland is rendered sympathetically, and even though the story takes place on a blistering summer day, the landscape is rendered neutrally; the distant bluffs "were vibrating and dancing with the heat," and the panting cattle were hidden under the shelving banks of the draws. The land is not hostile here as it had been in "Lou, the Prophet" or "On the Divide."

II

After a year on the *Home Monthly* Willa Cather returned to Nebraska for the summer. Apparently she intended to go back to Pittsburgh and resume her editorial duties in the fall, but during the summer she received word that the magazine had been sold. Whether or not her job vanished in the transaction the records do not say. She merely reported that she had severed her relationship, and she began casting about for a newspaper position. Meantime she settled down to write in Red Cloud. She told her old friend Will Jones in Lincoln that her writing was going better than it ever had before. Free of her official duties and away from Pittsburgh social life, she was getting a great deal accomplished. Yet when she received a wire from the Pittsburgh *Leader* offering her a job on the telegraph desk at seventy-five dollars a month, she accepted quickly. She was flattered to be offered a job when Pittsburgh was full of unemployed male reporters. Besides, she had no confidence in her ability to free-lance, and a salary seemed essential. Rationalizing her return to Pittsburgh by saying that she would be able to hear Emma Calvé and see Sarah Bernhardt, she packed her bags once again and left Red Cloud on September tenth.

When she reached Pittsburgh a few days later, she began work immediately as assistant telegraph editor for the *Leader*. She edited the wire copy that came in between eight A.M. and three P.M., and wrote headlines. This was unexciting work, but her evenings were free for the theater, and the paper was eager to have her write drama criticism, for which it would pay extra. The theater reviews she had written for the *Leader* in her spare time the year before eventually lengthened into an informal history of the Pittsburgh stage by the time she left the paper in 1900. She also reviewed concerts, recitals, musical comedy, as well as the legitimate theater, and later she did a great deal of book reviewing. She even continued writing for the *Home Monthly,* contributing a book column under a pseudonym, and she regularly sent her column, "The Passing Show," back to Lincoln, though she transferred it from the *Journal* to the *Courier.* There was no slackening in the enormous productivity she had demonstrated during the preceding year. She had good health and unflagging industry.

One can follow her activities during the next several years through this prolific output. She interviewed Anthony Hope Hawkins when he lectured in Pittsburgh, and she covered President McKinley's visit to the city. She was captivated by Minnie Maddern Fiske's performance in *Tess of the D'Urbervilles,* but was not enchanted with Maude Adams in *The Little Minister.* The Pittsburgh Symphony's performance of Dvorak's *New World Symphony* was a thrilling experience; so was Melba as Rosina in *The Barber of Seville.* And so it went: Julia Marlowe in *As You Like It,*

Richard Mansfield in *Cyrano de Bergerac,* Nordica, Schumann-Heink, and Jean de Reszke all in one glorious cast in *Lohengrin,* Helena Modjeska in *Mary Stuart.* And her reading, as extensive as ever, is revealed in her book columns, which discuss old favorites and reveal new enthusiasms. Henry James, whom she previously had called "the greatest living English master of the counterpoint of literary style," continued to receive praise. Kipling's new books pleased her as they appeared. She liked Kate Chopin's *The Awakening,* though she did not particularly care for the *Madame Bovary* theme. Maurice Hewlett's *The Forest Lovers* delighted her; so did Mary Johnston's *To Have and To Hold.* She never lost an opportunity to extol the virtues of various French writers, and she discovered A. E. Housman almost as soon as *A Shropshire Lad* appeared. She hailed Eden Phillpotts as a worthy successor to George Eliot and Thomas Hardy, but Booth Tarkington's first novel, *The Gentleman from Indiana,* was in general "puerile and sophomorically sugary," although the first few chapters were "exceedingly well written." Some of her literary passions of this era are surprising in view of her fondness for the old romancers. She showed great respect for Zola, and when Frank Norris's *McTeague* appeared, she devoted several columns to its warm approval. She also embraced Harold Frederic's *The Damnation of Theron Ware* as the "work of a literary artist and of a vigorous thinker."

When Willa Cather returned to Pittsburgh in September 1897, she was going on twenty-four, a very marriageable age. Her social life, which she already had described as pleasanter than she ever had thought possible, included a good deal of squiring about by eligible young bachelors. For the girl who formerly had worn her hair short and dressed like a man, it was, as she termed it, a new life. There is scant evidence that she had any love affairs in college, though she wore throughout her life a gold snake ring given her by Charles Moore, son of her father's Lincoln business associate; but when she got to Pittsburgh, the men apparently lined up for dates. She had not been in the city more than nine months before she was writing Mariel Gere that a young doctor had proposed to her. She had not decided whether to marry him, though it would be a good match, she thought. Dorothy Canfield had come over from

Columbus, had met and approved of him, and he had been very nice to her; but Willa was not in love.

She escaped that entanglement and finished out her first year, but by the following April there was a Mr. Farrar in her life. This presumably was Preston Farrar, English teacher at Allegheny High School, whose friendship she kept and whose job she later filled after he moved on to other things. He had broken his leg playing football, she wrote, so that she only saw him in plaster, but it was rather fun now that he was no longer in any pain. He too apparently had proposed, but again she did not feel very deeply about him. His friendship was so warm and comforting that she really did not want to exchange it for matrimony. And she added significantly that she had grown enamored of liberty. To be wholly free, to do with her money what she wanted, to help those who had helped her, to pay the debts of her loves and hates, this was what she wanted.

There is no evidence that Willa Cather ever came close to getting married. The men in this world that she loved most dearly were her father and her brothers Douglass and Roscoe. She had the deepest sort of devotion to all three, especially her brothers, and it is significant that one of her favorite novels was *The Mill on the Floss*. In that book George Eliot had captured more successfully than anyone else "that strongest and most satisfactory relation of human life, the love that sometimes exists between a brother and a sister . . . who have laughed and sorrowed and learned the world together from the first, who have entered into each other's lives and minds more completely than ever man or woman can again." She also loved her younger brothers passionately, but because they were so much younger, she was more aunt than sister to them. It seems perfectly clear that she simply had no need for heterosexual relationships; she was married to her art. Although she lavished much affection and perhaps her maternal instinct on her nephews and nieces, her literary offspring served adequately as surrogates for children of her own. The one great romance of her life was Isabelle McClung, whom she met some months after rejecting Mr. Farrar.

Throughout her life Willa Cather was convinced that art and marriage did not mix. As early as her Carlyle essay she had said so, and she kept repeating it. Liberty and solitude were necessary for the artist, and marriage was incompatible with either. When the actress Mary Anderson retired from the stage to domesticity, she pondered the demands of career and marriage. Mary Anderson was not a consummate artist, and for her perhaps the happiness of married life was the better choice. Yet for the greatest of women artists, women like "Sappho and the two great Georges [Sand and Eliot]," only art could satisfy. On another occasion, when Helena von Doenhoff retired from the operatic stage to marry, Willa Cather wrote a sort of obituary. The artist, she declared, must love his art above all things and must say to it, as Ruth said amidst the alien corn: "Where thou goest, I will go, and where thou lodgest I will lodge . . . thy people shall be my people, and thy God my God." To this she added: " . . . married nightingales seldom sing." When actress Marie Burrough's divorce was announced in the papers, she wrote in her column that Marie wanted to be free for her work and free from the obligation of matrimony. The fact that her husband had been her teacher and coach made her ungrateful, but then all actresses are ungrateful. "If they are actresses worthy of the name, they always have a *premier amour* to whom they return, their work." Another sentence she was fond of quoting: "He travels the swiftest who rides alone."

Thus it is no wonder that Willa Cather never married. Nor is it surprising to find that in her fiction artists never have happy marriages. Sometimes the heroine, like the author, avoids marriage, as Kitty Ayrshire does in "A Gold Slipper," but usually artists marry and suffer, as Cressida Garnet does in "The Diamond Mine." So strong was this conviction that Willa Cather on one occasion converted a happy artistic marriage in real life into a disastrous fictional union. This was in "Uncle Valentine," a tale inspired by her friendship with the composer Ethelbert Nevin. This attitude she may have got from one of her idols, Alphonse Daudet, for *Les Femmes d'Artistes* argues the point; yet she knew that Daudet himself had been happily married for thirty years to Julia Allard, also a writer. Her conviction about the hazards of artistic marriages even seems to have colored her feeling about marriage in general. It is a rare novel or story of hers in which there is not an

87

there is not an unhappy marriage either at the core or the periphery of the work. From *Alexander's Bridge* through *Sapphira and the Slave Girl* her fictional marriages are unhappy, marred by infidelity or at least incompatibility. The blasted marriages come to the outer limit of a kind of parabola in *The Professor's House* and *My Mortal Enemy,* both written at the peak of her career. There even is a brutally unhappy marriage vignette in *Death Comes for the Archbishop.*

Willa Cather had no need in Pittsburgh to get married to have companionship, for she quickly acquired a large circle of devoted friends. The first friend, however, was an old one, Dorothy Canfield, who then was an undergraduate at Ohio State University. She stopped off frequently on trips east, and Willa occasionally ran over to Columbus for a visit. Once after a long bout with influenza, she recuperated at the Canfields', and another time Dorothy and her mother both spent Christmas in Pittsburgh. For Dorothy there was a glamor about her older friend, who by now was earning her own living and making one hundred dollars a month, and the schoolgirl crush of Lincoln days lingered. Dorothy remembered long after: "My occasional brief stopovers in Pittsburgh were golden days for me. When people talk about Pittsburgh as a dirty, dark, noisy, grimy city, I can't imagine what they are talking about. Over it hangs, for me, a shining cloud of young memories."

Other early friends were librarians and devotees of music. There was May Willard, head of the children's department at the Carnegie Library, who remained a close friend until her death in 1941, and Edwin Hatfield Anderson, the head librarian, and his wife. Then there were the Litchfields, Ethel, an accomplished pianist, and Lawrence, one of Pittsburgh's leading physicians. Ethel had given up a career as a concert pianist for marriage but maintained a lively interest in music, entertained visiting musicians, and often played chamber music with members of the Pittsburgh Symphony. Willa Cather loved to go to her house, and she and Ethel became such close friends that after Lawrence's death Ethel moved to New York to be close to Willa. There is a suggestion of Ethel Litchfield in the character of Caroline Noble in "The Garden Lodge," one of the stories in *The Troll Garden* written in this period. Another musical friend was Mrs. John Slack, who lived lavishly in suburban Sewickley and gave musical parties to which she frequently invited Willa Cather. Her house and music room, which appear as part of the setting for "Uncle Valentine," were next door to Vineacre, the home of Ethelbert Nevin.

The great experience of Willa Cather's second year in Pittsburgh was meeting Nevin. Whether she met him at Mrs. Slack's or through his brothers, who turned out to be the owners of the *Leader,* the record does not say, but the meeting took place in the fall after Nevin had returned from living in Europe to settle down at his boyhood home at Vineacre. Willa Cather was simply charmed. He was her first real artist friend and in every way fitted her image of the Artist. He had begun composing songs as a child before he ever had studied music. His practical father had given him a musical education but then had forced him to go into business. Escaping from this bondage, he had become a restless world traveler, but wherever he went, Venice, Algiers, Boston, he composed incessantly, turning out hundreds of musical compositions, often working all night, suffering poor health most of the time. In an article for the *Ladies' Home Journal* she wrote: "Temperamentally Mr. Nevin is much the same blending of the blithe and the *triste* that gives his music its peculiar quality, now exultantly gay, now sunk in melancholy, as whimsical and capricious as April weather."

Nevin apparently found Willa Cather attractive and turned on all his charm for her. When she wrote Mariel Gere, reporting on the interesting people she had met during her second year in Pittsburgh, she listed Nevin as prince and king of them all. He had gone shopping with her that very afternoon, carried her bundles for her, and then bought her (in January) a bunch of violets as big as a moon. Think of it, she wrote, the greatest of American composers and a fellow of thirty with the face of a boy and the laugh of a girl. He actually was thirty-five but represented for her youth, gaiety, golden talent. The shopping scene appears very much as she remembered it in "Uncle Valentine," and when Nevin died three years later, his death was a bitter blow. Keats, Poe, Crane, Nevin—all geniuses doomed to die young.

Music and the theater were not the only facets to Willa Cather's life in Pittsburgh. When a young free-lance journalist named

George Seibel walked into the *Home Monthly* office with an article on Richard Wagner, she bought it and began another fruitful relationship. Soon she was visiting the Seibels in their modest South Side home once or twice a week for evenings of reading. Although the Seibels were part of the German-American population of Pittsburgh, the readings were French—Daudet, de Musset, Flaubert, Anatole France, Hugo, Pierre Loti, Théophile Gautier. They ran the gamut of recent and contemporary authors and accompanied their soirées with suppers of plain German cuisine, noodle soup, potato salad, sliced cucumbers, and homemade cookies. As long as she was in Pittsburgh, Willa Cather spent her Christmases with the Seibels, and on the first Christmas Eve after she had begun working for the *Leader,* she took Dorothy Canfield with her to help trim the tree. Dorothy, who would later take a doctorate in Romance languages before becoming a novelist, remembered vividly the cosmopolitan atmosphere and wonderful talk at the Seibel home. She also recalled George Seibel standing against a background of Christmas greens and reciting a Heine Christmas poem in his rich, resonant voice:

> *Der Stern blieb stehn über Josephs Haus . . .*

The Seibels and Willa Cather got on very well together, and they kept in touch after she left Pittsburgh. About the only serious disagreement they ever had was over Henry James, whom George did not like, but when it came to Balzac, Sand, Mérimée, de Maupassant, and other French writers, they shared a common enthusiasm. George Seibel remembered Willa Cather at this period as a person with eyes in every pore: "She was avid of the world, always wondering, always questioning, always digging, a prospector in the deep and quiet lodes of the soul."

Her interest in human nature and the artistic temperament were further served by her friendship with the leading lady of the Pittsburgh Stock Company, Lizzie Hudson Collier, an actress she had seen in Lincoln and perhaps had met there. When she arrived in Pittsburgh, Lizzie Collier was the star of the repertory company and a great favorite of Pittsburghers. She was a charming, kind woman, a competent actress, and not at all a prima donna. Society matrons and bootblacks alike vied for her attention, and Willa Cather was flattered to be her friend. On one occasion when Willa dropped in backstage, suffering from a severe bronchial cold, hoarse and feverish, Mrs. Collier put her in a cab, took her back to her suite in the Schenley Hotel, put her to bed, and nursed her for several days. Willa Cather wrote in the *Leader:* "I never come out of the theater with her after a matinee that there is not a string of carriages lined up in front of the stage entrance full of worshipful girls, who wave and smile at her and gaze at me with green-eyed jealousy and deep-seated loathing. . . . Here I am walking coolly with this 'popular idol' with my sordid, mundane little spirit fixed for nothing loftier than where we will go for dinner."

One night backstage in Mrs. Collier's dressing room she met one of those worshipful girls. It was a meeting that quite literally changed her life, for the other Collier fan was Isabelle McClung, the tall, handsome daughter of a socially prominent family. Isabelle and Willa were immediately drawn to one another, and the friendship that began that night grew to be a great love that lasted a lifetime. Not only did Isabelle become the most intimate friend of her life, but the two women were inseparable companions for the balance of the years Willa Cather lived in Pittsburgh. When Isabelle died in 1938, Willa did not think she could go on living, and after she recovered from her grief and reflected on the relationship, she believed that Isabelle had been the one person for whom all of her books had been written. This eventful meeting took place during the 1898–1899 theater season.

Isabelle McClung was the daughter of a dour Pittsburgh judge, a man of stern Scotch Presbyterian background who was as conservative in his tastes as the Pittsburghers Willa Cather earlier had satirized. The McClungs lived expensively in a large house on Murray Hill Avenue and expected their children to conduct themselves as well-bred young socialites. Isabelle, however, had her father's strong will and character but not his tastes. She was interested in art and music, and consorted with strolling players and drama critics. Although she had no artistic talents herself, she found proper Pittsburgh stuffy and stultifying, and needed an outlet for her energies and interests. In Willa Cather's career she found a cause that she could promote with enthusiasm.

sources or from occasional comments in letters Willa Cather wrote other friends. All of the hundreds of letters that passed between the two women were destroyed. The main outlines, however, are clear enough. The friendship developed rapidly enough so that by the time Willa Cather returned from a summer in Red Cloud to begin her third year on the *Leader,* she went to stay temporarily with Isabelle. The intimacy grew steadily during 1900, and after Willa spent the winter of 1900–1901 in Washington free-lancing and working as a government translator, she returned to Pittsburgh to live with the McClungs. By this time she had left journalism and was teaching Latin at Pittsburgh's Central High School.

A family battle apparently preceded this change in Willa Cather's living arrangements. E. K. Brown, whose chief informant was Edith Lewis, herself a rival for Willa Cather's affections, reports this: "Isabelle McClung's parents at first wondered at the propriety of having Willa Cather come to reside in their household, though they welcomed her as their daughter's friend. The daughter promptly threatened to leave home if she could not have her way; her parents yielded." The concession, however, was that Willa Cather could come to stay temporarily; the actuality was that she lived with the McClungs until she left Pittsburgh to join the staff of *McClure's Magazine* more than five years later.

The McClungs lived at 1180 Murray Hill Avenue in a fashionable East End residential area that overlooked the Monongahela River. It had solidity, elegance, comfort. Operated by a staff of servants, it provided luxuries that Willa Cather never before had known from the inside. The contrast with her boardinghouses, where cooking odors permeated the bedrooms and one stood in line to use the bathroom, was very sharp. Dorothy Canfield remembered: "There was a good deal of stately entertaining carried on in the McClung house too, the many-coursed dinners of the most formal kind, which seemed picturesque (and they really were) to Willa." There was nothing spartan in her nature, and the friends in Lincoln who feared she might go bohemian never had anything to worry about. Her career as a novelist actually was long delayed by her inability to cut loose and live in a garret while she was learning the craft of fiction.

A good picture of Willa Cather and her new friend at this time is supplied by Elizabeth Moorhead, a Pittsburgh writer who knew them both: "The two young women would forsake the family group soon after dinner, and evening after evening would go upstairs to the bedroom they shared to read together in quiet. This room was at the back of the house and its wide low window gave on a downward slope across gardens and shaded streets towards the Monongahela River and green hills rising beyond. There were no close neighbours to destroy their sense of privacy. Here the friends spent many happy and fruitful hours." To facilitate Willa's writing, Isabelle fixed up a study in the attic, a former sewing room, to which she could retire on week ends and work without being disturbed. Many of the poems in *April Twilights* and all of the stories in *The Troll Garden* were written there.

III

After a few months on the *Leader* in 1897, Willa Cather must have been dissatisfied with her job and her prospects. She was writing thousands of words of human interest features, drama criticism, and book reviews, but she was not getting on with her real career. Even the excitement of covering theatrical events could not last, and after she met Nevin she turned her attention more and more to reporting musical events, especially piano recitals. In February 1898 she broke the monotony of the Pittsburgh grind by visiting New York, but it was a busman's holiday, and she spent part of it writing guest drama reviews for the *Sun.* Seeing Helena Modjeska in *Mary Stuart* and having lunch with her, however, were well worth the trip, and she went back to Pittsburgh able to last until May, when she found an excuse to visit her cousin Howard Gore in Washington. Her cousin was professor of geodesy at Columbian University (now George Washington) and was preparing to go off on the Wellman polar expedition. He was full of fascinating stories and busy entertaining friends before leaving. Some of his guests were equally interesting: the Norwegian ambassador, the secretary of the German Embassy, and assorted diplomats. Her cousin's wife turned out to be a famous Christiana belle, daughter of a former Norwegian ambassador and a cousin of the king of Sweden. Willa Cather was much impressed by her; in fact, she had such a gay time that she hated to go back to the *Leader* office. But she was needed there, and the telegraph desk kept her sweltering away in the steamy Pittsburgh heat through June and July. She wrote Frances Gere that the horrors of war seemed to be a good deal worse in newspaper offices than in the field. She was grilling away in the heat and writing headlines all about Cervera's being bottled up in Santiago Harbor, but she hoped to get away for a vacation in the West by the first of August. She subsequently managed this and after visiting friends in Lincoln and family in Red Cloud went on to the Black Hills and Wyoming to see her brothers.

Back in Pittsburgh in the fall of 1898 she began the same old routine over again and probably wondered how much longer she could stand it. In all of 1898 and 1899 she published only two stories, neither of them work that she could be proud of. But she had to support herself, and there seemed no alternative. So she plugged away at the *Leader* for two more years. The second year on the paper began with a severe case of influenza, but she had a happy time in Columbus with Dorothy Canfield at Thanksgiving. She saw a great deal of Nevin, and after knowing him for a year he seemed about the most lovable man she ever had met. Then Isabelle McClung entered her life. On balance, the year was a social success, even though the newspaper work was no longer challenging. She rewarded herself at the end of the second year by returning home for the summer via the Great Lakes and stopping briefly at Mackinac Island. By the time she was well into her third year, the job had become a real grind, and she was about ready to take the plunge into free-lancing.

It is not clear just when she made the break, but she probably did little for the *Leader* after mid-March 1900, when her last regular drama review appeared there. She still was writing letters on *Leader* stationery as late as September twenty-ninth, but during the summer she was contributing to a new Pittsburgh literary magazine. A young man named Charles Clark had inherited twenty thousand dollars and with his inheritance had begun publishing the *Library*. But this journal only lasted from March to August, and by fall she rather expected to return to Lincoln for the winter. Her family wanted to move to the state capital, she wrote Will Jones, and since her mother was too ill to attend to loading the cookstove in the wagon, she would have to do it. She asked Jones if he could use her on the *Journal* part-time. She wanted to write stories three or four days a week and work on the paper the rest of the time. Nothing came of this plan, however, and her family did not move to Lincoln. Instead of returning to Nebraska, she went to Washington for the winter, got a job as a translator in a government office, and began sending columns of Washington news to the *Journal.* She also contributed a column to the *Index of Pittsburgh Life,* which had absorbed the *Library* when its young publisher's inheritance ran out.

It seems likely that she dared to quit her job on the *Leader* only after she had broken into the eastern magazine market. Somehow during her last year on the paper, or perhaps during her summer back in Nebraska, she had managed to write "Eric Hermannson's Soul." She had sent it to *Cosmopolitan,* which had bought it and published it in April 1900. This was her most important sale to date. Although the *Overland Monthly,* which had published "On the Divide" in 1896, was a national magazine, it was published in San Francisco and lacked the prestige and circulation of the New York based *Cosmopolitan.*

Willa Cather never reprinted "Eric Hermannson's Soul," but it is a very competent piece of fiction and marks a steady advance in her narrative skill. It is a long story and a subtle one. Eric is a blond giant, a young Siegfried, who has emigrated to Nebraska at eighteen, worked in the fields, played his fiddle at all the dances, hugged the girls, and visited Lena Henson, a woman of dubious reputation. When a passionate exhorter from the fundamentalist Gospellers captures Eric's soul, he puts away his violin and becomes another one of the dull clods from the Old World, "sobered by toil and saddened by exile." At this juncture beautiful Margaret Elliot comes out of the East to visit on the Divide. She meets Eric, is attracted to him, rides with him, and plays the organ for him, "probably the first good music he had ever heard." The hold of the Free Gospellers loosens, Eric falls in love with the accomplished Margaret. He agrees, at her urging, to play his fiddle again and to attend a dance she is giving before her departure for home. In doing so, he barters his soul, as he believes, for one evening of pleasure. The story ends with Margaret getting on the train and Eric, in possession of his soul, deaf to the reproaches of the Free Gospeller preacher.

A bare plot summary does great injustice to this tale. It is the way the material is handled and the careful management of detail that make the story interesting. One notices first of all that Willa Cather is beginning to possess her material and to handle it with a measure of aesthetic distance that makes one both see and feel the world of immigrant farmers on her Divide. The prairie, the grass, the fields of wheat and rye, the western sky—all are evoked, not simply described. In one particularly effective scene Eric and Margaret climb the windmill, as Willa and her brother had done in 1891, to view the clear night sky stretching away to the distant horizon, "which seemed to reach around the world." As they watch, the weary wind carries the heavy odor of the cornfields to them and the music of the dance sounds faintly from below. There is tension in this scene and a skillful development of the conflict between East and West. The author's sympathies lie with the West, but she understands the pull of culture and civilization. Also, her developing technique is nowhere better shown than in a scene depicting powerful sexual emotion without exceeding the limits permissible in magazine fiction of that day. In a ride across the prairie one afternoon Eric and Margaret meet a pack of wild horses and Margaret's pony nearly stampedes. Eric jumps off his horse, grabs the bit of Margaret's rearing pony, and while it is biting and kicking like the devil he subdues it. The scene, which has an orgastic intensity, is followed immediately by Eric's declaration of love. But the entire story is well conceived and executed, and it is significant to note too that Willa Cather could treat the same basic plot Owen Wister used in *The Virginian* two years later without resorting to a sentimental ending.

Her other stories published in 1900 are less impressive. The short-lived *Library* took five of them, but two were reworkings of earlier tales, and a third was "The Sentimentality of William Tavener," previously mentioned. The fourth was "The Affair at Grover Station," a psychological detective story with a railroading background. This story no doubt resulted from Willa Cather's summer visit with her brother Douglass in Cheyenne, where he was a railroad station agent. The most interesting of the stories is "The Dance at Chevalier's," a Nebraska tale that prefigures in some of its incidents both *O Pioneers!* and *My Ántonia.*

Willa Cather's winter of free-lance journalism in Washington in 1900–1901 was her last period of newspaper writing. When she returned to Pittsburgh about the end of February, she began her new life as a member of the McClung household and a teacher at Central High School. Journalism finally had proved too distracting and energy-consuming; teaching offered an income and three months' freedom in the summer for writing. Although she made only $650 a year when she began teaching, less than the *Leader* had paid her, the McClungs were subsidizing her living arrangements and she did not have extravagant tastes.

During her first semester at Central High School she taught Latin, and although she had taken a lot of classics in college, her Latin was very rusty and she found it hard work. By summer she had lost twenty pounds. She stuck it out, however, and after visiting her family and friends in Nebraska and going camping in Wyoming, she returned to her school. That fall there was an opening in the English department, and she happily decamped from the Latin classroom. For the next two years she taught English at Central High School, and when there was a vacancy due to the resignation of her friend Preston Farrar at Allegheny High School across the river, she applied for and received the position. Then she taught for the next three years at Allegheny.

When Willa Cather began teaching, she was twenty-seven years old, a veteran journalist of more than seven years' experience. She still was a good-looking young woman, though a bit plump, and her face showed what one of her students remembered as "intermittent dimples." She had begun wearing her hair parted in the middle and combed back into a bun, as all her later pictures show her. She continued to wear severely tailored clothes, skirts shorter than average and shirtwaists with stiff collars and cuffs. Mannish four-in-hand ties were also a prominent feature of her wardrobe.

She was determined to succeed as a high-school English teacher and put the same energy and vitality into her teaching that she had poured into her journalism. Her school was the classical high school, the school for Pittsburgh children who planned to go to college, and she was expected to give her students a rigorous training. "She knew that the only way to learn to write was to write," remembered one of her students, "and she set us to writing themes, one every class day, usually in the first ten or fifteen minutes of the period." She described her pupils perfectly in her later essay on writing, "The Novel Démeublé," when she spoke of "that drudge, the theme-writing high-school student." Her standards of marking were as low as her standards of English were high. "Seldom did she grade beyond 85, and that only rarely. Mostly we got 70s and occasionally achieved an 80 on our themes, which were all carefully corrected and returned to us." Remembering her own youthful rhetorical flights, she was ruthless in redpenciling "fine writing." She was greatly admired by some of her students and heartily disliked by others.

She did not have a natural talent for teaching, but her classes were not dull. She had read far more than most teachers and passed on her literary enthusiasms to her students. One of them remembered that she often praised Sarah Orne Jewett and frequently embellished her class discussions with anecdotes about Lillian Nordica. Her most famous pupil, critic and teacher Norman Foerster, recalled that "her voice was deeper than is usual; she spoke without excitement; her manner was quiet, reposeful, suggesting reserves of energy and richness of personality. Her teaching seemed natural and human, but without contagious sparks." She got better and better as she continued teaching and enjoyed it more every year. After she transferred to Allegheny High School, she even had two assistants to help her as readers and apprentice teachers. When she left Pittsburgh to join *McClure's Magazine*, she departed with real regret. She wrote in an open letter to the students in her home-room class on June 2, 1906: "One always has to choose between good things it seems. So I turn to a work I love with very real regret that I must leave behind, for the time, at least, a work I had come to love almost as well." Her career as high-school teacher already had been recorded in fiction in her best-known story, "Paul's Case."

CHAPTER 4

Literary Debut

I

AFTER A YEAR and a half of teaching, during which she sold a story to the *Saturday Evening Post*, Willa Cather had saved enough money to go to Europe. For any educated American the periodic need to visit Europe to water his cultural roots is a compelling imperative, and for Willa Cather the urge was doubly strong. The European immigrants she had met on the Divide, the German-French culture of the Wieners in Red Cloud, her early love for the classics, and her intense absorption in French literature—all these things drew her like a magnet to the Old World. Soon after school was out in June 1902, she and Isabelle McClung sailed from New York for Liverpool. They embarked on the *Noorland* on the fourteenth and planned a three-months' tour of England and France that would not bring them back until several weeks after school opened in September. To supplement her savings, Willa arranged to send back weekly travel letters to the *Journal*.

The two young women had the good luck to land in the grimy English Midlands on a radiant June day when the city of Liverpool was gaily decorated for the coronation of Edward VII. From their hotel they could see St. George's Hall across a square in which countless Union Jacks were fluttering in the breeze. At the foot of the Duke of Wellington's statue a blind man played a concertina while in the square were throngs of bobbies, red-coated soldiers, and people in holiday spirit. From the hotel window it was all gay and picturesque, a tourist poster, but when they went into the street they encountered the usual shocks that Americans going abroad for the first time experience. The shabby, tasteless dress of the working class, the stoop-shouldered, unhealthy physical appearance of the people, stood in marked contrast to the American reality. Willa Cather was enchanted by the sound of British English, however, and wrote that "after hearing only English voices for a few days, the first American voice you hear . . . is apt to suggest something of the nature of burrs or sandpaper."

They did not stay in Liverpool long but departed soon for Chester, where Willa Cather wrote delightedly on July first of the quaint red-brick houses, the majority very old, with diamond windowpanes and high-walled gardens behind. The walls were beautifully toned and colored by age and overgrown with ivy and Virginia creeper. Hedges of holly or alder trees rose above the walls, and under foot was the matchless English green of the sod. They promenaded along the top of the old walls of the city and peered into the tidy walled gardens. Chester was an authentic bit of the Old World they had come to find. When they went out to Hawarden Castle, they spent nearly half a day of utter solitude at the foot of the splendid ruined Norman tower originally built in 1075. The rains and winds of nearly a thousand years had given the masonry of the tower a clean-washed look. She wrote: "One can understand, lying a morning through at the foot of the Norman tower, why there are Maurice Hewletts in England." It seemed to her an overwhelming temptation to try reconstructing old ruins in historical fiction. She later did it, of course, in *Death Comes for the Archbishop* and *Shadows on the Rock;* and when she died she was at work on a novel laid in medieval Avignon.

Willa Cather's highest priority of business on her trip to Europe was to visit Shropshire and to meet A. E. Housman. She had discovered Housman's poems when they first appeared, and reprinted some of them in her columns. She later described herself as "Housman's bond slave" ever since *A Shropshire Lad* had appeared, and she wanted to see the places he wrote about. Her letter to the *Journal* of July eleventh is datelined "Ludlow" and describes both Ludlow and Shrewsbury, the latter surrounded by a loop of the Severn River, "which is nowhere more green and cool and clear." As the pilgrims looked across the stream towards the meadows on which the lads had played football in Housman's boyhood, a group of boys trooped out with a ball. It was a perfect experience: Housman's poems come to life.

But there was no trace of the poet in Shrewesbury. Willa Cather told her *Journal* readers that she had gone to the library and had seen "old files of the little country paper where many of his lyrics first appeared as free contributions signed 'A Shropshire Lad.' " This was sheer invention, as the poems never had been published in such a manner. It is true, however, that she could not find out anything about Housman there, and she wrote a friend the following year that no one in Shrewesbury she talked to ever had heard of him. The public library had a copy of his book with uncut pages. When she got to London, she battered the doors of his publishers until they gave her his address. Then she, Isabelle, and Dorothy Canfield, who had joined them in London, all went to call on Housman.

She did not describe her visit to Housman in her newspaper letters, but she told people about it later, and garbled versions got into print and vexed her the rest of her life. One of them, by Ford Madox Ford, whom she called the prince of prevaricators, had her going to Housman as the representative of the Pittsburgh Shropshire Lad Club and presenting him with a solid-gold laurel wreath. They did take a bus out to his lodgings in Highgate and found him living in a horrible boardinghouse in a miserable suburb. When they arrived, Housman, a bachelor, was expecting some Canadian cousins and came racing down the stairs to greet them. It was only after they were seated in his drab little hole of a study that the mistaken identity became apparent. Housman was a teacher of Latin at University College, a great classical scholar, and, as he said, more interested in his Latin texts than poetry. When Willa Cather tried to tell him what his verses had meant to her, he was covered with embarrassment and could think of nothing to say.

Fortunately Dorothy Canfield saved the day by mentioning that she was working at the British Museum on a doctoral dissertation dealing with Corneille and Racine in England. Scholarly research was a topic Housman could talk about, and for the rest of the visit he and Dorothy carried on a dialogue. Meantime Willa sat on his couch with broken springs, brooding about Housman's shoes and cuffs and shabby carpet and wondering how the gaunt and gray and embittered figure before her could have written the magical lyrics that had moved her so deeply. When the three young women finally got out of Housman's boardinghouse and onto a bus headed back for London, they all burst into tears. No doubt it was her great disappointment that kept her from sending an account of the visit to the *Journal.* In her old age she always intended to write about the experience someday in order to set the record straight, but she never did. One of the last letters she wrote was to Dorothy Canfield Fisher, asking for memories of the visit.

The last three weeks of July were spent in London, and besides visiting Housman the travelers saw a great deal of the British capital. They explored the gin-soaked East End, which looked just like Hogarth's "The Harlot's Progress," watched an Italian religious procession, visited galleries, parks, and the usual tourist attractions. They were especially interested in painters' studios, visiting several, and one entire letter to the *Journal* described the studio of Edward Burne-Jones. Shortly before crossing the Channel to France, they saw Beerbohm Tree's production of *The Merry Wives of Windsor.* Another entire column was devoted to the play, for it not only had Tree in the cast, but it also brought together two feuding leading ladies, Madge Kendal and Ellen Terry.

Willa Cather had been a Francophile from early childhood. The *joie de vivre* of the French community on the Divide and Mrs. Wiener's stories of France had made a deep impression, and she empathized completely with the passengers on board the Channel steamer who were getting home.

Above the roar of the wind and thrash of the water I heard a babble of voices, in which I could only distinguish the word "France" uttered over and over again with a fire and fervor that was in itself a panegyric. . . . All the prone, dispirited figures we left [on deck] two hours before were erect and animated, rhetorical and jubilant. They were French people from all over the world. . . . Above all the ardent murmurings and the exclamations of felicity, there continually rose the voice of a little boy who had been born on a foreign soil and who had never been home. He sat on his father's shoulder, with his arms locked tight about his neck, and kept crying with small convulsions of excitement, "Is it France? Is it France?"

Then the dawn began to come. The sky was black in the direction of England, and the coast of France began to grow gray ahead of them. Soon the high chalk cliffs of Normandy were a pale purple in the half light, and fishing boats began to pass the ship. When they touched the dock, the sky, the gravel beach, and the white town were all wrapped in a pale mist, and the narrow streets were canals of purple shadows. Everyone was speaking French, "clear voices that phrased the beautiful tongue they spoke almost as music is phrased." In a sense she too had come home.

The next six weeks in France were a deeply moving artistic and literary pilgrimage. Before getting to Paris, they stopped in Rouen, where Flaubert had been born and raised, and paid their respects to a monument to the master. Just across from that was the statue of his pupil and friend de Maupassant, another of Willa Cather's mentors. In Paris they visited the cemetery of Père-Lachaise, where the tomb of de Musset touched her profoundly. She was pleased that his grave was carefully tended and that the Parisians cared enough for his memory to keep fresh flowers on his tomb. Balzac's grave seemed ugly and deserted in contrast, but that did not matter much, for Balzac "lives in every street and quarter; one sees his people everywhere." Outside of Paris they visited at Barbizon to see where Millet, Rousseau, and fellow artists of that school had worked. As they wallked in the forest, Willa Cather remembered that this was where Robert Louis Stevenson had fallen in love with the woman he later married in California. After a month in Paris they departed for the South of France, and presently they were in Avignon staying in a hotel that once had lodged Henry James.

Willa Cather's emotional response to France was further intensified when she reached Provence. She hardly had words to describe Avignon. The papal palace, a huge, rambling Gothic pile, dominated the town, and from the marvelous gardens on the rock above the palace one could look down to the Rhône where the ruins of the old Roman bridge still reached out into the river. In another direction the snowy peaks of the Alps shimmered in the smog-free air of 1902. Everywhere she went in Provence, she saw Daudet, the writer of all French authors she loved most. When she got to Arles and close to the site of Daudet's *moulin,* her travel letters were peppered with allusions to the master.

The trip also included a visit to Marseilles and the Mediterranean coast. Again the points of reference were literary. While she was dining in a hotel overlooking the Château d'If, where Edmond Dantès had been imprisoned, a small squall came up with blue lightning, wild gusts of rain, and metallic thunder. She wondered where she had seen just such a storm before and then remembered: "It was on the stage of the Funke Theatre, when Mr. James O'Neill used to be sewn up in a sack and flung by the supers from the Château d'If into the Mediterranean." Two hours later they took a train for Hyères and later spent some time in the tiny fishing village of Le Lavandou, where the coast for a hundred miles on either side was as wild as when the Saracens held it. After traveling as far down the Riviera coast as Monte Carlo with its "oppressive splendor," the tourists began retracing their steps and heading back towards the Channel coast and home. When Willa Cather returned to Central High School in September, she was ready to begin assembling her first book.

II

Her first book, however, was not a collection of stories but a volume of poems. Ever since she had been in college, she had been writing and publishing verse, first in undergraduate publications, then in the *Home Monthly,* the *Courier,* and the *Library.* Beginning in 1900 she began placing her poems in national magazines—the *Critic, Lippincott's, Harper's Weekly,* and the *Youth's Companion.* Richard Badger of Boston, who headed a vanity press, heard of her and apparently sent her a seductive letter offering to publish a volume of her poems. Of course, the author had to put up a certain sum. Willa Cather accepted the proposal, and arrangements were made to bring out a slender little volume of thirty-seven recent poems in April 1903. She wrote Will Jones in January that Badger was putting out a lot of new verse by such people as Clinton Scollard, Edith M. Thomas, and Harriet Prescott Spofford, and had made her very liberal terms. She hoped to make some money from the book and wanted to borrow a Lincoln directory for the purposes of circularizing her friends. But in such august company and under such an imprint, it is no wonder that

April Twilights attracted little attention. Had she known more about the commercial side of publishing, she would have shunned Badger, but then Badger knew how to flatter young poets. He previously had captured E. A. Robinson in his net.

She probably never recovered her subvention, but she did get a good many favorable reviews. Her friend George Seibel, who conducted the book page in the Pittsburgh *Gazette,* gave her a glowing notice; "a book of genuine poetry in unpretentious guise . . . singing its way straight to the heart of every one who looks within its covers." *The New York Times* also praised her work, finding that her poetic gift was genuine and that the book gave "promise of an unfolding to be looked for with eagerness." She got a full-page review in *Poet Lore,* complete with picture and bio-graphical data; but that magazine was published by the Gorham Press, which also printed Richard Badger's books.

"I do not take myself seriously as a poet," Willa Cather said in 1925, and that was generally her attitude once she had begun to publish novels. Nine years after *April Twilights* had appeared, a new friend, Elizabeth Sergeant, wanted a copy, but Willa wrote her that she had bought up and sunk in a tarn all the copies she could get. She did not want her friend to read them, as they belonged to the time when she was young and inexperienced and had been nowhere. This, of course, was not at all true, but she did not write much poetry after her book came out, only sixteen more poems during the rest of her life. She did reprint her poems in 1923, dropping thirteen and adding some new ones, and again in 1937 in her collected works with two more deletions from the original group. Eunice Tietjens, who reviewed the 1923 edition of *April Twilights,* states the case judiciously:

This is a book of poems by a great literary personality, who well deserves the Pulitzer Prize—but not by a great poet. . . . Her stories are unforgettable. They etch themselves into your con-sciousness. . . . Much of herself comes through. . . . The same sense of humanity, the same sense of drama, the same directness of vision. . . . Eighteen or twenty years ago I read several of these poems . . . and as I read them now they are as familiar as old friends. Yet now, examining them in the cold light of later knowl-edge, I see that I have loved and remembered them because of the humanity, not because of the poetry.

Yet one also must agree with Bernice Slote, who believes that readers "interested in her major fiction and its interpretation will find the 1903 *April Twilights* wholly relevant." The subjects of Willa Cather's poems parallel the subjects of her stories, her newspaper columns, and her reading. The opening poem, "Grandmither, Think Not I Forget," is a love poem that invokes the memory of Grandmother Boak. There are poems with classical subjects such as the pastoral "Arcadian Winter," the lines on the statue of Antinous, "Winter at Delphi," and "Eurydice." Shakespeare furnished the inspiration for "Paradox," in which she plays off Caliban and Ariel to suggest the contradictions inherent in art. There are poems derived from her recent trip to Europe, "Mills of Montmartre," "Provençal Legend," and "London Roses." In the last the "slatern girls in Trafalgar" cry, "Rowses, Rowses! penny a bunch!" The echoes of Housman also are strong, particularly in "In Media Vita," where she sings of

> *Lads and their sweethearts lying*
> *In the cleft o' the windy hill;*
> *Hearts that hushed of their sighing,*
> *Lips that are tender and still.*

There are many good lines and occasionally striking figures, but in general the poems are bookish, drawing their metaphors from reading rather than from living. She was quite aware of this failing in her verse, and when she disparaged her poetry to Elizabeth Sergeant, she remembered that one poem, "White Birch in Wyoming," had begun by evoking the Pre-Raphaelite painter Burne-Jones:

> *Stark as a Burne-Jones vision of despair,*
> *Amid the painted glare of sand and sky,*
> *She stands. . . .*

This nature poem also goes on to allude to the Valkyries and Brünnhilde. Occasionally, however, there are lines that readers today can admire, such as "Prairie Dawn," which is as good a poem as any of the Imagists of the early twentieth century were writing:

A Crimson fire that vanquishes the stars;
A pungent odor from the dusty sage;
A sudden stirring of the huddled herds;
A breaking of the distant table-lands
Through purple mists ascending, and the flare
Of water ditches silver in the light;
A swift, bright lance hurled low across the world;
A sudden sickness for the hills of home.

Good as this poem is, the land described is not Webster County, Nebraska, but Wyoming, where she had visited her brother; and the hills of home would have to be in her native Virginia, in her adopted Pittsburgh, or in her imagination. She had not yet discovered the Divide as a poetic subject, even though she was beginning to treat it affirmatively in her fiction. Nebraska does appear in *April Twilights,* but as a setting for another purpose. This is in "The Night Express," a poem that was inspired by the return to Red Cloud of a local boy who had been killed in a railroad accident east of town:

From out the mist-clad meadows, along the river shore,
The night express-train whistles with eye of fire before.
. . . .
While lads who used to loiter with wistful steps and slow,
Await to-night a comrade who comes, but will not go.

This is undistinguished verse, but the story that was partly inspired by the event, "The Sculptor's Funeral," transmutes the material into a memorable piece of short fiction.

In addition to the characteristic subjects that Willa Cather uses in her poems, the elegiac note that pervades her mature fiction also is strongly evident here. The François Villon theme, *"Où sont les neiges d'antan,"* recurs again and again, as in "Aftermath," which apostrophizes the vanished past:

Thou art more lost to me than they who dwell
In Egypt's sepulchres, long ages fled;
And would I touch—Ah me! I might as well
Covet the gold of Helen's vanished head,
Or kiss back Cleopatra from the dead!

It is myth and romance, lost youth, golden opportunities, and Arcady that Willa Cather mourns as a Pittsburgh English teacher at the age of thirty. By the time she wrote *O Pioneers!* in 1913, however, the elegiac tone included Nebraska, as in the poem she wrote to be an epigraph for the novel. There she sings of "Evening and the flat land,/Rich and sombre and always silent"; against which "Youth,/Flaming like the wild roses" is "Singing like the larks over the plowed fields."

Willa Cather's taste in poetry remained classical and romantic. When she reviewed an anthology of younger poets in 1902, she saw a great deal of Emersonian influence in American verse and a trend towards shorter forms, chiefly the lyric. She thought American poetry was characterized by perfection of form and intensity of spiritual experience. She approved of this trend because it reinforced her own principles and practice; yet paradoxically she also was fascinated and attracted by Whitman's "barbaric yawp." Her nominations for American masterpieces were Thomas Bailey Aldrich's "Memory," Emerson's "April," Poe's "To Helen," and Lanier's "A Ballad of Trees and the Master." There is no evidence that she ever discovered Emily Dickinson. Of her older contemporaries she liked Louise Imogen Guiney very much, but there is no proof that she ever read E. A. Robinson. Even after she knew him in Greenwich Village, she never found anything to say about his poetry. Among her exact contemporaries Robert Frost was a genuine enthusiasm. When *North of Boston* appeared, she wrote Elizabeth Sergeant that he was really and truly a poet with something fresh to say. Sara Teasdale was an acquaintance whose poetry she admired, and when she wrote in 1931 asking Sara to send her a collection of her poems, she admitted that the new crop of poets did not please her. She did not like analytic poetry, but thought that something should flower in a poem.

III

While Willa Cather was basking in the glow of being a published poet, a momentous chain of events was taking place. H. H. McClure, head of the McClure Syndicate, passed through Lincoln scouting for talent, and Will Jones urged him to look at the work of his former columnist. H. H. McClure told his cousin, S. S. McClure, the magazine editor and publisher, and that volatile genius wrote soliciting her stories for possible use in his magazine. She mailed them to him sometime about the middle of April 1903, but without much confidence that anything significant would happen. She already had submitted some of her stories to *McClure's Magazine,* and they had come back with rejection slips. A week after the parcel left Pittsburgh, however, she received a telegram from McClure summoning her to his office immediately. As soon as she could get away from her school, she took the train for New York and presented herself to McClure on the morning of May first.

Life was never the same for her after that interview. She walked into the offices of S. S. McClure at ten that morning, not worrying much, she later wrote, about streetcar accidents and such; at one o'clock she left stepping carefully. She had become a valuable property and worth saving. McClure with characteristic enthusiasm for his discoveries had offered her the world. He would publish her stories in book form. He would use them first in his magazine, and those he could not fit in, he would place in other journals for her. He wanted to publish everything she wrote from that point on. When she told him that some of the stories already had been rejected by *McClure's,* he said he never had seen them and called in his manuscript readers and asked them in her presence to give an accounting of their stewardship. She wrote Will Jones afterward that she sat and held her chin high and thought her hour had struck.

But that was not the end of the interview. McClure took her out to his home at Ardsley in Westchester County to meet his wife and children and Mrs. Robert Louis Stevenson, who was visiting him. Mrs. Stevenson already had read the stories and they talked them over together. McClure accepted the tales without any revisions and then wanted to know all about his new discovery, who she was, where she came from, what she had done up until then. There was no circumstance of her life that he did not inquire into, and he began to plan her future for her. She wrote afterward that if he had been a religious leader he would have had people going to the stake for him. What a genius he had for proselyting! He took a hold of one in such a personal way that business ceased to be a feature of one's relationship with him.

Unfortunately Willa Cather had promised to visit the Canfields, who then lived in New York, and she could stay only one day with the McClures, though they pressed her to stay longer. But when she left McClure, she was in a state of delirious excitement, his captive for life. Her future seemed assured, her first volume of fiction would be published the following year. Publication actually was postponed until 1905 so that two of the tales could be published in *McClure's Magazine* before the book's appearance, but that was a small matter. She was fairly launched at last, ten years after her debut as a newspaper columnist and drama critic. She still had a great deal to learn about writing, but never again would she have to worry about rejection slips. Meantime, she had to come down to earth and return to her Pittsburgh classroom.

The collection of stories that had so excited McClure appeared as *The Troll Garden* under the imprint of McClure, Phillips, and Company in 1905. Readers found seven tales arranged in a thematic design and introduced by two epigraphs, one from Charles Kingsley and the other from Christina Rossetti. If they were magazine readers, they might have read four of the stories already, for "'A Death in the Desert'" had been in *Scribner's* even before Willa Cather met McClure, "A Wagner Matinee" had appeared in *Everybody's Magazine* in February 1904, and *McClure's Magazine* had used "The Sculptor's Funeral" and "Paul's Case" shortly before the book appeared. The first three of these are in a sense western stories; "Paul's Case" and the three previously unpublished ones are laid in Pittsburgh, New York, and London. All concern in some way the world of art. One might have wondered at the collection, had he remembered that Willa Cather wrote in 1901 when she was beginning to create these tales: "The world is weary unto death of stories about artists and scholars and aesthetic freaks, and of studies of the 'artistic temperament.'" But she still was in her Henry James period, and the lives of artists and musicians fascinated her.

The key to the design of the book lies in the reinforcing epigraphs. The quotation from Kingsley is taken from *The Roman and the Teuton,* a series of historical lectures given at Cambridge. It is part of a parable he tells to introduce a discussion of the invasion of Rome by the barbarians: "A fairy palace, with a fairy garden; . . . inside the trolls dwell, . . . working at their magic forges, making and making always things rare and strange." The forest people, the barbarians, are attracted to the troll garden, Rome, and covet it and finally overrun it; but they find afterwards that they have destroyed the marvels they sought. The other epigraph comes from "The Goblin Market":

> *We must not look at Goblin men,*
> *We must not buy their fruits;*
> *Who knows upon what soil they fed*
> *Their hungry thirsty roots?*

In Christina Rossetti's poem one sister tastes the fruits and one does not. The fruits of the goblin men are related in Willa Cather's mind to the magical things rare and strange made by the trolls in their garden. The things desired are not only delightful and marvelous but also dangerous and capable of corrupting. Throughout her life Willa Cather made these juxtapositions: East against West, experience against innocence, civilization against primitivism. They were built into her life from her Virginia origin contrasted to Nebraska, from her study of history, literature, and the classics, in which the lure of Latin civilization drew her away from her native Anglo-Saxon Protestant culture, and from her life in Pittsburgh and the East after a prairie childhood. She loved art like a religion, but by the time these stories appeared, she was able to see that one might mistake Baal for the true god.

The first of the stories is "Flavia and Her Artists," a tale that concerns the pursuit of false art. Though it is laid in Westchester County, New York, it derives from her experiences in the homes of music patrons in Pittsburgh. Flavia, a collector of artists, fills her house with just the sort of aesthetic freaks that Willa Cather had complained about, but Flavia does not know that her artistic menagerie holds her in contempt. The story turns on the vicious profile of Flavia that M. Roux, a famous French novelist, gives to an interviewer after leaving the establishment. Flavia's patient, unhappy husband insults the guests in order to empty the house and save Flavia from finding out about the interview. She, of course, believes her husband to be a barbarian incapable of under-standing art.

The Jamesian flavor of this story is quite obvious, and Willa Cather never reprinted it. The irony of the relationship between the husband and wife, however, is very well managed, and al-though satire was a mode that Willa Cather never employed very effectively, or tried to, there are some pleasing satiric barbs in the story. They are delivered by a successful young actress, who hap-pens to be Flavia's second cousin. She is a sensible girl who does not take her stardom seriously and comments acutely on the go-ings-on to Imogen Willard, daughter of one of Flavia's old friends. Flavia finds Imogen interesting because she has written a doctoral dissertation on a "well-sounding branch of philology at the Ecole des Chartres." Dorothy Canfield must have suggested this charac-ter.

The second story in the collection is "The Sculptor's Funeral," one of her frequently anthologized tales. It contrasts with the first one by having a Red Cloud locale, though the stated setting is a little Kansas town. Where "Flavia and Her Artists" deals with false art, "The Sculptor's Funeral" concerns the inability of the Western barbarians to appreciate true art. Because it exposes the philistin-ism of the prairie town, the story often has been classified under the literary rubric "revolt from the village." In that respect it invites comparison with the earlier work of E. W. Howe and Ham-lin Garland and later books like *Spoon River Anthology*, *Wines-burg, Ohio*, and *Main Street*. It really fits into the larger pattern, however, of Willa Cather's consideration of the forest children versus the trolls. The story also derives in part from the poem previously mentioned, "The Night Express," and the author's at-tendance in Pittsburgh at the funeral of the local artist Charles Stanley Reinhart. She wrote in a column at the time that Rein-hart's family had not appreciated him, no one in Pittsburgh knew anything about him, or cared, and it passed all understanding how he could have come out of that commercial city.

The story begins with the arrival in Sand City of the body of Harvey Merrick, world-famous sculptor, who is regarded by his fellow townsmen as one local boy who did not amount to much. As the various characters sit about the mean and tasteless Merrick

house during the wake, Banker Phelps expresses the general sentiment: "What Harve needed, of all people, was a course in some
first-class Kansas City business college." Then he might have
amounted to something and helped run the family farm; instead,
his father had indulged him and sent him off East and to France
to study art. One man in town, however, knew, loved, and appreciated the sculptor, and voices scathing denunciation of the
meanness of Sand City. He is Jim Laird, a free spirit who never
got away from Philistia, and when the sculptor's body is brought
home he has become a drunken wreck. The contrasts are further
heightened by the creation of Henry Steavens, student and fol-
lower of the sculptor, who brings the body home for burial and
provides a sympathetic audience for Laird.

This is an excellent story that Willa Cather never repudiated,
though she did believe in her old age it was exaggerated in feeling
and carelessly executed. Ultimately she directed Alfred Knopf to
refuse to let it be anthologized any more; but she did not do this
until she had reprinted the story unchanged in *Youth and the
Bright Medusa* in 1920 and again with a few revisions in her
collected works.

"The Garden Lodge" concerns Caroline Noble, who gives up
preparation for a concert career for marriage, as Ethel Litchfield
had done, and marries a Wall Street tycoon. Caroline had grown
up in an artistic household where there had been intense devotion
to art but never enough money to pay the bills. "Caroline had
served her apprenticeship to idealism and to all the embarrassing
inconsistencies which it sometimes entails, and she decided to
deny herself this diffuse, ineffectual answer to the sharp questions
of life." After six years of marriage this practical, sensible woman
is surrounded by children, wealth, and an indulgent, loving husband. One day she invites the great Wagnerian tenor Raymond
d'Esquerré to stay with them, and they spend hours together in
the garden lodge. He feels the need to get out of Klingsor's Garden occasionally and to work in a quiet place, and he knows Caroline Noble is no lion hunter but a serious nonprofessional artist.
After he leaves, she goes to the garden lodge alone, plays the first
act of *Die Walküre,* the last of his roles they had practiced
together, and the memory of his presence overwhelms her: "It was

not enough; this happy, useful, well-ordered life was not enough." A storm breaks, rain beats in, as Caroline passes the night alone in a dark agony of the soul. The next morning, however, she awakes, despises herself for her weakness, crawls back to the main house from the garden lodge, and resumes her life. This story also was never reprinted.

" 'A Death in the Desert'," which takes its title from a poem by Browning, occupies the middle position in the book. The chief character does not appear on stage but provides the focus of the story. He is a brilliant composer just reaching the pinnacle of his creative powers, a character inspired by Ethelbert Nevin, whom he resembles in many details. Willa Cather must have written the story within a year following Nevin's death in mid-career, for it was originally published in January, 1903. It is not only her tribute to him but also a vehicle to examine three different kinds of artists in one story.

The story takes place on a ranch near Cheyenne, Wyoming, where one can see from the ranch house "a blinding stretch of yellow, flat as the sea in dead calm, splotched here and there with deep purple shadows; and, beyond, the ragged blue outline of the mountains." Katherine Gaylord, singer, is dying of tuberculosis on her brother's ranch. On to the scene comes Everett Hilgarde, younger brother of the great composer, who stops in Cheyenne en route to the West Coast. He accidentally discovers that Katherine is there dying and stays with her several weeks until the end. Years before when she had been on her way to stardom, a pupil of his brother's, he had loved her with a schoolboy's passion.

Nothing very much happens in this story. Everett and Katherine talk, mostly about the great Adriance, and in their talk the lives of all three are reconstructed. Adriance sends the score of his latest sonata, "a tragedy of the soul," a tragedy of "effort and failure," his greatest composition yet written. As Everett plays it over, she dissolves: "This is my tragedy, as I lie here spent by the race-course, listening to the feet of the runners as they pass me." Adriance, still gay, youthful, charming, and exuberantly creative, still leads the race. While Katherine is dying, Everett reflects on his own life. If her life is tragedy, his is pathos. He had the bad luck to resemble his brother, to aspire to an artistic career, but to be endowed with only average talent. As Katherine looks at him sitting at the piano, she thinks that his resemblance to his brother is as though a sculptor's finished work had been rudely copied in wood. But Everett long since has accepted his fate and resolved "to beat no more at doors he could never enter." Thus in this middle story of *The Troll Garden* Willa Cather considers one forest child who entered the garden and lived, another who was destroyed there, and a third who was denied entrance.

" 'A Death in the Desert' " occupies a significant place in Willa Cather's publishing history. It is the first story she published that she ever reprinted, but she never was satisfied with it. Before reprinting it in *The Troll Garden* following the publication in *Scribner's*, she revised it extensively, making approximately one hundred substantive changes, many of them extensive cuts. Then when she reprinted the story in *Youth and the Bright Medusa* in 1920, she revised extensively again, this time making 179 substantive changes of all sorts. Finally, for her collected works seventeen years later the story still dissatisfied her, and rather than revise again she did not reprint it. Dorothy Canfield Fisher, who reviewed *Youth and the Bright Medusa,* remembered the original version and compared it with the latter. She recommended that anyone who wants to see how a real artist "smooth[es] away crudeness without rooting out the life" should study these revisions. "To see her do it gives me complete and rounded pleasure that only fine craftsmanship can give."

"The Marriage of Phaedra," also never reprinted, is the most Jamesian tale in *The Troll Garden* and was suggested by Willa Cather's trip to Burne-Jones's studio in Kensington. For the story she created an American painter-author who visits the studio of the recently deceased English painter Hugh Treffinger in order to gather material for a biography. He strikes up a friendship with James, the painter's valet, who is custodian of the studio. From James comes the story of the painter's life and marriage—marriage in a double sense, for it was his two marriages that killed him, his last unfinished painting, "The Marriage of Phaedra," and his relationship with his wife, the socialite Lady Treffinger. It is interesting to note that this piece of fiction began taking form as early as the travel letter to the *Journal* describing Willa Cather's visit to

115

the studio. There she invents James, the valet-custodian, who in real life never existed. Here again is a study of an artist in relationship to society, the painter destroyed by his wife, one of the barbarians. Again the notion that art and marriage do not mix is exemplified, and the story contrasts interestingly with "The Garden Lodge," in which an artist and a barbarian are happily married, but only after the artist has given up her career.

"A Wagner Matinee" is another tale that treats Nebraska roughly and invites comparison in this respect with "The Sculptor's Funeral." It also has biographical interest, because readers familiar with Willa Cather's life always have assumed that Aunt Georgiana in the story was suggested by Aunt Franc, whose farm at Catherton Willa often visited and who had come from New England as a bride to pioneer Nebraska. The story deals with the return to Boston of the narrator's aunt to collect a legacy. She is a tired old farm wife, worn out from too much cooking, too much childbearing, too much housework on her husband's homestead in Nebraska. Because she had taught music before her marriage, the narrator takes her to a concert. The music awakens the memories of her youth and makes her realize what she has missed during all the grueling years of toil on the prairie. At the end of the concert she breaks down and cries, "I don't want to go, Clark, I don't want to go!" To this the narrator adds: "I understood. For her, just outside the door of the concert hall, lay the black pond with the cattle-tracked bluffs; the tall, unpainted house, with weather-curled boards, naked as a tower; the crook-backed ash seedlings where the dish-cloths hung to dry; the gaunt moulting turkeys picking up refuse about the kitchen door."

When this story appeared in *Everybody's Magazine* in 1904, it had repercussions. Willa Cather's old friend Will Jones rapped her on the knuckles in the *Journal:* "The stranger to this state will associate Nebraska with the aunt's wretched figure, her ill-fitting false teeth, her skin yellowed by weather. . . . If the writers of fiction who use western Nebraska as material would look up now and then and not keep their eyes and noses in the cattle yards, they might be more agreeable company." She replied promptly to defend herself, denying that she ever had any idea of disparaging the state. She had placed the story back in pioneer times and she thought everyone admitted that those days were desolate. She also thought she was paying tribute to those uncomplaining women who weathered those times. Farm life was bad enough when she knew it, and what must it have been like before that? She had to admit, however, that she had used the farmhouse where she and her family had lived, and some of her recollections. And it all was so beastly true that her own family felt quite insulted. They already had told her that it was not nice to tell such things. Yet, she added, a story is a personal impression, a sort of mood, not a real estate advertisement. To Viola Roseboro' she wrote that the whole affair had been the nearest she had come to personal disgrace. She seemed to have done something horrid without realizing it, but someday, she supposed, it all would seem humorous. That she could not have intended any disparagement of her aunt is perfectly clear from the warm, affectionate tone of all her letters to Aunt Franc.

This story underwent many revisions in subsequent reprintings and even survived in her collected works, but she did not soften the description of Aunt Georgiana or the bleak view of Nebraska when she reprinted it in *The Troll Garden.* She made 102 substantive changes, but they are mostly stylistic improvements. Some of the description of the aunt is cut, but what was trimmed had been a superfluity. The skin "yellow as a Mongolian's from constant exposure to a pitiless wind" and the "ill-fitting false-teeth" both remain. In 1920, however, she made extensive revisions again, this time to modify the portrait. The entire paragraph describing the aunt was cut, and the view that remains is similar in tone to the heroic descriptions of the pioneers in *O Pioneers!* and *My Ántonia.* The final version in 1937 made a few more substantive changes that further modify and soften the portrait.

The final story in the collection is "Paul's Case," the best known of all her stories and at the end of her life the only one she would allow to be anthologized. The wheel comes full circle with this tale of the Pittsburgh high-school boy who commits suicide in New York. Like Flavia in the opening story, Paul is not an artist but is seduced by art. As a schoolboy he is uninterested in Latin and math but lives for Carnegie Hall, where he has a job ushering. He hates his life in a prosaic, conventional, middle-class residential area. "It was at the theatre and at Carnegie Hall that Paul really lived; the rest was but a sleep and a forgetting. This was Paul's fairy tale, and it had for him all the allurement of a secret love." Paul's principal and his father decide that he must leave school, go to work, and stop hanging about the theaters and Carnegie Hall. But Paul cannot stand life in a business office and steals a thousand dollars from his employer. He goes to New York, buys himself elegant clothes, rents a suite at the Waldorf, lives for a while his dream life in actuality; then when his money is gone and his father is about to come after him, he goes to Newark and quietly drops under the wheels of an oncoming locomotive. Another forest child destroyed by the lure of the Troll Garden.

"Paul's Case" has been justly admired. It is a polished story that needed very few revisions in its subsequent reprintings. It captures the very tone of Pittsburgh in 1905 and is a remarkable psychological portrait. It was compounded, as she wrote in 1943, of two elements: the first was a boy she once had in her Latin class, a nervous youth who always was trying to make himself interesting and to prove that he knew members of the local stock company; the other was herself, particularly the feelings she had about New York and the old Waldorf-Astoria when she was teaching in Pittsburgh and occasionally visiting New York. As a college girl in Lincoln, she first had felt the pull of New York on her aspirations and desires, and as a newspaperwoman in Pittsburgh, she had been drawn into orbit by the gravitational force of the metropolis. Had it not been for the lure of the big city, Willa Cather's apprenticeship might have ended sooner, for "Paul's Case" attains a high level of artistry. She was not to go beyond it for another seven years, six of which she would spend in a literary detour editing *McClure's Magazine.*

CHAPTER 5

McClure's Magazine: 1906-1912

I

AT THE BEGINNING of 1906 *McClure's Magazine* was a fabulously successful enterprise under the editorial direction of an erratic genius. For the past three years the magazine had led the muckraking movement in exposing graft, corruption, dishonesty, and venality in big business, government at all levels, and even in the labor unions. In January 1903, S. S. McClure had written an editorial announcing the movement, and simultaneously he published the third in Ida Tarbell's sensational series on the Standard Oil Company, Lincoln Steffens's exposure of municipal corruption in Minneapolis, and Ray Stannard Baker's article on lawlessness in the mine workers' union. Tarbell, Steffens, and Baker, all working on the staff of *McClure's* at the same time, gave the journal a brilliance perhaps unsurpassed in American magazine history. McClure had a genius for discovering talent and directing it. He had a passion for facts and an old-fashioned missionary zeal to cure the ills that infected the body politic. As an impoverished Irish immigrant whose career had been an Horatio Alger hero come to life, he had worked his way through Knox College, married a professor's daughter, invented the newspaper syndicate, and gone on to create *McClure's Magazine.*

Yet despite his genius McClure was a hard man to work for. His ebullient and captivating personality left its mark on Willa Cather when she met him in May 1903, but at that very moment he was philandering with a third-rate poetess, leading his devoted wife a merry chase, bouncing across the country and back and forth to Europe, throwing off editorial ideas, mostly impractical, like a Fourth of July pinwheel, spending the company's money like

Croesus. The hard work of getting out the magazine was left to Ida Tarbell and others, and the business affairs fell to John Phillips, his former college classmate, who had been with him for years. Eventually the strain of living and working with McClure, of trying to keep his indiscretions from causing scandal, of thwarting his schemes for bankrupting the company, proved too much for Miss Tarbell and Phillips. When McClure insisted on going ahead with plans to start a new magazine, the crisis came.

Spring 1906 was an eventful era in the history of the magazine. McClure returned from one of his many trips to Europe in late March and was confronted by his associates with an ultimatum. Either he would have to sell out to them or they would sell out to him. They could not stand working with him any longer unless they could control the company's affairs. Both sides thrashed about during April. McClure wrote Phillips that he could not give up his magazine: " . . . kings who have come to the end of their tether, as a rule suffer death rather than give up part of their power." He felt the same way. The outcome was that McClure made arrangements to buy out Miss Tarbell and Phillips. His former associates then left him for good, taking with them Steffens, Baker, and a good many other members of the staff, even McClure's own cousin whom he had put in charge of the syndicate. On May tenth the rebels cleaned out their desks and departed. Late that afternoon Witter Bynner, who had been hired as office boy after graduating from Harvard four years before, found McClure sitting alone in the editorial department. "Bynner," he asked, "are you leaving me too?" Bynner could not speak. McClure broke into sobs.

McClure bounded back immediately, however, and even before the exodus, had begun putting together a new staff. One of the first things he did was to remember that Willa Cather was teaching at Allegheny High School. He apparently rushed to Pittsburgh, went to see her at Judge McClung's house, stayed to dinner, enchanted everyone with his talk, and when he left he had signed on a new mate for his disabled ship. Three days after the May tenth debacle the Nebraska State *Journal* reported that Willa Cather was now with *McClure's*.

When the call came, she did not hesitate. After seven years of journalism and five and one half of teaching, she was eager to move on. There was not even time to manage a trip back to Nebraska, and she boarded the Pennsylvania Railroad for New York as soon as school was out. It must have seemed that New York always had been her goal. The city had been the capital of the publishing industry for many years, and it long since had succeeded Boston as the national literary center. She had been to New York a good many times before joining *McClure's*, and the winter scene that the title character in "Paul's Case" contemplates so avidly must have been the New York that she saw in February 1898. Subsequent visits included stops en route to and from Europe in 1902, the memorable meeting with McClure the following year, a summer visit to Edith Lewis in 1904, and two trips during her last year of teaching.

A recent visit had been the gala occasion of Mark Twain's seventieth birthday dinner on December fifth. Given by Colonel Harvey of Harper and Brothers in the Red Room of Delmonico's, it brought out 170 literary and quasi-literary notables. Her invitation no doubt was the result of her authorship of *The Troll Garden*, then a new title on McClure, Phillips, and Company's trade list. Twain and Howells were the great celebrities of the evening, but there were many lesser notables that Willa Cather must have been excited to meet or at least to see: Mary E. Wilkins Freeman, Alice Brown, George Ade, Julian Hawthorne, and Owen Wister. Charles Major and Rex Beach, neither of whom she had any use for, also attended; so did Andrew Carnegie and Emily Post. Somehow Dorothy Canfield also had managed an invitation, but viewed in retrospect, the only important writer there besides Howells and Twain was Willa Cather. No one had thought E. A. Robinson, Ellen Glasgow, Edith Wharton, or Theodore Dreiser worth inviting, even though they all had begun publishing. It was a glittering evening nonetheless, and six months later Willa Cather, Pittsburgh English teacher, was to be a member of that establishment, an associate editor of a powerful magazine.

There was plenty of action in the offices of *McClure's Magazine* that summer when Willa Cather reported for work. In rapid succession McClure hired Perceval Gibbon, George Kibbe Turner, Henry Kitchell Webster, Will Irwin, Ellery Sedgwick, George

Kennan, and Cameron Mackenzie. Young Bynner, who stayed with the boss, found himself managing editor for five days until Irwin was lured away from the New York *Sun* to take command. Gibbon, a Welsh journalist whom McClure hoped would be another Kipling, stayed only a few weeks, though he became a contributor, and Webster, a novelist, remained only a couple of months. Ellery Sedgwick, an experienced editor, lasted a year before going on to the *Atlantic Monthly.* Kennan, uncle of the diplomatist and also a Russian expert, was dispatched to San Francisco to carry on Lincoln Steffens's muckraking activities in city government, and Turner, a veteran reporter, was sent off to Galveston to investigate the creation of the city-commission form of government. Of all the new employees only Willa Cather and Mackenzie survived the vicissitudes of the magazine. She resigned a few months before McClure himself was forced out by his creditors, and Mackenzie, who married Bess McClure, remained on as managing editor even after his father-in-law's downfall. The new team was augmented further by one other "loyalist," Viola Roseboro', chief manuscript reader, who began the new game by discovering a new writer, Damon Runyon.

Ellery Sedgwick in his autobiography reports that a week at *McClure's* "was the precise reversal of the six busy days described in the first chapter of Genesis. It seemed to end in a world without form and void. From Order came forth Chaos." The staff worked under some natural law of desperation. The chief was continually interrupting, cutting, revising, and efforts were periodically made to circumvent him by hiding out in nearby hotel rooms in order to finish articles to meet deadlines. "Yet with all his pokings and proddings the fires he kindled were brighter than any flames his staff could produce without him. . . . the intensity of McClure's enthusiasm would bring any project to a white heat." Edith Lewis, who was a proofreader on the magazine and later Willa Cather's apartment-mate, remembers that "working on *McClure's* was like working in a high wind." The boss, of course, was the tornado and seemed to be everywhere at once. He was full of ideas, all of which he wanted acted upon at once. Yet he was patient and gentle, never lost his temper, and treated everyone courteously, office boys and managing editors alike.

Long after both she and McClure were out of the magazine, Willa Cather wrote a story, "Ardessa," laid in a magazine office reminiscent of *McClure's*. The editor in this tale is named O'Mally, who has come out of the West like McClure and has built a great muckraking magazine in six incredible years. On his staff are five famous men, every one of whom he has made ("it amused him to manufacture celebrities"); but no amount of recognition can make a stuffed shirt out of O'Mally. He is a born gambler and a soldier of fortune: "O'Mally went in for everything; and got tired of everything; that was why he made a good editor." It is restful, however, when O'Mally is in Nevada tending to his silver mine. Then the great men of the staff are left alone "as contemplative as Buddhas in their private offices, each meditating upon the particular trust or form of vice confided to his care."

Willa Cather must have wondered sometimes what she was doing there. She had absolutely no interest in muckraking, found social reformers very dull people, took the dimmest possible view of literature that had a message. But there was another side to *McClure's*, the literary content of the magazine. McClure not only had the talent for directing the work of great reporters like Steffens and Baker, but he also could sniff out good fiction. Much of Kipling's best work had appeared in the magazine; McClure published Stevenson, Hardy, Arnold Bennett, Crane, O. Henry, London, Twain, and Conan Doyle. He thought he probably had lost more money publishing Conrad than anyone else. He was open-handed with his profits and never regarded a dollar he had made as anything more than an opportunity to buy something better for the magazine. Willa Cather had as one of her duties reading the flood of manuscripts that poured in from hopeful authors, nearly all of which were uniformly bad and unpublishable. She also had to help whip into publishable form articles by semiliterate fellows who knew all about copper mines in the West but could not write.

Life in New York was exciting, and once she settled down there, she never left the city except to travel or to spend the summers in cooler climates. She often complained about the noise and dirt and the ever-increasing vulgarity of the city, but she never could give it up. She moved into a studio apartment at 60 South Washington Square, in the same building that Edith Lewis lived in, and commuted daily from Washington Square to the magazine office on East Twenty-third Street. Greenwich Village at that time was a pleasant place to live. Few automobiles yet marred the urban scene, and on the north side of the square the long row of mellow brick houses gave the area an aristocratic look. On the south side of the square were less pretentious buildings occupied by writers and artists. The studio apartments that painter Don Hedger and singer Eden Bower occupy in the story "Coming, Aphrodite!" draw on Willa Cather's memory of her first days in New York. They live on the top floor of an old house and share a grubby bathroom at the end of the hall. Hedger's single room with a cheerless northern exposure looks out on a court and the roofs and walls of other buildings. He had a sink, a table, and two gas burners in one corner. Eden Bower's apartment is somewhat pleansanter—two rooms facing west on the square.

But down below, the square was lovely that summer. It was almost the last summer of the old horse-stages on Fifth Avenue. The fountain threw up mists of rainbow-water, occasionally spraying Italian babies playing on the rim, and robins hopped about on the blindingly green grass, newly cut. "Looking up the Avenue through the Arch, one could see the young poplars with their bright, sticky leaves, and the Brevoort [Hotel] glistening in its spring coat of paint, and shining horses and carriages,—occasionally an automobile." Farther uptown were the theaters and the Metropolitan Opera House. It was great to be thirty-two years old and finally a part of this marvelous city.

But what New York and *McClure's Magazine* did to her writing career is another matter. During the years she was actively involved in editing the magazine, she had very little time to write. She published four stories in 1907, but it is likely that they had been written before she left Pittsburgh. In 1908 and 1909 she wrote just one story each year, and the following year is a total blank. During 1911, the last year in which she gave the magazine her full attention, she managed to publish one tale and write a short novel.

The stories of 1907 break no new ground and represent no advance beyond the tales published in *The Troll Garden*. It seems likely that some may have been written about the same time as the stories collected in the book. Three are stories of artists, and the fourth is a tale so Jamesian that it might have been written by Edith Wharton. The first of these is "The Namesake," previously discussed, and the second is "The Profile," a story laid in Paris about a painter who marries a woman badly disfigured by a scar on her face. Its denouement is a tragedy growing out of the painter's obsession with his wife's scar. The psychological drama enacted reminds one of James in its narrative technique and Hawthorne in its theme and subject, particularly such a story as "The Birthmark." The third story is "The Willing Muse," also very Jamesian, about a writer who marries a writer. The husband is a perfectionist; the wife is a hack with astonishing fecundity, who produces two novels a year. The husband's ability to write is destroyed by his wife's Niagara output. Bertha Gray in this story reminds one of Jane Highmore in James's "The Next Time," and Kenneth Gray seems compounded of Paul Overt in "The Lesson of the Master" and Ray Limbert in "The Next Time." The final member of this quartet is "Eleanor's House," the most Jamesian of all, a tale of a husband so devoted to his first wife that he cannot bear to take his second wife to the home created by the first. The story is psychological drama in which the second wife manages to exorcise the influence of the first.

Willa Cather never reprinted any of these stories, regarding all of them as unsound apples and apprentice work. When F. L. Pattee wanted to anthologize "The Willing Muse" in 1926, she refused out of hand. The story, she wrote, was so tepid and bloodless that she would not consider under any circumstances letting it be reprinted. Yet all of these stories are competent, and as they now appear in her *Collected Short Fiction*, one can see that her later disparagement is unduly severe. She had not yet found her own material and did not wish to be reminded of her Jamesian period, but in the handling of narrative techniques such as the use of minor-character point of view and in the subtle control of psychological conflict they are skillfully done.

II

Willa Cather had not been in New York more than six months before McClure gave her an assignment that took her to Boston for most of 1907 and part of 1908. He had bought a manuscript that was full of interesting, even sensational material, but it was badly in need of rewriting and checking. This was Georgine Milmine's *The Life of Mary G. Baker Eddy and the History of Christian Science*. Mark Sullivan, the first member of the staff to work on this manuscript, had made several trips to New England checking facts about Mrs. Eddy's remarkable life and had prepared the first few installments for the magazine. Willa Cather took over the task, moved into the Parker House in Boston, later an apartment on Chestnut Street, and also traveled about rural New England to verify details of the series. McClure had a passion for accuracy. and did not mind paying a writer for months of painstaking research for a single article. The assignment involved interviewing many of Mrs. Baker's early associates, looking up records, working over the manuscript with Mrs. Milmine.

The articles began appearing in January 1907, the month Willa Cather went to Boston to work on the April installment. The series was a sensation and ran in the magazine, with a few breaks, until the middle of the following year. McClure had not lost his talent for filling the magazine with provocative and interesting material. While the Christian Science series was being prepared, the magazine ran a serial by Kipling, Carl Schurz's memoirs, and Burton Hendrick's exposure of the life-insurance industry. While Milmine's manuscript was running, *McClure's* published fiction by Conrad and began Ellen Terry's memoirs. McClure could get along without his star writers, and circulation went up in 1906; but as it turned out, he could not do without the business acumen of John Phillips, and his downfall in 1911 was due to financial mismanagement.

The Boston assignment was a marvelous stroke of good fortune for Willa Cather. If New York was an exciting, lively place, Boston had charm and a rich literary past. Many of the familiar bearded schoolroom poets of her youth had lived in and about Boston. Indeed, she had played the game of authors with their pictures and book titles, and Emerson had long been one of her sources.

During this stay in Boston she made a number of literary friends: Ferris Greenslet of Houghton Mifflin, later her publisher, Margaret Deland, writer, and Louise Imogen Guiney, poet. She also met Louis Brandeis, future Supreme Court justice, his wife, and her sister Pauline Goldmark, social worker.

Her most important friendships began, however, one day in the late winter of 1908 when she set out from the Parker House to call on Mrs. Brandeis in Otis Place. When she arrived, her hostess said she wanted to take her to visit a very charming old lady, Mrs. James T. Fields, widow of the former Boston publisher, who lived in nearby Charles Street. Together they set out on what for Willa Cather was a moving journey into the past. To the girl from Red Cloud the firm of Ticknor and Fields was literary history, an imprint on the books she had read in her father's bookcase. That Mrs. James T. Fields could still be living in Boston in 1908 seemed incredible. Her husband had been the friend and publisher of Hawthorne, Emerson, Lowell, Holmes, an early editor of the *Atlantic Monthly,* and a key figure in New England's golden age. Annie Fields was in fact living at 148 Charles Street in the same house that had entertained Dickens, Thackeray, Matthew Arnold, and a host of other literary notables. She had married Fields when he was a middle-aged widower and had survived him by many years.

Although Mrs. Fields was over seventy, she did not seem old when Willa Cather was conducted into her drawing room. "Frail, diminished in force, yes; but, emphatically, *not* old." She was still a gay, vital spirit, a woman with a merry, musical laugh, a hostess of consummate skill and grace. In her presence Willa Cather relived literary history of the nineteenth century. She had talked to Leigh Hunt about Shelley. She had known Joseph Severn, who had given her a lock of Keats's hair. The house was full of treasures: rare editions, manuscripts of great authors, association copies of books written by her guests. If one did not "go at" her, Mrs. Fields would talk of her famous visitors just as though they were people who had dropped in for tea last week. For the first time in her life, Willa Cather later wrote, she felt that Americans had a past of their own, and she went away with an exultant feeling:

It was at tea-time, I used to think, that the great shades were most likely to appear; sometimes they seemed to come up the deeply carpeted stairs, along with living friends. At that hour the long room was dimly lighted, the fire bright, and through the wide windows the sunset was flaming, or softly brooding, upon the Charles River and the Cambridge shore beyond. The ugliness of the world, all possibility of wrenches and jars and wounding contacts, seemed securely shut out.

Willa Cather loved going to that house on Charles Street and she loved its occupant, though she never quite got over her awe. She also visited Mrs. Fields at her Massachusetts summer place at Manchester-by-the-Sea and wrote her frequently, but in her letters she was always afraid of touching on one of Mrs. Fields's prejudices and letting the noisy modern world in on her. When DeWolfe Howe disposed of Mrs. Fields's correspondence, she insisted that her letters be destroyed because they were too unrepresentative. When she was with Mrs. Fields, however, she did not feel constraint and their relations were natural. She delighted in the contrasts between her world of *McClure's Magazine* and the surviving bit of the Victorian era on Charles Street. It was delicious to have Mrs. Fields look up from the paper and ask gravely who Rex Beach was and did he have anything to do with letters? Mrs. Fields was the soloist and she was the accompanist, she wrote Howe, and she did not mind learning from her hostess. One day Mrs. Fields quoted a line of poetry that Willa Cather did not recognize.

"'That's very nice,' said I, 'but I don't recognize it.'"

"'Surely,' she said, 'that would be Dr. Donne.'"

She never pretended with Mrs. Fields, and so she asked: "And who . . . was Dr. Donne?" Mrs. Fields, she recalled, was patient with her ignorance and sent her up to bed with two fat volumes of Donne to read.

She learned a great deal from Mrs. Fields, not just the anecdotes of literary history or who and what John Donne was. It was her manner, her complete faith in the great tradition, her life-style, to use a contemporary term, that instructed Willa Cather. She was an exemplary figure, a model, even though Willa regarded herself as a "new woman," emancipated and progressive. When she reiewed Howe's edition of Mrs. Fields's diaries, *Memories of a Hostess,* she quoted a sentence from Aristotle that Mrs. Fields had copied in her diary as a young woman: "Virtue is concerned with action; art with production." The problem of life, she added, was to harmonize the two. In a long life, wrote Willa Cather, "she went far toward working out this problem." Willa Cather too pondered this maxim and believed in it.

Even more important than meeting Mrs. Fields, however, was meeting Sarah Orne Jewett, one of the most prepotent forces in her literary development. Mrs. Fields and Miss Jewett were old friends, and the beginning of Willa Cather's friendship took place at 148 Charles Street during one of Miss Jewett's periodic visits to Boston from her home in South Berwick, Maine. Willa Cather had discovered Sarah Orne Jewett at least as early as her Pittsburgh period and had come to rank her among the three greatest American writers, in the company of Twain and James. An immediate friendship sprang up between the two women, and Willa Cather saw her several times during the balance of 1908 in Boston and with Mrs. Fields at Manchester. Her unexpected death in June 1909, while Willa Cather was in London on business for McClure, was a bitter loss. Immediately afterwards she wrote Mrs. Fields, in one of two letters that have survived, that everything she had been doing and undertaking had been done with the hope of interesting Miss Jewett. And now all the wheels stood still and the ways of life seemed very dark and purposeless. Mrs. Fields, knowing the shock her death would cause, wrote an immediate consoling letter, which reached London two days after Willa had heard the news. Mrs. Fields would never know, she wrote, what a kind thing she had done. Meantime, the *Kaiser Wilhelm der Grosse* of the North German Lloyd Line was bringing her back through heavy seas to resume her editorial duties on *McClure's.*

She had been promoted to the editorial desk of the magazine the year before on finishing her assignment in Boston with the Christian Science manuscript. She and Kibbe Turner succeeded Will Irwin, whose tenure as managing editor had lasted about a year. Whether he quit or was fired is not clear, but he admitted: "As a curb on genius, I was not a success." McClure actually was his own managing editor as well as editor-in-chief, and the person or persons who sat on the editorial desk were merely expected to handle routine editorial correspondence, dispose of would-be con tributors who insisted on calling in person, recognize any talent that swam into view, and keep McClure informed of what was going on. By about 1909 Willa Cather actually was managing edi tor, but she never listed herself as such in *Who's Who* and the magazine carried no masthead to indicate who was what. She was able to get along with McClure better than anyone else, and oc cupied her uneasy editorial seat for more than three years. Under McClure's training she became a competent magazine executive

Before she settled down to that job, however, she had an other trip to Europe with Isabelle McClung. The two friends sailed in April 1908 and this time visited Italy. Willa Cather' long love affair with Virgil, Rome, and Latin civilization finally could feed at the original sources. They spent a week in the Apennines and went on to Rome and Naples. From the lovely Gulf of Salerno Willa Cather wrote Sarah Orne Jewett that the camellias were all in bloom in the Rufolo Garden and her hotel in Ravello was covered with yellow roses. She had a room over looking the sea. Apparently Miss Jewett had stayed there, for she wrote that her correspondent no doubt would remember the view. The land dropping down to the sea looked like ho green porcelain whose flow had been checked by the jagged cliffs along which ran the Salerno road. It was surely a sea of legend, a sea that glimmered centuries away with the opaque blue water that Puvis de Chavannes painted. The day before there had been a religious festival at nearby Amalfi, and she had started out gaily in the company of Italians along the foot path that ran along the carriage road. Just at a point where the path became visible to the road, she met some people from Nebraska who recognized her. She had to go back to Ravello with them and lose her Italian companions and the fiesta.

The trip to Italy was only an interlude, however, and by July she was back in the office. There was no visit home that sum mer, though she did get up to Manchester to see Mrs. Field and Miss Jewett. Sometime that summer she managed to write a pretty good story ("On the Gulls' Road") that *McClure* scheduled for publication in December. In the autumn she an

Edith Lewis took an apartment together at 82 Washington Place and began living arrangements that were to last a lifetime.

Edith Lewis had met Willa Cather in Lincoln in the summer of 1903 just after returning home from an eastern college. She then had gone to New York to work, had entertained Willa Cather there twice in succeeding years, and since 1906 they both had worked for *McClure's*. The friendship grew during the year Willa Cather spent in Boston working on the Christian Science articles, for Edith Lewis was sent up from New York with proof which they read together—a practice they continued after Willa began writing novels. The relationship between the two women was a warm, close, lasting friendship that endured through all vicissitudes. Elizabeth Sergeant, who met them both in this period, wrote of the relationship: "A captain, as Will White of Emporia said . . . must have a first officer, who does a lot the captain never knows about to steer the boat through the rocks and reefs." Edith Lewis was Willa Cather's first mate. But she never supplanted Isabelle McClung in the captain's affections, even after Isabelle deserted her for matrimony.

Willa Cather had misgivings about the story that appeared in the December issue of *McClure's*. She wrote Sarah Orne Jewett as she finished reading proof that the scent of the tuberose still clung to it and it rather screamed. Stories like that, by which she meant stories in her Jamesian manner, did not seem to matter very much any more, but she was working on another one that Miss Jewett might like, a western story that McClure sniffed at and thought all introduction. From her description it is clear that this story was "The Enchanted Bluff," a splendid tale that breaks out of her Jamesian bondage and foreshadows her best later work. One infers from her letter that she enclosed a copy. *Harper's* published the story in April 1909, but there is no record of Miss Jewett's comment on it.

The story that came out in December, "On the Gulls' Road," is another Jamesian yarn that takes place on board a ship sailing from Italy to New York. The narrator, a young man, meets the beautiful Alexandra Ebbling, invalid wife of the ship's chief engineer. He falls in love with her during the voyage and in the course

of his attentions to her learns of her loveless marriage. She permit
him to love her because she knows she cannot live long. The stor
ends with Mrs. Ebbling going back to her native Norway and th
narrator cherishing his memories.

Though this story barely escapes maudlin sentiment, it brough
immediate praise from Sarah Orne Jewett. She had read the stor
with "deep happiness," and it made her feel very near to th
writer's "young and loving heart." The wife and her husband ha
been drawn with "unerring touches and wonderful tenderness fc
her." And she added: "It makes me the more sure that you are fa
on your road toward a fine and long story of very high class." Th
lover, however, she thought was flawed, though it was done a
well as it could be when a woman writes in the man's characte
Yet it is always a masquerade, she noted, for a woman to try t
adopt a man's point of view in fiction. It is better to write abou
male characters than to be them.

Although Willa Cather had great respect for Miss Jewett's opir
ions, she never took this advice very seriously. She already ha
written a good many stories from a male point of view, and eve
since her youthful masquerade as "William Cather, M.D.," she ha
been disposed to do this. She never recognized that she could nc
write like a man. When she wrote *My Ántonia* her narrator wa
Jim Burden, and when she wrote *A Lost Lady* the story was see
through the eyes of Niel Herbert. It is true, however, that most c
her great characters are female: Alexandra Bergson, Ántonia, The
Kronborg, Marian Forrester.

Miss Jewett was not satisfied with the letter she had writte
about "On the Gulls' Road." She thought about the story and he
young friend for the next two weeks and then wrote a long secon
letter which really said what was on her mind. She saw enoug
potential in Willa Cather that she felt obliged to level with her. "
cannot help saying what I think," she began, "about your writin
and its being hindered by such incessant, important, responsib
work as you have in your hands now." She thought it impossib
for her to be a magazine editor and at the same time have he
writing talent mature properly. Although *The Troll Garden* co
tained some good work, especially "The Sculptor's Funeral," "yc
are older now than that book . . . but if you don't keep and gua;

and mature your force, and above all, have time and quiet to perfect your work, you will be writing things not much better than you did five years ago."

Then she went on to review Willa Cather's background and career to date: "You have your Nebraska life,—a child's Virginia, and now an intimate knowledge of what we are pleased to call the 'Bohemia' of newspaper and magazine-office life. These are uncommon equipment, but . . . you stand right in the middle of each of them when you write, without having the standpoint of the looker-on who takes them each in their relations to letters, to the world." Willa Cather also had a good education, which was necessary and important to her. But at this point in her career (she was just thirty-five) she needed a quiet place to write: "Your vivid, exciting companionship in the office must not be your audience, you must find your own quiet centre of life, and write from that to the world . . . in short, you must write to the human heart, the great consciousness that all humanity goes to make up." Otherwise, she added, what might be strength in a writer is only crudeness, what might be insight is only observation, and what might be sentiment is only sentimentality. "You can write about life, but never write life itself. And to write and work on this level, we must live on it."

This remarkable letter from a great old writer to an aspiring young one touched Willa Cather deeply. She responded with an eight-page reply a day or two after receiving it. In her answer she analyzed herself, her prospects, her ambitions, her talents, more profoundly perhaps than ever before. The letter is extremely revealing of her state of mind two and one half years after joining *McClure's* staff. She admitted that she was deeply perplexed about her life. She was not made to have to do with what McClure called "men and measures." In order to get on with that kind of work, she had to go at it with the sort of energy most people had to exert only on rare occasions. Consequently she was living from day to day much like a trapeze performer on the bar. It was catch the right bar at the right time or onto the net you go. Her mind was off doing trapeze work all day and came back to her only at night when she was exhausted.

Then the reading of so many poorly written manuscripts had a deadening effect. This part of her job made her dread everything made out of words. She felt diluted and weakened by it, as though she were living in a tepid bath and could no longer stand heat or cold. She often thought of trying to get three or four months a year free to write, but then planning articles for the magazine was pretty much in her head and she had become a sort of card catalogue and could not turn the notes over to anyone else. McClure was trying to make her into a carbon copy of Ida Tarbell and wanted above all else clear-cut journalism, something she did not despise, but she got no satisfaction from it.

It seems clear from this letter that McClure exerted a sort of Svengali-like influence on her. He had been telling her that he did not think she ever would amount to much as a writer but that she had the makings of a good magazine executive. He thought she had better let it go at that, and she was beginning to think that maybe he was right. Yet despite the opinion of the "chief" she felt that perhaps she should consider her immortal soul. McClure thrived on the perpetual debauch of editorial life, but five years more of it were sure to make her fat, sour, ill-tempered, and— worst of all—fussy.

When Miss Jewett had said that she needed a quiet center for her life or her writing would not improve, she touched an exposed nerve. Willa Cather was much disturbed that her writing did not seem to be improving. If she had been making any progress at all in the past five years, she wrote, it had been progress of the head, not of the hand. In her editorial duties she could do what she wanted and could learn by experience, but in her writing she was a newborn babe every time she started something new. She came to it naked, shivery, and without any bones, and never seemed to learn anything at all.

Why, one asks, did Willa Cather continue nearly three more years living this "perpetual debauch"? She admitted to Miss Jewett that she could stop working the next summer and have enough money saved to live simply for three or four years. She still sent money occasionally to her family, but that was not the reason she did not break loose. The answer must lie in the hold McClure had on her, the attractions of New York, the pleasures of being a Red Cloud girl who had fought her way to the top, and the genuine self-doubt that her letter to Miss Jewett displays. Whatever the reason, she conceded that she had something like a split personality.

There is no doubt that McClure appreciated Willa Cather's work and rewarded her generously. "I have been greatly pleased with your work," and "I am awfully proud of your splendid work," he would write her when she was out of town on magazine business. He had another way of holding on to her, perhaps even more effective than praise. He sent her to Europe in May 1909 and again two years later to hunt manuscripts for the magazine. He believed in frequent trips to Europe and thought that a roving editor was more likely to discover talent than a sedentary one. During her first trip to London she went to hear Vera Figner, a Russian political prisoner who had been released after twenty-two years of mostly solitary confinement in the dread Schlüsselburg Prison in the Neva River near St. Petersburg. From this experience came a series of articles by David Soskice, *The Secrets of the Schlüsselburg,* for which she wrote the introduction.

On these trips she met many interesting theatrical and literary people. She got to know William Archer, London drama critic, writer, and contributor to *McClure's,* who took her to the funeral of George Meredith and to the first London performance of the Abbey Theater. They sat with Lady Gregory in Yeats's box and saw Synge's *The Playboy of the Western World.* Through Archer she met various London stage people and gathered the background material that went into her first novel, *Alexander's Bridge.* She also met H. G. Wells, Ford Madox Ford (then Hueffer), Edmund Gosse, and made friends with Katherine Tynan.

For the next twenty months following her return from Europe in 1909 Willa Cather was pretty well chained to her editorial desk. She squeezed in a six-weeks' visit to Red Cloud in September and October, and then McClure went to Europe, leaving her to run the magazine alone. She wrote her Aunt Franc in January that she had been so tired by Christmas that she had gone to bed for the holidays. During most of 1910 she drudged away on Twenty-third Street while McClure remained away. In July she wrote her former Pittsburgh pupil Norman Foerster, then a new Harvard graduate, that she was editing the magazine by herself and expecting no vacation until October. She did get away in the late fall but was back at her desk from December until she went to the hospital with severe mastoiditis at the end of February. The results of her industry were reflected in the circulation figures, however, and each year the sales increased. The issue for June 1910 was the largest in the magazine's history.

The articles and stories that *McClure's* published in the period of her managing editorship, however, do not seem remarkable sixty years later. Mrs. Humphry Ward was the serialized novelist in these issues, and Willa Cather bought fiction from Arnold Bennett, O. Henry, Theodore Dreiser, and Jack London. She also bought stories from Rex Beach and Kathleen Norris, three from the latter within six months. Nonfiction articles included muckraking pieces by Turner, a series on Grover Cleveland, and work by Jane Addams. William Archer wrote on the theater, and there were more reminiscences by Ellen Terry. One day she bought an article on the sweated workers in the tenements by a brisk young woman just out of Bryn Mawr.

This was Elizabeth Sergeant, who walked in to *McClure's* offices with her manuscript and a letter of introduction from Pauline Goldmark. Articles on social problems did not interest Willa Cather, but buying them was part of her trapeze act, and this one was publishable. She took the contribution and admitted Miss Sergeant to her circle of friends. It was a friendship that was very close for the next two decades. It never was broken off, but the two women did not see each other very often after the twenties. Willa Cather's friendships—and also her hates—usually were formed on the basis of intuitive reactions to people. She knew right away if she wanted to bother with a person, and if she did, a warm relationship was likely to flower. Elizabeth Sergeant met the test, despite the fact she had written on slum problems. She was, moreover, perhaps the only political liberal Willa Cather ever was close to, but their friendship was personal and literary and they steered clear of what McClure called "men and measures."

The woman that Miss Sergeant met in *McClure's* office in January 1910 was a buoyant, rather square woman with no trace of the feminist about her. She shook hands in a direct, almost brusque manner and led her visitor through the jostle of the noisy outer office to her private office. Her boyish, enthusiastic manner was disarming. Her voice had a western resonance about it (Miss Sergeant was from Boston), and her clothes were informal, as if she rebelled against urban conformities. She wore a bright striped blouse and a loud Irish-tweed skirt that cut her sturdy legs in half. When McClure came into the office, Miss Sergeant could see at once that they were made to work together. "Their Midwest voices harmonized, their seething inner forces supplemented each other. There was an inspirational quality about the dynamic unspoiled assistant that kept the older man afloat on his sea of discovery—the only sea he was interested in navigating."

Another lifelong friendship began at *McClure's* when the future playwright Zoë Akins submitted verse to the magazine. Although the verse was not up to Willa Cather's standards, she found the author a delightful young woman of twenty-three who had come to New York from St. Louis to be a writer. In sending back her verses Willa Cather wrote Zoë Akins that she really ought to try playwriting, but whether or not she was responsible for making a playwright out of her new friend is a moot point. She did begin writing plays, however, and after achieving a great success in *Déclassée* in 1919 went on to write one successful play after another until she won a Pulitzer Prize in 1935. Willa Cather and Zoë Akins carried on a lifelong correspondence, writing each other warm and affectionate letters several times a year. Although Zoë settled in California in the thirties, she came to New York on theater business every year and the two friends always got together. Willa had no hesitation in telling Zoë when her plays were bad, and Zoë always took her criticism good naturedly. Zoë also had a genius for sending her friend gifts that pleased her, often flowers, sometimes extravagant ones, like a blooming apple tree at Christmas time. Nothing ever marred this relationship, and Willa Cather wrote Zoë in 1936 that she was one of her comforts and one of the very few people she trusted. On another occasion she wrote that she envied Zoë's natural ability to enjoy life and her courage to take chances. For Willa Cather there was a golden glow about this friend.

Besides Elizabeth Sergeant and Zoë Akins, there was a steadily widening circle of New York friends. Although her fondness for the theater diminished greatly after she went to *McClure's*, she maintained a lively interest in George Arliss, who lived with his wife near Washington Place. She thought his characterization of Disraeli was one of the great performances of the era, and she often went to after-theater parties at his apartment. She also was a friend and neighbor of Viola Roseboro' of *McClure's* staff and came to know and admire Ida Tarbell, even though the latter had left McClure in the celebrated break. (McClure's former employees seldom left the "chief" with any rancor.) Another friend and neighbor was Mrs. Clara Potter Davidge, who had built E. A. Robinson a studio behind her house at 121 Washington Place. Willa Cather met Robinson there but apparently did not care for him and never solicited any of his poems for *McClure's*.

The year 1911 opened with a sudden, terrifying illness—a case of mastoiditis that put her in the hospital for several weeks and left her weak and exhausted for several more. While she was recuperating, McClure sent her to Europe again to hunt for manuscripts. But by early May she was back in the office at her old editorial desk, and by the end of the month she was in Boston on business. Her years of editing the magazine were about to end, though she did not yet know it. When she visited Boston, she spent a very pleasant week with Mrs. Fields, one of her best visits, and was in good spirits. Mrs. Fields herself, then seventy-six, had come down to the South Station to meet her, the first time in years she had been there, and the charm of that magically haunted house was never so potent. That other rare spirit, Sarah Orne Jewett, seemed not far away, and the house was full of things that had belonged to her. A lift had been installed for Mrs. Fields's use, and Willa wrote that she had become an expert elevator boy. If she failed as managing editor, she wrote Louise Guiney, she always could get a job with the company as an elevator operator.

The euphoria revealed in this letter lasted well into the summer. She had fully recovered from the mastoid infection of the winter, and her trip to London must have provided her with more than manuscripts for the magazine. She had by this time gotten the idea for a three-part serial for *McClure's* that would appear in book form the following year as her first novel, *Alexander's Bridge*. When and where she wrote this story is uncertain, but after returning to New York on June third she made another trip to New England later in the month to visit Mary Jewett in South Berwick, Maine. She may have begun the story there, or if she did not, at least the memory of Sarah Orne Jewett must have inspired her. She wrote Elizabeth Sergeant on the twenty-seventh that she was saluting her from the little desk where it all happened. With her enthusiasm for Miss Jewett rekindled, and fresh from her visit to Charles Street, she must have written fairly rapidly. The novel was finished by the end of the summer, and somewhere along the way she also found time to write "The Joy of Nelly Dean," a Nebraska story that the *Century* would publish in October. It was a very productive summer despite the fact that McClure was in Europe and she had the entire editorial burden of the magazine on her shoulders.

III

Although it was her first novel, *Alexander's Bridge* marks the end of her beginning rather than the beginning of her end. The story is Jamesian, the world of Boston and London. The characters are Bartley Alexander, bridge-builder; his wife Winifred, young Boston society matron; Hilda Burgoyne, London actress, beautiful, talented, single; and Professor Lucius Wilson, one of Alexander's former teachers, who appears occasionally as observer, a sort of Jamesian *ficelle*. The materials out of which this novel is fashioned are the settings and people of Willa Cather's years at *McClure's:* the Boston of Chestnut Street where she had rented an apartment briefly, and Mrs. Fields and her house on Charles Street, the theater world of London to which she had been introduced by William Archer on her business trips for the magazine, and a news event of 1909—the collapse of a new bridge under construction across the St. Lawrence River at Quebec.

The novel tells the story of Bartley Alexander, who at the age of forty-three already is a world-famous engineer. Glowing with strength and cordiality and rugged, blond good looks, he is the bridge-builder whose picture the Sunday supplement editors always want "because he looked as a tamer of rivers ought to look." He is happily married to a woman who has brought him wealth and position, but despite the outward appearance of success, he is a restless soul, a man who has found no happiness. When the story opens, he is building a great bridge across the St. Lawrence. On one of his business trips to London he meets Hilda Burgoyne, an actress he once had been in love with in his student days. They resume their former relationship, and for the next year Bartley lives a double life. After an agonizing struggle he makes the decision to leave his wife for Hilda, but at that moment he is summoned to Quebec by his subordinates in charge of the bridge construction. The bridge has developed alarming symptoms of strain, and as Alexander inspects the structure, it collapses into the river, killing him and many of the workmen.

Bartley Alexander is an interesting characterization, a man with a flawed moral nature. As Professor Wilson tells him at the beginning: "I always used to feel that there was a weak spot where some day strain would tell. . . . The more dazzling the front you presented, the higher your façade rose, the more I expected to see a big crack zigzagging from top to bottom." This had been Wilson's feeling when Bartley was in college, but at the moment of relating it he believed he had been mistaken. He had not, of course, and Alexander's life comes crashing down at the end, just as his bridge comes crashing down. He had put too much stress and strain on his life, and he had figured too closely the stresses and strains in his bridge. He had loved his wife, who even at the end "still was, as she had always been, Romance for him, and whenever he was deeply stirred he turned to her." But Winifred with all her charm, taste, and wealth lacked one vital thing, "the energy of youth." This missing élan vital he found in Hilda Burgoyne. The opposing forces of his wife and his mistress ultimately opened the fissure that Wilson had foreseen.

At the end of the novel it is Bartley's dalliance with Miss Burgoyne that prevents his getting to the bridge in time to head off the final disaster. Thus the novel concludes by bringing into appropriate conjunction the bridge collapse as symbol of failure and the tragic end of Bartley Alexander. To give the novel a Jamesian twist at the end, the tragedy that takes place is a lesser tragedy than the one Bartley can foresee as the train rushed him toward his stricken bridge. Bartley in planning to leave his wife for Hilda realizes that he will become an outcast doomed to drag out a restless existence on the Continent, far from the world of men and action. He perceives the crack in his moral nature before the crack in his bridge hurls him into the abyss.

Although the world of Bartley Alexander is not the characteristic world of Willa Cather, one should not, as she did, relegate the book to a sort of limbo outside the canon of her works. It fits into the pattern of her life and total accomplishment quite well. The character Bartley foreshadows other characters, and in him the author subconsciously reveals herself. Thematically the book is linked to the reading of her formative years and to her lifelong preoccupations. In its plot *Alexander's Bridge* uses materials that look both forward and backward.

Bartley Alexander is a westerner, a self-made man who has come from somewhere out in Willa Cather's country and successfully stormed the eastern citadels. As he reaches forty-three, the specter of middle age looms ahead, and he realizes that he has not got from life all he wants. The crack in his moral nature is caused by his inability to harmonize desire with possibility, and the resultant inner conflict looks ahead to the similar struggle of Godfrey St. Peter in *The Professor's House.* Alexander's restless dissatisfaction with his eastern life also anticipates Jim Burden, the narrator in *My Ántonia.* Willa Cather, managing editor of a great magazine, might have spoken for herself the words she gives Bartley when Professor Wilson comes to visit: "You work like the devil and think you're getting on, and suddenly you discover that you have only been getting yourself tied up. A million details drink you dry. Your life keeps going for things you don't want, and all the while you are being built alive into a social structure you don't care a rap about." Bartley has a divided personality, just as Willa Cather admitted having, as she toiled on at *McClure's* and yearned to escape to something nobler. Although she managed to harmonize *her* conflicts, characters divided against themselves always fascinated her.

The dominant theme in *Alexander's Bridge,* the theme of Bartley's yearning and seeking, runs like a leitmotiv through her fiction. Basically it is a part of the author's temperament, for she had been searching and questing up to the time she wrote the

novel. Bartley's desires are partly her desires, and later the yearning and seeking that corrupt Marian Forrester in *A Lost Lady* and
destroy Myra Henshawe in *My Mortal Enemy* carry on this preoccupation. How deep-seated this theme is in Willa Cather's life and
writing may be seen in the way she goes back to classic myth to
reinforce this motif. Her wide reading is thoroughly assimilated in
her adult writing, but it always is present as an unobtrusive under-
pinning. As Bernice Slote notes in *The Kingdom of Art*, one of the
"most deeply affective and complex symbols in Willa Cather's
writing" is the moon myth, that is, the myth of the unattainable
moon goddess Diana, the object of man's desires. Like Keats's
youth Endymion, who searches for the moon goddess, Bartley
Alexander quests for Hilda Burgoyne, who embodies for him
youth and vitality. The novel contains ample moon imagery and
allusions to the myth to make it clear that Willa Cather inserted
this material deliberately. The moon imagery occurs again with
this theme of yearning in *A Lost Lady* and *My Mortal Enemy*. The
moon myth is woven inextricably into the fabric of Willa Cather's
personality.

The plot of *Alexander's Bridge* is no less a part of the whole
design of her fiction than is character and theme. The skeleton of
the story is the eternal triangle, a basic plot that she already had
tried with variations in "Death in the Desert" and "On the Gulls'
Road" and would use again in "The Bohemian Girl," *O Pioneers!*,
and *A Lost Lady*. Bartley Alexander's story also is the tale of a
person killed by his inability to reconcile the contradictions in his
character, and in this respect the novel foreshadows the stories of
Myra Henshawe in *My Mortal Enemy*, Claude Wheeler in *One of
Ours*, and the heroine in *Lucy Gayheart*. In both the triangle and
the tragedy the plot is structured by the use of another myth, this
time the story of Helen of Troy. Bartley-Paris (who also is called
Alexander in the *Iliad*), Winifred-Oenone, and Hilda-Helen act
out a drama that bears resemblance to the ancient myth.

Willa Cather began disparaging this novel almost as soon as she
finished it. The month after it appeared in book form, she wrote
Louise Pound not to bother reading it but to wait for "The
Bohemian Girl," which would be out in August. That, she thought,
was *real*. When Houghton Mifflin reissued *Alexander's Bridge* in

1922, and asked her to write an introduction for the new edition, she did so, but she could find nothing at that time to praise in her first novel. She had been a beginner, she wrote, and as a novice had felt that knowledge of life could be gained by going out to look at it, as one goes to a theater. The beginner has to "work through his youthful vanities and gaudy extravagances," she continued, "before he comes to deal with the material that is truly his own." After another nine years passed, she looked back on the novel as a "studio picture" that had been the result of meeting some interesting people in London. "Like most young writers, I thought a book should be made out of 'interesting material,' and at that time I found the new more exciting than the familiar. The impressions I tried to communicate on paper were genuine, but they were very shallow."

It would be hard to describe Willa Cather as a young writer or an inexperienced one at this time. She was thirty-eight when the novel appeared, and had published at least three dozen stories since leaving college. It also is not true that she was unable to tell the difference between stories in her best vein and tales in her Jamesian manner. When she had written Sarah Orne Jewett in 1908, she had made a clear distinction between "On the Gulls' Road" and "The Enchanted Bluff." She knew then that the western material was the real thing for her. The reason she did not mine her mother lode extensively until after writing *Alexander's Bridge* is probably the obvious one: She was indeed absorbed in her life as managing editor of *McClure's*, and that life was for her then the most interesting subject for fiction. It was only after she made the break from the magazine, partly through accident, that she began to devote herself extensively to western settings and characters. She was being quite disingenuous in her 1922 preface to *Alexander's Bridge* when she quoted the advice she once received from Sarah Orne Jewett: "Of course, one day you will write about your own country. In the meantime, get all you can. One must know the world *so well* before one can know the parish."

Later when she was writing her next novel, *O Pioneers!*, she wrote Aunt Franc a revealing letter about *Alexander's Bridge*. Apparently accused by her aunt of allowing a moral flimsiness in Bartley Alexander, she admitted the charge and defended herself by asserting that one can not always write about what one most approves of. A writer has to have either an unusual knowledge of or a peculiar sympathy for a character. He must by some accident have seen deeply into his character, and it is this intense realization that gives his writing the tone and distinction that lifts it above the commonplace. Alexander, with his flawed character, was at this point in her career a person she felt she knew. She had tried, she said, writing about several of the people she most admired, simply because she admired them, and the results had been utterly flat and commonplace, just like hundreds of other stories.

Rereading the novel today, one is inclined to agree with Edith Lewis, who discovered after Willa Cather died that the book is really pretty good. The work is contrived and somewhat artificial, but "when it at last moves into its true theme, the moral division in a man's nature, it gathers an intensity and power which come from some deeper level of feeling, and which overflood whatever is 'shallow' or artificial in the story." The novel is in fact a very competent piece of work, tightly written, well organized, very professional. Theme and symbol are carefully worked out, and the concentration on the main character never gets out of focus. One has to admit, however, that the novel is somewhat bloodless, a performance of the head rather than of the heart, and does not take hold of the reader the way Willa Cather's later books do. And it is no doubt true that the novel would have been forgotten long ago if its author had not gone on to write *My Ántonia* and *A Lost Lady.* She never again laid a novel in Boston or London and did not try another novel with a male protagonist until she wrote *One of Ours* ten years later.

Willa Cather's dissatisfaction with *Alexander's Bridge* came chiefly from the change in her life that was taking place. Within two or three months after finishing the novel she no longer would be managing editor. She would be facing west at last, having got out of the magazine mill that had ground her up so fine. The end of the old life came suddenly and unexpectedly. Circumstances quite out of her control ended the agonizing ambivalence that had kept her living a double life in the antithetical worlds of journalism and literature. When she stepped out of the eastern world of Bartley Alexander, she immediately stepped into the western world of Willa Cather.

The new life was precipitated by a financial reorganization of the McClure company. The "chief" finally had gotten himself into impossible financial straits, and Mackenzie, his son-in-law, had to raise outside capital. The outcome was a reorganization in which McClure lost financial control of his empire. He signed a contract for the lease of his magazine with an option to buy. The contract provided that he was to be retained as editor-in-chief, at least outwardly, but as Curtis Brady, the business manager, later said: "What was going to happen ... was so clear a blind man could have felt it with his cane." At this juncture both Brady and Willa Cather retired from their positions, and Mackenzie, who moved over from the business office, and Frederick Collins, editor of the *Woman's Home Companion* and one of the reorganizers, took over the real editorial reins. A year later McClure was ousted from his position by new owners—unhorsed after twenty years as founder, editor, and guiding genius. Thus one reorganization unexpectedly whisked Willa Cather from Pittsburgh to New York, and another shake-up pried her loose from her managing editorship. She did not sever her connection with the magazine, however; she took a leave of absence and planned to come back as a staff writer rather than as an editor.

The escape from organized chaos came just in time. The euphoria of June had been only a brief interlude. She nearly had become the sour, ill-tempered, fussy woman she had written Sarah Orne Jewett she was afraid of turning into. After she got away, she wrote McClure asking him to forget how cranky she used to get when she was tired. She could not bear to have either McClure or Miss Roseboro' remember her like that, as it all seemed so foolish in retrospect. Her rest and rehabilitation center was Cherry Valley, New York, near Cooperstown in the beautiful Finger Lakes area. She and her devoted Isabelle McClung rented a house in the village about the first of October and settled down for three months of quiet and seclusion. Mrs. McClung had grown up in Cherry Valley, and Isabelle, who loved the place, had selected their retreat. After they had been there several weeks, Willa Cather wrote McClure that she had been tramping about in the rain for four days. But stormy autumn weather was the kind she always liked best, and after hiking through the wet woods she was able to sleep nine hours without turning over. And in a later letter she wrote that nothing ever happened in Cherry Valley except the weather, but when one was resting that was quite enough.

The first literary chore that she performed in Cherry Valley was the revision of part of *Alexander's Bridge*. The first of the three installments needed reworking before the serial began appearing in *McClure's* in February. She made the necessary changes in October and sent off her manuscript to Mackenzie on November third. Meantime her Boston friend Ferris Greenslet of Houghton Miffllin had persuaded his company to bring out the serial in book form in May. Sometime between magazine publication and book version she made a few cuts and rewrote a few passages, but the alterations were not extensive. Already she had lost interest in the book, though she was glad enough to be launched at last as a novelist.

While she was working over the manuscript of *Alexander's Bridge,* McClure stopped off in Cherry Valley on his way to Battle Creek, Michigan, for some dental work. He apparently was worried about his former assistant's state of mind and wanted to look in on her new surroundings. The two had grown very close to each other in the years they had worked together, and outside of her father and brothers, there was no man Willa Cather loved more than McClure. She seems to have left New York feeling guilty about leaving McClure back in the office naked unto his enemies. He tried to allay this feeling by writing her just before going to see her: "You must dismiss the magazine from your mind entirely and forget it exists and when you come back I hope you will not let yourself be tied up in office machinery." After he had been to see her, she wrote gratefully that the long talk she had had with him had straightened her out more than anything else could have done.

After McClure's visit and the revision of the novel there was nothing to stop her from losing herself completely in her writing. One can perhaps date the turning point in her career precisely on November 4, 1911, for she sent off her manuscript to Mackenzie on the third and wrote McClure on the fifth that she was working on a new story, which would be about the length of the bridge-builder tale. She was thoroughly enjoying her work and greatly relieved to be writing again. She was not even going to think about magazine work. With the "chief's" blessing and the seclusion of Cherry Valley to assist her, she worked for the next two months with a great burst of creative energy. She finished the first story, "Alexandra," which was the original version of *O Pioneers!*, and immediately began another "foreign" tale laid on the Divide, "The Bohemian Girl." Thus in two months she turned out about fifty-thousand words of fiction in her best vein of western material. In quantity this was more than all of *A Lost Lady* and two-thirds of *My Ántonia*. In a real sense she was beginning her new literary life, and it is not surprising that she developed an immediate distaste for *Alexander's Bridge*, the last product of her old life.

Willa Cather did not end her relationship with *McClure's* until the middle of 1913, but she never again was involved in office routine and editing. She spent very little time in the office during 1912, but she gave her former employers five or six months the following year, during which she wrote four articles, two on drama, one on opera singers, and a fourth on "Training for the Ballet." A fifth article on drama, not written until 1914, ended her assignments for the magazine, and for the rest of her life she wrote principally novels and occasionally short stories. The work she had done during the three-months' leave at Cherry Valley convinced her finally that she could safely afford to give up the security of a salary.

The year 1912 began nearly as badly as the previous year, however, and she had to spend another several weeks in the hospital with some unspecified complaint. She wrote Zoë Akins early in February that she was in Boston staying with Margaret Deland and recuperating, but by the first of March she was back in New York to attend Howells's seventy-fifth birthday dinner. She still had no enthusiasm for poor dear gentle Mr. Howells, but despite *Silas Lapham* and other dreadful things, she was rather pleased at the storm of applause and affection displayed for the old novelist by the four hundred guests at the dinner.

She had been in a mellow mood when she attended the dinner. She wrote Elizabeth Sergeant the day before that Mackenzie had taken her to lunch recently and had asked her if she did not have something to show for her sojourn in the country. She told him she had a story too long and too highbrow for *McClure's*, but he guessed he would like to read it. She gave him "The Bohemian Girl" and the next day met him for tea at the Brevoort. He astonished her by offering $750 for the story. She laughed and told him *McClure's* never paid such prices for fiction and that her story could not possibly be worth more than $500. He replied that she was silly not to take what he offered, but if she insisted, he would pay her $500, providing she agreed to accept the larger figure next time. Mackenzie was no fool. The magazine had been getting a good many letters praising *Alexander's Bridge*, which still had one month to run, and "The Bohemian Girl" was an excellent story. Willa Cather also thought it a pretty good tale, as she admitted to Zoë Akins, who wrote congratulating her after it appeared in the August issue of the magazine.

Despite the fact "The Bohemian Girl" never was reprinted, it is undeniably vintage Cather. "The Enchanted Bluff" (1909) with its rich evocation of her youth in Red Cloud is also an excellent tale, but this story is longer and more ambitious, and it leads directly to *O Pioneers!* The story details the return of Nils Ericson to his boyhood home on the Divide. He has been off in the world seeking his fortune while his brothers and his mother remain on the farm. By the time he returns, the pioneering days are over, and the whole tribe of Ericsons are prosperous farmer-capitalists. Nils finds that the girl he had loved, Bohemian Clara Vavrika, has married his older brother Olaf, a smug, self-satisfied, materialistic farmer. Clara is handsome, vivacious, musical, too rare a spirit to be buried on a Nebraska farm. She takes after her father, the *bon vivant* Joe Vavrika, who operates the tavern in the Bohemian settlement. The denouement of the tale is the elopement of Nils and Clara.

There are a number of interesting things about this story. It foreshadows in the Nils-Clara relationship the Emil-Marie subplot of *O Pioneers!*, and the time of the story is approximately that of the second and succeeding parts of the novel. In addition, the materialistic brothers in the story look ahead to Alexandra's unimaginative, plodding, and scheming brothers in the novel. What is most interesting about "The Bohemian Girl," however, is the character Nils, who returns to the Divide after an absence of twelve years. His responses are those of Willa Cather returning home after living in Pittsburgh and New York. Nils, who had to get away from the farm when he was eighteen, is ready to love the land at the age of thirty:

He gave the town, as he would have said, a wide berth, and cut through a great fenced pasture, emerging, when he rolled under the barbed wire at the farther corner, upon a white dusty road which ran straight up from the river valley to the high prairies where the ripe wheat stood yellow and the tin roofs and weather-cocks were twinkling in the fierce sunlight.

The country is beautiful, the farms well cared for and productive, and Nils thinks he might like to settle down there. But this is a passing feeling. His brothers disgust him, and one finds in his reaction to the people, at least the second generation, whom Joe Vavrika describes as "a tame lot," the same critical attitude that appears in the characterization of the Bergson brothers in *O Pioneers!* Nils's real enthusiasm is for the old women. At Olaf's barn-raising party Nils watches a group of the old women preparing the food for the guests:

They were a fine company of old women, and a Dutch painter would have loved to find them there together, where the sun made bright patches on the floor and sent long, quivering shafts of gold through the dusky shade up among the rafters. There were fat, rosy old women who looked hot in their best black dresses; spare, alert old women with brown, dark-veined hands; and several of almost heroic frame, not less massive than old Mrs. Ericson herself.

This is Willa Cather herself observing the women of the heroic period of Nebraska's history, even though, characteristically, she insists on seeing them through the eyes of a male character.

As soon as Willa Cather completed the sale of "The Bohemian Girl," she made plans for a long vacation in the West. She would visit her brother Douglass, now a brakeman on the Santa Fe, who worked out of Winslow, Arizona, and see a part of the country she never had visited. She left New York in March, stopped off to visit Isabelle McClung in Pittsburgh on the way, then continued on toward the Southwest. This was to be a journey deep into the American past. It would have important ramifications in her literary career, and when she returned to New York she would be light years away, emotionally and psychologically, from the magazine world of *McClure's*.

CHAPTER 6

$=\!\!\!\!=\!\!\!\!\infty\!\!\infty\!\!\text{\textcircled{O}\textcircled{O}}\!\!\infty\!\!\infty\!\!=\!\!\!\!=$

Triumphant Years: 1912–1919

I

IN HER INTRODUCTION to a new edition of *The Song of the Lark* in 1932, Willa Cather characterized her opera-singer heroine as a person "wholly at the mercy of accident." But to persons of such "vitality and honesty" as Thea Kronborg, she added, "fortunate accidents will always happen." This was an article of faith with her, for her own life demonstrated its truth. Her trip to the Southwest, like her release from *McClure's*, was another of the lucky accidents. Nebraska and France already had taken hold of her; now it was to be the ancient peoples of pre-Columbian Arizona and New Mexico. The literary consequences of her visit were great: Part IV of *The Song of the Lark*, "Tom Outland's Story," which is the core of *The Professor's House*, and all of *Death Comes for the Archbishop*. That the region already had pulled on her imagination is demonstrated by "The Enchanted Bluff," in which the Red Cloud boys around their island campfire in the Republican River promise each other one day to climb the bluff to find the lost Indian civilization. The Southwest acted powerfully on Willa Cather's creative imagination, and she went back five times during the next fifteen years. She discovered there a part of America with a past. Nebraska had only a geologic history.

When she boarded the Pennsylvania Railroad in March 1912, she had been in the West only once in the past five years. She had managed to visit Red Cloud for six weeks in 1909, but otherwise her managing editorship had kept her in the East. Now she was to experience the West all over again, particularly its bigness, which always had paralyzed her a little. She wrote Elizabeth Sergeant that when she was away from the West she remembered only the tang on the tongue, but back there again she was experiencing the same tightness of the chest that she recalled as a child. It had been stronger when she was young, but it persisted. She never could let herself go in the West but was always resisting a little, like a person who could not swim fighting the water instead of going with the current. She was feeling the old dichotomies again: Virginia versus Nebraska, New York versus Red Cloud, East versus West, desire versus possibility, that had tugged her in opposite directions all her life.

The first two weeks in the West were not particularly promising. Early in April she reached Winslow, Arizona, which she thought an ugly western town. She found her brother living in a little eggshell house by the Sante Fe Railroad with a tediously dull brakeman named Tooker and a drunken Cockney cook. But the desert was very fine—bright red sand like brick dust and the eternal sage and rabbit bush—after one had crossed two miles of tin cans and old shoes to get to it. She reported on April twentieth that she did not plan to stay very long because she would not be able to write there. Her brother could not understand this, but she would visit him a while, see the surrounding country, and then fade away in search of a place to work.

Then things began to happen. She was enchanted by a visit to an Indian mission with a local priest; she spent three marvelous days exploring canyons and cliff-dwellings; then she went on to the most colossal spectacle of all—the Grand Canyon. She did a great deal of horseback riding and hiking, climbed down one cliff hand over hand, and enjoyed herself immensely. During the days they were exploring canyons, they started out at daylight in a light wagon with canteens, cooking utensils, and food, spent the entire day tramping about, dined around a campfire, and returned each night to hotel beds and hot baths. Even her brother's roommate, the impossible Mr. Tooker, turned out to be a splendid companion in the hills. All his miserable information, gained from reading thousands of magazines, fell away like a boy dropping his clothes to go swimming, and he was a strong, active climber, full of verve and stories.

But the most wonderful event of all was meeting Julio, a Mexican from Vera Cruz, too beautiful to be true and different from anyone else in the world. She was charmed by him, then completely infatuated. He was simply wonderful, Antinous come to earth again, a marvelous singer of Mexican and Spanish songs. Her letters to Elizabeth Sergeant for the next three months are filled with Julio. It took her days to get over the day she spent in the Painted Desert with him, and even after getting back to Red Cloud she could not stop writing about him. He was without beginning and without end. He had a personal elegance, the like of which she never had known, and a grace of expression that simply caught one up. She said she hated to get letters raving about the beauty of untutored youths of Latin extraction, such as people wrote when they went to Italy, but she could not help herself. Julio, however, was not soft and sunny like an Italian; he was indifferent and opaque. He had the long, strong upper lip seen in Aztec sculpture, somber eyes filled with lots of old trouble, and the pale yellow skin of very old gold and old races. She wrote Elizabeth Sergeant that she must come to the Southwest, and if she did, she was certain to pick up a Mexican sweetheart, who would take as much time and strength as she would give him.

A couple of weeks after leaving Winslow and Julio, she wrote that she still might go back for him. He would look lovely at Mrs. Fields's, but then Mrs. Isabella Gardner would sweep him up and take him to Fenway Court, which he would like better than her apartment. Two months later she was still on this subject and thought that she really must get Julio to New York, where he could make an easy living as an artist's model. But she had gotten away from him. Julio was wonderful, she wrote, but he could not take the place of a whole civilization. One could play with the desert, love it, go hard night and day and be full of it and quite tipsy with it, but the moment came finally when one had to kiss it good-by and go—go bleeding, but go.

Before she left Winslow, Julio took her to a Mexican dance where she was the only Anglo-Saxon present. The music and dancing later furnished the setting for the Mexican dance that Thea Kronborg attends in *The Song of the Lark*. There is a suggestion of Julio in Johnny Tellamantez and the Rama Boys in the same novel, but her poem "Spanish Johnny" was written before she ever visited Arizona and was inspired by a man she had known as a child. Julio also told her the story of an Aztec Cleopatra, "The Forty Lovers of the Queen," which Don Hedger tells Eden Bower in "Coming, Aphrodite!" But Julio was perhaps too intense an experience to furnish literary capital, for he never appears as a character in her fiction. Yet the feeling about him must have lasted. It is suggested in the remark Elizabeth Sergeant reports she made when someone asked how Mabel Dodge could have married Tony Luhan, an Indian.

"How could she help it?" Willa Cather replied.

The experience in the Southwest supplied important material to *The Song of the Lark*. At a critical point in her career Thea Kronborg leaves Chicago for Arizona to rest, recuperate, and think. She has been ill with tonsillitis during the winter and spring, as Willa Cather was, and needs the dry air of the Southwest. But more important, she needs to get "out of the stream of meaningless activity and undirected effort." Ever since leaving home for Chicago to study music, she has always been "a little drudge, hurrying from one task to another." But on the ranch she visits near Flagstaff "the personality of which she was so tired seemed to let go of her" and as she climbs into her big German featherbed the first night, she feels "completely released from the enslaving desire to get on in the world." All of these reactions are autobiographical, and while Willa Cather actually began her new life in Cherry Valley six months before, the two months she spent in Arizona and New Mexico made the break with her past irrevocable. She planned to go back to *McClure's* in September, but she did not. Like Thea Kronborg, who made the crucial decision to study music in Germany while vacationing in Arizona, Willa Cather there pointed herself towards her future vocation as novelist. Also like Thea, after she had time to think and plan and rest, she was ready to return to civilization. When she got back to Pittsburgh in July, she wrote that she was glad to be out of the West. For the first time in years she had her fill of it. It was too big and too consuming—full of swift yellow excitement—and the pace finally had tired her. One day outside a beautiful Indian village she saw written in the sands a sentence from Balzac: "*Dans le désert, voyez-vous, il y a tout et il n'y a rien; Dieu, sans les hommes.*" She had been sitting mournfully beside the Rio Grande

153

that day wondering what was wrong with her. When she saw that sentence, she knew that it was time to go.

The McClung home in Pittsburgh was her headquarters for the next six months. There she could write happily in her old attic sewing room, as she had during her teaching days. She went to work with great enthusiasm, feeling that her mind had been washed and ironed and readied for a new life. She had gotten her second wind and never again would she let herself be tortured by little things. She had returned with a head full of stories that she was dreaming about at night. The first was "The White Mulberry Tree," a tale she thought would terrify Mr. Greenslet. It had come to her, she told Elizabeth Sergeant, on the edge of a wheat field in the Bohemian country when she had visited Nebraska on the way back from the Southwest. Her excursions on the Divide, which included watching a wheat harvest for the first time in years, had acted as a powerful stimulus to her imagination.

She settled down with her new ideas and fresh memories of Red Cloud and Webster County and began working on the new story. This was the most tragic tale she ever had written, a version of Paolo and Francesca among the corn rows. In it Frank Shabata, a Bohemian farmer, surprises and kills his wife Marie and her lover Emil Bergson under a white mulberry tree. As in the *Divine Comedy*, the fate of the young lovers is sealed by a chance kiss, but unlike Dante's telling, the deformity of the outraged husband is moral rather than physical. When she finished this story, she got out "Alexandra," which she had written the year before in Cherry Valley, and examined the two tales together. What happened at that point, she explained later, could only be described "as a sudden inner explosion and enlightenment." It was like bringing together two chemicals that produced a powerful reaction. The result was a new compound combining both stories: the novel *O Pioneers!*

She worked steadily during the fall, though she had to make two trips to New York on business, but by December she was nearly finished. She thought the new work was superior to "The Bohemian Girl"; it was much more closely knit and the most ambitious thing she had tried. She wrote Zoë Akins that the country itself would be the hero, but she thought the Swedes and the

Bohemians in it also were interesting. She was pleased with her book and completely happy while working on it. Only after Houghton Mifflin accepted it for publication and she began reading proof did she begin having doubts.

She sent the manuscript to Elizabeth Sergeant, whose judgment she trusted, and was greatly bolstered by her friend's approval. She admitted that the weak spot in the novel was that the skeleton did not stand out. The modeling was soft and without bold features, but she defended herself by saying that the form was dictated by the land. The country itself had no skeleton, no rocks, no ridges. Its fine light soil ran through one's fingers, and its softness somehow influenced the mood in which one wrote of it and structured the story. Later when she wrote of *O Pioneers!*, she recalled that there had been no arranging or inventing. Everything was "spontaneous and took its own place, right or wrong." And she added: "Since I wrote this book for myself, I ignored all the situations and accents that were then generally thought to be necessary." This memory is true enough, but she did not approach publication day with any great assurance.

Consequently, she was delighted when the people at home read the novel and pronounced it genuine. She admitted to Zoë Akins that one liked to shine a little for the home folks. In her youth she never was able to make much of an impression in Nebraska, because there was not much she could do then that the people would admire, except excel in horseback riding. One cannot get a rise out of a cow with a sonnet, she said. In 1913, however, she succeeded in putting Nebraska on the literary map, and as she recalled later, she succeeded despite the unfashionableness of her locale and the fact that Swedes had not appeared in American literature before except in humorous sketches. She defied the New York critic whom she quoted: "I simply don't care a damn what happens in Nebraska, no matter who writes about it." She might well have quoted Virgil here, as she does in *My Ántonia*: " '*Primus ego in patriam mecum . . . deducam Musas*'; 'for I shall be the first, if I live, to bring the Muse into my country.' " *Patria* to Virgil had meant his native Mantua, and to Willa Cather it meant Webster County and the Divide.

She recognized from the first that her success was partly the result of not violating the integrity of the material. She later wrote in a presentation copy of the novel for Carrie Sherwood: "This was the first time I walked off on my own feet—everything before was half real and half an imitation of writers whom I admired. In this one I hit the home pasture and found that I was Yance Sorgeson and not Henry James." Yance Sorgeson was one of the prosperous Norwegian immigrant farmers of Webster County, a man who died rich but who refused to give up the old ways or to be impressed with his own success. Willa Cather had indeed found her own stance in this novel, although it was not actually her first hit in the home pasture. It was, however, her first home run.

When Thea Kronborg in *The Song of the Lark* goes to Arizona, she spends her summer days in Panther [Walnut] Canyon. The ranch she visits is adjacent to the canyon, and each morning she climbs down to the ancient cliff-village below the rim of the mesa. One morning she is struck by the significance of the shards of broken pottery that she has been admiring in the ruins. She has wondered why the Indian women lavished such loving care in decorating the jars used in their daily routine to carry water from the floor of the canyon to their cliff-dwellings. As she stands in the stream bathing, it comes to her. The world of the mesa Indians centered on water, the life-giving liquid that she was pouring over herself. "The stream and the broken pottery: what was any art but an effort to make a sheath, a mould in which to imprison for a moment the shining, elusive element which is life itself." Life is hurrying past us, too strong to stop, too sweet to lose. The Indian women held it in their jars. The sculpture she had seen at the art institute caught it in a flash of arrested motion. In singing one made a vessel of one's throat and caught the stream in a scale of natural intervals.

The same principle applied to literature. One made a sheath with words to capture the rushing flow of life. The structural principle of fiction must be organic. Form must follow function. Thus when she came to write of Nebraska and the Swedes and Bohemians on the Divide she worked out a form that was loosely episodic and let the tale pace itself. When she felt like digressing, she did, as in the chapter introducing Old Ivar near the beginning of the novel. When she finished sketching in the background of the novel

156

in the first seventy-one pages ("The Wild Land"), she did not hesitate to skip sixteen years before resuming the story. After the tragedy in the orchard in which Emil and Marie are killed by Marie's husband, she wrote another entire section, all anticlimactic, to finish off the novel. Yet she succeeds brilliantly in creating in about sixty thousand words a saga of Nebraska extending from pioneering days to about 1900. Birth, growth, love, death—it is all there.

Although "The Sculptor's Funeral," "Paul's Case," "The Bohemian Girl," and a few others of Willa Cather's early works achieve excellence, *O Pioneers!* is the first of her productions to strike the characteristic note of nostalgia. The tone is uniformly elegiac, as it would be in all of her best work of the future. The poignancy in her best fiction derives from the remembrance of things past, the evocation of a departed grandeur seen in contrast with a lesser present. The novel begins in 1883, the year that the Cathers moved from Virginia to Nebraska. The pioneer days are sketched briefly but lovingly with the focus on Alexandra, then about twenty years old, whose father is dying and on whose shoulders falls the burden of subduing the wild land. She is the great earth mother, one of the heroic pioneer women, like old Mrs. Ericson in "The Bohemian Girl," the Cathers' neighbor Mrs. Lambrecht, or Ántonia Shimerda. Her courage, vision, and energy bring life and civilization to the wilderness. As Alexandra faces the future confidently, Willa Cather writes: "For the first time, perhaps, since that land emerged from the waters of geologic ages, a human face was set toward it with love and yearning. . . . The history of every country begins in the heart of a man or a woman."

This often-quoted passage is important. It sets the tone of the novel and its successors. The pioneer times are always a frame of reference and provide the contrast that becomes in Willa Cather's fiction a key structural device. When the novel picks up sixteen years later, the Nebraska farmlands are prosperous. Instead of the shaggy red buffalo-grass in all directions the land is a "vast chequer-board, marked off in squares of wheat and corn; light and dark, dark and light." Telephone wires crisscross the country and again, as in "The Bohemian Girl," the "gilded weather-vanes on the big red barns wink at each other across the green and brown and yellow fields." But though the times now are prosperous, the contrast between the pioneers and the tame second generation is painfully apparent. Alexandra has not changed, like Yance Sorgeson, but her brothers are mean little men cast in a smaller mold than old John Bergson, who had died in the struggle to subdue the wild land. Prosperity divides Alexandra and her brothers, who had toiled together during the lean years of struggle. When Carl Lindstrum, the friend of Alexandra's youth, comes back to visit, he misses the old land and the old days, despite the fact his family gave up and sold out. Now, "when I come back to all this milk and honey," he tells Alexandra, "I feel like the old German song, '*Wo bist du, wo bist du, mein geliebtes land*?' "

For Willa Cather the struggle was always more interesting than the achievement. She was fond of quoting the French historian Michelet: "*Le but n'est rien; le chemin, c'est tout.*" For Alexandra success was not very sweet. It brought the bitterness of blasted hopes in the tragedy of her beloved younger brother Emil, for whom she had struggled to give advantages that she had never had. He returns from college with no vocation, falls in love with their neighbor's wife, and dies with her, like the legendary Pyramus and Thisbe, under the white mulberry tree. He is an attractive young man, full of promise, not like his crass older brothers; but he is cut off at the beginning of his manhood, another victim of the new times. Alexandra and the earth remain, however, and Willa Cather gives her heroine the promise of a serene middle and old age. Carl returns to her when he hears of the tragedy, and they plan to marry. The land remains the ultimate heroine of the story, as the author closes the book: "They went into the house together, leaving the Divide behind them, under the evening star. Fortunate country, that is one day to receive hearts like Alexandra's into its bosom, to give them out again in the yellow wheat, in the rustling corn, in the shining eyes of youth!"

The transcendental echoes of the closing sentence make it particularly appropriate that the title of the novel should have come from Whitman's poem. The tone of the novel is similar, and the theme of life everlasting is close to one of Whitman's themes in *Leaves of Grass*, especially Part 6 of "Song of Myself":

TRIUMPHANT YEARS: 1912–1919

What do you think has become of the young and old men?
And what do you think has become of the women and children?
They are alive and well somewhere,
The smallest sprout shows there is really no death.

Emerson to Whitman to Willa Cather: The line in American literature is direct and clear. Although her methods were modern and her subjects the immigrant farmers of Nebraska, she belongs to the tradition of American romanticism.

When Willa Cather sent her manuscript to Elizabeth Sergeant, she wrote that the book would be pretty good or an utter fizzle. Anyway she had done what she intended, and to commemorate that fact she dedicated it to the memory of Sarah Orne Jewett, "in whose beautiful and delicate work there is the perfection that endures." It is significant that *Alexander's Bridge* carries no dedication at all and that *O Pioneers!* is offered to the memory of her friend and literary mentor. The material in the novel fulfills the prescription that Miss Jewett wrote and which Willa Cather quotes in her introduction to *The Best Stories of Sarah Orne Jewett:* "The thing that teases the mind over and over for years, and at last gets itself put down rightly on paper—whether little or great, it belongs to literature." She told Elizabeth Sergeant that this was a story she always had wanted to write. This statement is not literally true, but it is a fact that the material had been a part of her for many years. When she elaborated on Miss Jewett's statement, she differentiated sharply between literary material long in hand and story subjects worked up for the moment: "The shapes and scenes that have 'teased' the mind for years, when they do at last get themselves rightly put down, make a very much higher order of writing, and a much more costly, than the most vivid and vigorous transfer of immediate impressions." It would be safe to say that *O Pioneers!* belongs to literature, while *Alexander's Bridge* is a sort of higher journalism.

The reviewers treated *O Pioneers!* very kindly. Ferris Greenslet had been right when he told his colleagues at Houghton Mifflin that the novel "ought to . . . definitely establish the author as a novelist of the first rank." Willa Cather's career follows an ascending curve, with some aberrations, for the next fourteen years and through the next seven novels. Then the curve levels off, and the novelist in her last two decades writes with continued skill and dedication but does not surpass herself. Floyd Dell, who had yet to become a novelist himself, reviewed the novel as "the most vital, subtle, and artistic piece of the year's fiction." He thought it was touched by genius and saw in it "an attitude toward life, that in its large and simple honesty has a kind of nobleness."

II

When Willa Cather carried her finished manuscript from Pittsburgh to New York early in 1913, she began her new literary life in a new apartment at 5 Bank Street. The apartment had been rented the previous fall, and Edith Lewis already had moved in. They took half of the second floor of a large brick house that had been converted to apartments with only a few structural changes. A wide staircase ran up the center of the house, large windows pierced the sturdy walls of the building, and high ceilings gave the place a spaciousness that made up for a lack of central heating. They had seven rooms, the front three of which they used as one huge living room. Furniture mostly came from secondhand dealers on University Place, and an Italian carpenter built them low open bookshelves. Over the white marble mantel in the living room Willa Cather hung a large etching of George Sand, and on it later she placed a bust of Keats that Mrs. Fields willed her. The apartment had charm and comfort, and Willa Cather lived and worked there happily during her best years, until 1927 when the construction of a subway forced her to move.

One of the great attractions of 5 Bank Street, however, was not the physical charm of the place but Josephine Bourda, their cook and housekeeper. She went to work for the new tenants as soon as she arrived from France and was with them for many years. She spoke no English when she arrived, and even after she had learned a little, refused to speak anything but French. Her father had kept a restaurant in Pau, and she was an accomplished cook; but she also was a vital personality, warmhearted, humorous, perceptive. Edith Lewis writes: "Her personality was so pervasive and uncompromising that she created a sort of French household atmosphere around us; and I think there is no question that this contributed, to a certain extent, to such novels as *Death Comes for the Archbishop* and *Shadows on the Rock*." She also made possible a great deal of entertaining during the succeeding years.

Once Willa Cather had settled down in the new apartment, she turned her attention to fulfilling a promise she had made to her old friend and former boss McClure. His letter announcing his dismissal by the new owners of the magazine had caught up with her in New Mexico the summer before, and she had replied indignantly. Surely his news could not be so bad as he thought it. Surely they could not keep a man of his ability and experience down long. And how could they have the nerve to take his salary to pay the magazine's debts? McClure always had been so generous with other people that it made her fighting Irish mad to have him tormented and deviled by his creditors. She promised to do anything she could to help him. Unfortunately, the only thing she was able to do was to help him write his autobiography. The new owners had offered to apply the fee for serial rights to his life story against his debts if he could get someone like Willa Cather to assist him. She gladly undertook the project and refused to accept any compensation for it. The task was a labor of love.

She had some doubts about her ability to write the autobiography just the way McClure would like it. Some of the Christian Science articles she had not been able to do exactly as the "chief" had wanted them. And so it might be with the autobiography: The events that sang one tune to McClure might sing another to her. She might not be able to catch step with him, but she was willing to try. If, as the old song said, "a willing heart goes all the way," they would succeed very well. She was never more willing about any piece of work. She need not have worried about the results, however, for the portrait she drew is S. S. McClure himself, an autobiography written with all the skill of a thoroughly professional writer who also is a great novelist. It may be the best ghost-written autobiography ever produced.

There is no suggestion on the title page that Willa Cather wrote the book, but in the front matter appears this statement: "I am indebted to the cooperation of Miss Willa Sibert Cather for the very existence of this book." Whether or not readers ever suspected that McClure did not write it is uncertain, but as the life began appearing serially in the magazine, McClure began getting fan letters such as this one from Josephus Daniels, Secretary of the Navy: "Your opening chapter . . . is charming in its simplicity and beauty. I can almost see the route you took to school and hear the voices of the children. The only good history is autobiography, and I am hungry for your next chapter." Willa Cather wrote her old editor Will Jones that she had enjoyed writing the autobiography because McClure had been so honest about it and had not wanted the truth dressed up. If he had wanted the account of farm life in Indiana ornamented or softened, the story would have been dull to write and dull to read.

The autobiography deals mostly with McClure's boyhood and early struggles, and stops at the point where his magazine becomes a big success. Struggle was always more interesting than success, and McClure's Horatio Alger rise was what really interested Willa Cather. The narrative also is kept simple, which was consistent with McClure's personality and speech, but it also suggests that the ghost-writer was putting into practice her theory that the essence of art is to simplify. Finally, there is a strong empathy with the subject, just as there is between Willa Cather and her fictional characters like Alexandra Bergson or later Thea Kronborg and Ántonia Shimerda. It is clear from the autobiography that Willa Cather and McClure understood each other well. They shared many ideas and ideals, and both had a sense of destiny. The picture of McClure arriving at Knox College in 1874, penniless but with a consuming desire for an education, is drawn vividly and with complete sympathy. Willa Cather understood the earnest striving of the immigrant boy as well as she understood herself.

While Willa Cather was reading proof on *O Pioneers!* and wondering what her next novel would be about, she set to work fulfilling her promise to write five articles for *McClure's*. She already had done one, "Plays of Real Life," a review of the current theater season, in which there had been plays by Shaw, Pinero, and Arnold Bennett, and she decided to do her next piece on opera singers. She picked three Americans, Louise Homer from Pittsburgh, the Metropolitan Opera's leading contralto; Geraldine Farrar of Melrose, Massachusetts, who had made her operatic debut at nineteen; and Olive Fremstad, Swedish-born immigrant and reigning Wagnerian soprano at the Met. Opera continued to be one of her great interests, and she and Edith Lewis went often to hear the great voices of that golden age of opera, singers like Caruso, Mary Garden, Tetrazzini, Chaliapin, and many others besides the three Americans chosen for the article.

One day Willa Cather made an appointment to interview Fremstad. According to Miss Lewis, she went to the singer's apartment and waited a long while until Fremstad returned from a motor ride. There had been some slight mishap, and the prima donna came in late. She was tired, pale, drawn. She also looked old, and her voice was only a husky whisper. Willa Cather excused herself and said she would return another day. That night she, Edith Lewis, and Isabelle McClung, who was visiting, had tickets for *Tales of Hoffmann*. The second-act curtain was unaccountably delayed, and after a long while the management announced that the soprano had been taken ill. Mme. Fremstad, however, had agreed to finish the opera. Then the curtain went up, and there before Willa Cather's astonished eyes was the woman she had left a haggard wreck several hours before. She now was singing "in a voice so opulent, so effortless, that it seemed as if she were dreaming the music, not singing it."

" 'But it's impossible,' Willa Cather kept saying. 'It's impossible.' "

Sometime later the interview did come off. About the middle of April she went to Fremstad's apartment again, and when she came away she was choked by things unutterable. She told Elizabeth Sergeant that if she could write all that Fremstad made one know, it would be worth-while. She was just like the women on the Divide—with suspicious, defiant, farseeing pioneer eyes. It came to Willa Cather in a flash that here was Alexandra Bergson with a voice. Even her apartment was furnished with Alexandra's taste in furniture. Willa Cather believed that the pioneer women on the Divide possessed many of the traits of the artist, the drive, the perception, the energy, the creative force. They had created a new country out of an idea, just as Fremstad created the roles of Elsa or Sieglinde or Brünnhilde out of her mind and personality.

163

A Swedish immigrant who had grown up in Minnesota and had fought her way to the pinnacle of artistic success—there was a character to write about.

A week later she still was full of Fremstad. To find a new type of human creature, to get inside a new skin, that was the finest sport there was, she told Elizabeth Sergeant. After her interview she also had another moving experience at the stage door of the opera house when she saw Fremstad come out after singing Kundry in the Good Friday performance of *Parsifal.* She wanted to go up to her and congratulate her, saying something like "Hurrah for Mrs. Ericson," but she merely bowed to her secretary. The singer's eyes were empty glass. She had spent her charge.

These three glimpses of Fremstad—pinch-hitting on a moment's notice, drained after a great performance, and talking like Alexandra Bergson in the midst of her Grand Rapids furniture—came together like the inner explosion that had produced *O Pioneers!* The result was an idea for a new novel, *The Song of the Lark.* The new novel would give Willa Cather a chance to combine her lifelong interest in art and artists and her maturing views of Nebraska and Red Cloud. It would be the story of an artist's struggle for recognition and would combine the careers of both Olive Fremstad and herself.

She did not begin writing *The Song of the Lark*, however, until October. After spending the summer in New York working on articles for *McClure's*, she and Isabelle McClung visited the Shenandoah Valley during September. Then she went to work in the attic study at 1180 Murray Hill Avenue and in four weeks produced the first twenty-eight thousand words—written in first draft and rewritten. She went back to New York in November and kept on writing, but the interruptions were maddening. If she could only nail up her front door, she wrote. She did have her phone disconnected, but all the good she got out of that was Fremstad wearing down her two-thousand-dollar Isolde vocal chords trying to get Chelsea 2036 and always getting a brewery instead. But the writing did go ahead, until in February she pricked her scalp with a hatpin and got a serious case of blood poisoning. This put her in the hospital for a week with a shaved and bandaged head. It infuriated her to be the victim of such a silly accident. She had no patience with herself or anyone else who had grotesque accidents. Such persons were clowns. But while she was in the hospital, Fremstad came sweeping in with a load of flowers and showed her how to do her hair to cover the bandages. This cheered her up a great deal, and then Isabelle came to spend a month while she recuperated. Finally she was able to work again, and the world looked brighter. In May she went back to Pittsburgh to work, and the rest of the novel was written there.

By this time she and Fremstad had become good friends. She went to the singer's apartment frequently for tea, and Fremstad often dined at Bank Street. In June Willa Cather visited Fremstad at her place in Maine, where she saw another astonishing side of her Swedish friend. She was a Viking dynamo from morning to night. She fished as though she had no other means of getting food, cleaned her own fish, swam like a walrus, rowed, tramped, cooked, and gardened. Willa Cather watched it all and felt as though she were living with the wife of the dying gladiator in deep German forests. These contacts with Fremstad acted like a bellows on the creative fires producing the new novel.

From September until February she was working in Pittsburgh, and the manuscript pages kept piling up. She took time off to visit the West in the summer, going all the way to New Mexico and Arizona and, of course, stopping off in Red Cloud en route. She brought her younger brother Jack back with her and enrolled him at Carnegie Tech, and when she was not writing that fall, she was rubbing the rough farmer edges off her brother. On February first the novel was almost done, two hundred thousand words, she wrote Zoë Akins, more than three times as much as *O Pioneers!*; and by the middle of the month she brought the manuscript back to New York. Before the end of July she had read proof, and the book appeared in the fall. It carried a dedication, "To Isabel McClung," which was followed by a verse:

> *On uplands,*
> *At morning,*
> *The world was young, the winds were free;*
> *A garden fair,*
> *In that blue desert air,*
> *Its guest invited me to be.*

Both *O Pioneers!* and *The Song of the Lark* had been written substantially at the McClung house in Pittsburgh under Isabelle's loving and protective eye. It was the place Willa Cather could work best, and she acknowledged her debt gratefully.

The Song of the Lark is an engaging and effective novel. Although the setting is Moonstone, Colorado, and the protagonist the musical offspring of a Swedish preacher, the background actually is Red Cloud and the Cather family. The first part of the novel, "Friends of Childhood," which is by far the longest of the six major subdivisions, evokes the memories of Willa Cather's childhood. Thea Kronborg spends her youth in the same nostalgic atmosphere that surrounds all of Willa Cather's best characters. Her relationships with her mother and younger brother, her room and the house, her friendship with Dr. Archie, who is a major character in the novel, her pleasure in Uncle Billy Beemer's cottonwood grove, all are created out of the Cather family background, the author's memory of Dr. McKeeby, and her reminiscences of Red Cloud. Scenes such as Thea's pneumonia and Dr. Archie's ministrations, Thea's piano lessons with the derelict German music teacher—these are materials that had teased the author's mind for many years.

At the age of seventeen Thea goes to Chicago to study the piano and at the end of the year discovers that her real vocation is singing. After an unsatisfactory summer in Moonstone she leaves home for good and returns to Chicago to study voice. There is a great deal of autobiography in the development of the character at this age, her yearnings, her aspirations, her determination. It is Willa Cather during her college years at Lincoln and Willa Cather at home during her summer vacations. This section of the novel occupies Parts II and III. Next is "The Ancient People," Part IV, the action that takes place in Arizona. It is richly evocative, not because the material had teased her mind a long time, but because the experience was so deeply felt that it became almost immediately available.

Part V, "Dr. Archie's Venture," is the shortest part of the novel and exists chiefly to wind up the first four sections and prepare for the conclusion. Part VI, "Kronborg," takes place ten years later and deals with Thea's operatic triumph in New York. Narrated by the omniscient author and seen through the eyes of Dr. Archie and Fred Ottenburg, the man she ultimately marries, this section is entirely constructed of immediate materials. According to Willa Cather's own theory, this part should be inferior. It is, although it creates a fascinating picture of a prima donna attaining the "frozen heights," as Willa Cather put it in her *McClure's* article. She had been observing artists for twenty years, and her understanding of the artistic temperament came out of long experience. She understood what it meant for Fremstad at the age of forty finally to achieve complete mastery of her Wagnerian roles. She herself was the same age when *O Pioneers!* finally brought her prima donna billing.

Although *The Song of the Lark* is a success story, Thea Kronborg's success is somewhat like Alexandra Bergson's, achievement at the expense of valuable things sacrificed. The same principle of contrast that Willa Cather used effectively in *O Pioneers!* again provides counterpoint. There is a moving scene between Thea and Dr. Archie when the latter visits her in New York. He says he is afraid that she does not have enough personal life outside her work. She looks at him and smiles:

'My dear doctor, I don't have any. Your work becomes your personal life. You are not much good until it does. It's like being woven into a big web. You can't pull away, because all your little tendrils are woven into the picture. It takes you up, and uses you, and spins you out; and that is your life. Not much else can happen to you.'

She had sacrificed everything for her career—family, friends, a private life.

Whether or not artists have to sacrifice everything might be debated, but Fremstad was the kind of artist who had, and Willa Cather had believed since she was seventeen that the god of art accepts only human sacrifices. She put it another way when she told an interviewer in 1921: "A book is made with one's own flesh and blood of years. It is cremated youth." Yet only from the ashes of youth could artistic maturity, Phoenix-like, arise. "Youth," she wrote in her review of Arnold Bennett's play *Milestones*, "is the only really valuable thing in the world. . . . It is force, potency, a physiological fact. . . . The individual possesses this power for only a little while, a few years. . . . If he devotes these years to self-sacrifice . . . God may reward him, but Nature will not forgive him."

"An inevitable dualism bisects nature," Emerson writes in his essay "Compensation." Willa Cather and Thea Kronborg both believed this and felt it within their own natures. The artist being human and yet propelled by the inner knowledge of his special election cannot help being at the start something of a split personality. When Thea prepares to leave Moonstone for Chicago, she feels "as if she were being pulled in two, between the desire to go away forever and the desire to stay forever." Willa Cather experienced the same tug of opposing forces, and like Thea concluded that one had so little time in life that one must keep moving.

The poignancy of the novel is heightened a great deal by the use of the Orpheus myth, which provides a structural framework and allusive richness for the narrative. The Orpheus theme is inserted early in the book by A. Wunsch (whose name means desire), Thea's first music teacher, who introduces her to Gluck's opera *Orfeo ed Euridice.* It is his favorite piece of music, and his battered score is his legacy to his talented pupil. As he drifts downward to an alcoholic oblivion, to be torn by the Thracian women and cast into the Hebrus, Thea goes on toward her destiny with his cherished gift. The myth of Orpheus, of course, is the eternal story of the striving artist whose reach exceeds his grasp, who must reconcile desire with possibility. He cannot always have his beloved Eurydice, for human frailty thwarts the realization of the ideal. At the end of the novel Thea's magnificent talent and tremendous will to achieve the heights have brought her to the perfection of Orpheus before his loss, but the reader's knowledge that Thea, after sacrificing her life for her art, must eventually lose her Eurydice haunts the ending.

The Song of the Lark displeased Willa Cather somewhat in later years after she went on to greater accomplishments. So strong was the impact of Fremstad that she was unable to leave anything out. When the novel actually appeared, the two hundred thousand words she originally wrote were pruned to one hundred sixty-three thousand, but even so she disregarded her own precept that the essence of art is to simplify. Her narrative technique here is closer to Theodore Dreiser's with its enormous accumulation of detail than it is to her other novels. Because Willa Cather's real gift is the power to evoke emotion through a process of severe selectivity, in this novel the reader is constantly wanting to use a blue pencil. It seems unnecessary to know all about Dr. Archie's unhappy marriage or to have extensive documentation of Fred Ottenburg's background. One is astonished to read about reform politics in Colorado in view of Willa Cather's normally impenetrable disinterest in the political process, and the epilogue could well have been amputated without loss. She should have remembered the quotation from the elder Dumas, which Thea learns and which she was fond of repeating: " . . . to make a drama, a man needed one passion, and four walls."

Willa Cather recognized later that her novel was overwritten, and when Houghton Mifflin decided to reissue it in 1932, she cut about ten per cent of the total wordage, all from the last two books. In her introduction to the new edition, she noted that the chief fault lay in the last part, which deals with Thea Kronborg at the peak of her success: " . . . the life of a successful artist in the full tide of achievement is not so interesting as the life of a talented young girl 'fighting her way,' as we say. Success is never so interesting as struggle." She might well have made further cuts in the earlier parts of the novel, but she was not really interested in rewriting the book. She did have another try at similar materials several years later in *Lucy Gayheart.*

She also was somewhat embarrassed over the title when the book was reissued. The novel had been given its title from a picture by that name in the Chicago Art Institute, a rather mediocre painting by Jules Breton, depicting a peasant girl on her way to work looking up at a skylark singing. Willa Cather intended, as she says in her 1932 preface, to suggest by the title "a young girl's awakening to something beautiful." Because the book chiefly concerns an artist's youth, the title is appropriate enough, though the Breton painting is inferior; but beyond this, the title has even greater significance. The singing lark is a motif that recurs many times in Willa Cather's life and fiction and always symbolizes desire, aspiration, and longing.

Willa Cather was sorry when she finished writing *The Song of the*

Lark. At the beginning she was excited by the experience of getting into another person's skin; by the time she finished, she reversed her metaphor, because of the novel's considerable autobiographical content, and wrote that she missed feeling Thea stretching inside herself. When the book appeared, she was well satisfied with it and pleased by the reviews. H. L. Mencken, for example, wrote in *The Smart Set* that "Miss Cather, indeed, here steps definitely into the small class of American novelists who are seriously to be reckoned with. . . . I have read no late novel, in fact, with a greater sense of intellectual stimulation. . . . Miss Cather not only has a desire to write; she also has something to say."

The greatest accolade, however, came from Fremstad herself. Willa Cather dreaded a little having the singer read the novel, and thought she might be furious about her fictional portrait. When she met Fremstad in Lincoln, the singer embraced her and exclaimed that she could not tell where Thea left off and she began. She was glowing with excitement over the book and even thought the tone of the last part was just right. She said it was the only book she ever had read about an artist in which she had felt there was something doing in the artist.

III

When *The Song of the Lark* finally was finished and all the proof read and returned, Willa Cather had been working on the book or thinking about it for well over two years. She was ready for a real change. S. S. McClure, who recently had become editor of the New York *Evening Mail,* invited her to undertake a writing assignment in Germany, and she agreed to go. Just what she was supposed to do, surviving records do not say, but McClure, noted for harebrained ideas as well as productive ones, then was treading a slippery path as the pro-British editor of a paper owned by a pro-German industrialist. He may have thought that someone like Willa Cather ought to be reporting from inside Germany. But the *Lusitania* already had been sunk, and anti-German feeling was beginning to run high. Another lucky accident saved Willa Cather from getting involved in writing articles from Germany during the latter part of 1915. Isabelle McClung was to go along on the trip, but her hardheaded father who held the purse strings, old Judge McClung, said no. Since Isabelle could not go and Willa did not want to go alone, plans were canceled. How much feeling surrounded this series of events one cannot determine now, but in the end Willa Cather went off to the Southwest with Edith Lewis.

This time she visited Mesa Verde for the first time. She wanted to see more cliff-dwellings than she had found in Walnut Canyon near Flagstaff. Mesa Verde had become a national park in 1906, and the huge Cliff Palace with its 223 rooms had been excavated only a few years before. She and Edith Lewis took the narrow-gauge Denver and Rio Grande Railroad over the Continental Divide from Denver to Durango and then continued on to Mancos. There was no auto road into the park then, and they had to hire a team and driver to take them in. Very few people were visiting the park that early, and for the week they stayed they had almost the exclusive services of the ranger who ran the government tourist camp. Also Willa Cather met the brother of Richard Wetherill, one of the two cowboys who had discovered the Cliff Palace in 1888, and heard the story of his adventures. She was thrilled by the tale of Wetherill's swimming the Mancos River in search of lost cattle and coming upon the hidden city just as it had been left when the mesa Indians abandoned it in the thirteenth century. Some ten years later this story and the visit to the ruins went into "Tom Outland's Story" in *The Professor's House.*

Just before returning to Mancos, they had the experience of getting lost in Soda Canyon in the company of a substitute guide. They visited an unexcavated cliff-dwelling called the Tower House and had to climb down to the bottom of Soda Canyon by a trail that only could be ascended by ropes. Their inexperienced guide planned to take them back up another trail, but by late afternoon after they had walked for miles and come to the opening of Cliff Canyon, the guide had to admit that they were lost. He then thought, though he was not sure, that there was an archeologist's camp about four miles up Cliff Canyon. Willa Cather told him to go alone and leave Edith Lewis and her there to wait for help. Miss Lewis remembers:

The four or five hours that we spent waiting there were, I think, for Willa Cather the most rewarding of our whole trip to the Mesa Verde. There was a large flat rock at the mouth of Cliff Canyon, and we settled ourselves comfortably on this rock. . . . We were tired and rather thirsty, but not worried, for we knew we should eventually be found. We did not talk, but watched the long summer twilight come on, and the full moon rise up over the rim of the canyon. The place was very beautiful.

Eventually there were shouts from up the canyon, and two men from the camp appeared. Their guide had been so exhausted that he could not come back himself. Cliff Canyon was a mass of broken rocks all the way, and they were pulled and pushed and led by their rescuers for four miles until they came to a place where they could climb out of the canyon by scaling the lopped-off branches of a huge pine that had been felled against the cliff like a ladder. They got to the archeologist's camp at two in the morning. When Willa Cather reported this adventure to Elizabeth Sergeant, she wrote that she was bruised and sore but happy and ready to go back and be mauled again by the big brutality of Cliff Canyon. She never learned so much as in the twenty-four hours of that experience. That country, she said, drives one crazy with delight.

From Mesa Verde they went on to Taos, where they stayed at a primitive adobe hotel run by a Mexican woman. This was long before Taos had become an artists' colony, and they had to drive a long way by horse and wagon over a rough road to get there. They spent a month in New Mexico, rode horseback a great deal, drank in the scenery, and observed life in the surrounding Spanish-speaking villages. Miss Lewis reports that Willa Cather "was intensely alive to the country—as a musician might be alive to an orchestral composition he was hearing for the first time. She did not talk about it much—but one felt that she was deeply engaged with it always, was continually receiving strong impressions from the things she saw and experienced." She was, of course, storing the material that eventually would go into *Death Comes for the Archbishop* twelve years later.

At the end of the eventful summer Willa Cather went back to Pittsburgh, and Edith Lewis returned to New York. There was no new novel taking shape, and a profound emotional crisis was about to engulf her. In November Judge McClung died, and since Mrs. McClung had predeceased him, Isabelle finally was free of parental domination and in possession of independent means. Willa and Isabelle spent a sad Christmas in the old house on Murray Hill Avenue, and Willa wrote Aunt Franc on Christmas Day that the kind and hospitable house which had been a home to her for fifteen years would probably be sold and that this was the last Christmas she ever would have there. To a person who clung to family ties and old friendships as strongly as Willa Cather, the end of this era cut deep. She wrote that never again would she feel so safe and happy in any other house, and even her New York apartment, which she liked very much, was never home in the same sense.

The shock of losing the old refuge, however, was only the lesser part of the crisis. Sometime during the winter months Isabelle told Willa that she was going to be married. The announcement was a thunderbolt. This was the end of the intimate relationship with Isabelle that had lasted since 1899. The paralyzing effect of this news may be judged by a letter she wrote in mid-March. She reported dryly to Dorothy Canfield Fisher that she was unable to start a new book because of the death of Judge McClung and Isabelle's marriage. Elizabeth Sergeant, who heard of Isabelle's defection as she walked with Willa Cather on an icy day in Central Park, reports that as Willa broke the news her face was bleak and her eyes vacant. "All her natural exuberance had drained away."

She picked herself up after the shock, however, and went west for a long sojourn. She and Edith Lewis returned to Taos in 1916 for a longer stay than the year before, and she visited her brother Roscoe in Lander, Wyoming. From Wyoming she wrote on August third that Isabelle's marriage was still a hard blow to take and always would be, but the rest of the world was beginning to look as it used to. She was having a great time with her brother and his family. They had two rivers flowing through their backyard, both full of trout, and were taking her on long horseback rides into the sand hills to the east and the Wind River range to the west. She would be in Red Cloud by the end of the month.

When she got home, she had to forget her own problems and

173

take over the household chores during her mother's serious illness. From September until nearly Thanksgiving Willa Cather served as cook and housekeeper and on the whole enjoyed it, though there were eight in the family all the time. She finally mastered the secret of good pastry and wrote that she never again would be intimidated by a kitchen range. When she returned to New York at the end of November, she told Mary Jewett that she was riotously well after her six months in the West. She must have recovered her spirits, because she already was at work on *My Ántonia*.

Thirty-three years after she began gathering the materials for *My Ántonia*, Willa Cather finally was ready to put the story on paper. As she looked back in her old age, she felt that the character of Ántonia was the embodiment of all her feelings about the early immigrants in the prairie country. The first story she heard in Nebraska was the account of Francis Sadilek's suicide, and it seemed in retrospect that she must have been destined to write that novel if she ever wrote anything. When Margaret Lawrence's *School of Femininity* appeared in 1936 with a perceptive chapter on Willa Cather's fiction, she admitted the thesis of this essay: She could only write successfully when she wrote about people or places she admired greatly or even loved. The characters she created could be cranky or queer or foolhardy or rash, but they had to have something in them that thrilled her and warmed her heart.

Annie Sadilek was such a girl. Willa Cather told an interviewer in 1921 that one of the people who had interested her most when she was a child was the Bohemian hired girl who worked for one of their neighbors. "She was one of the truest artists I ever knew in the keenness and sensitiveness of her enjoyment, in her love of people and in her willingness to take pains." On one of her visits to Red Cloud Willa Cather again saw Annie, now Annie Pavelka, on her farm surrounded by her large brood of children. The memories of her childhood came flooding back, and the idea for the novel was born. Edith Lewis says she brought the first two or three chapters back to New York when she returned from Red Cloud at Thanksgiving in 1916. E. K. Brown places the meeting with Annie in the same year, but it must have occurred earlier.

In the summer of 1914, while she was still writing *The Song of the Lark*, she spent two weeks driving around in the French and Bohemian country north of Red Cloud. She spent days on the road or in the threshing fields with the temperatures often up to 110 degrees. She was thoroughly happy, and only the eternal heat finally drove her away. She saw many old friends on this occasion and would have liked to stay for weeks. All of those people, she wrote at the time, were like characters in a book. The story had begun, she explained, when she was little, and it continued year after year, like *War and Peace*, always with variations, always much stranger than any invention. Whenever she went back, her friends filled her in on the details of the story that had taken place during her absence. It seems more than likely that she saw Annie during this summer. If one assumes that the novel begins in the year the Cathers moved to Nebraska, the time of Jim Burden's return from New York to visit Ántonia is 1914.

Elizabeth Sergeant first heard the idea for *My Ántonia* early in 1916, while Willa Cather still was emotionally distraught over Isabelle's marriage. She talked about the new novel one day while she was having tea with Miss Sergeant, but it was six months before she could pull herself together enough to begin writing it. During this tea she placed a Sicilian apothecary jar filled with flowers in the center of a bare table and said:

"I want my new heroine to be like this—like a rare object in the middle of a table, which one may examine from all sides . . . because she *is* the story."

This description of the concept makes clear that she was not planning to write another long novel like *The Song of the Lark*. William Heinemann, in rejecting that novel for British publication, had written her that "the full-blooded method, which told everything about everybody," was not natural to her. She recognized that he was right and went back to the method of severe selectivity she had used in *Alexander's Bridge* and *O Pioneers!* She was beginning to formulate consciously the principles she later would spell out in "The Novel Démeublé." "How wonderful it would be," she writes in that essay, "if we could throw all the furniture out of the window; and along with it, all the meaningless reiterations concerning physical sensations, all the tiresome old patterns, and leave the room as bare as the stage of a Greek theatre . . . for the play of emotions great and little."

Once she decided that Annie would be the central figure, she had to work out the narrative technique for presenting her. She chose a first-person point of view because she believed that novels of feeling, such as *My Ántonia* would be, were best narrated, while novels of action should be written in the third person. But who should her narrator be? She told her interviewer that she rejected Annie's lover as narrator because "my Ántonia deserved something better than the *Saturday Evening Post* sort of stuff." Then she explained that most of what she knew about Annie had come from talks with young men. "She had a fascination for them, and they used to be with her whenever they could. They had to manage it on the sly because she was only a hired girl." Thus Willa Cather created as her narrator Jim Burden, whose age, experience, and personal history closely paralleled her own. Sarah Orne Jewett perhaps would have faulted her for this, as she had for using a male viewpoint in "On the Gulls' Road." But Willa Cather's preference for male narrators in her fiction was inveterate and no doubt sprang from the strong masculine element rooted deep in her personality.

She felt obliged to defend her use of a male point of view, however, when she wrote her old friend and editor Will Jones. Because her knowledge of Annie came mostly from men, she explained, she had to use the male narrator, and then she rationalized that she felt competent to do this because of her experience in writing McClure's autobiography. She had captured McClure so effectively that even Mrs. McClure and John Phillips, McClure's college classmate, found the presentation completely convincing. When she first began writing the autobiography, she found it awfully hampering to be McClure all the time, but in the end it became fascinating to work within the limits and color of the personality she knew so well. Ever since then she had felt a sort of nagging wish to try the experiment again.

The story line in *My Ántonia* follows fairly closely the actual lives of Ántonia Shimerda Cuzak [Annie Sadilek Pavelka] and Jim Burden [Willa Cather]. The narrative begins on the Divide when Jim Burden and the hired man, Jake, arrive from Virginia to live with Jim's grandparents. Ántonia Shimerda is a neighbor, who is seen through Jim's eyes and who becomes his playmate, though she is four years older. Book I takes place on the farm and describes life both at the Burdens and the Shimerdas and includes the suicide of Annie's father, which in reality had taken place earlier. Willa Cather probably did not meet Annie before moving to town because she was not a close neighbor. But when the Cathers lived on Cedar Street in Red Cloud, Annie came to work for the Miners, who lived a block away, and Willa Cather's memory of her in Book II, "The Hired Girls," comes from her own experience as well as from mutual friends. When the novel moves to the state university in Book III, Annie drops out of the story, and the narrative recounts Jim Burden's life in Lincoln and his relationship with Lena Lingard, another of the "hired girls." Annie reappears in Book IV just after her railroading fiancé has deserted her, and then in Book V twenty years later with her family and her Czech farmer-husband Tony Cuzak. The narrator Jim Burden in the last two books is first a student at Harvard home for the summer and then a New York lawyer visiting Nebraska on business. The tremendously moving picture of Annie surrounded by her ten children in Book V is the scene that produced the inner explosion that inspired the book.

More than most writers, Willa Cather presents readers with the chance to compare literal fact with artistic imagination. There is a great deal more factual basis in *My Ántonia* than the bare story outline of the title character and the narrator. The town of Black Hawk is again Red Cloud, and the Nebraska farmlands again provide the locale. Jim's grandparents, of course, are drawn from life, the entire Miner family play roles in the drama, and Herbert Bates appears as Gaston Cleric. In addition to the major characters and incidents, minor characters and minor incidents also are rooted in actuality. The Negro pianist, Blind d'Arnault, who plays in Black Hawk, was drawn from a real Blind Tom, whom she heard in Lincoln, and a Blind Boone, whom she probably had heard in Red Cloud. The visitor to Red Cloud today can see the home of Wick Cutter, who in actuality was a moneylender named Bentley and apparently just as evil and unsavory as the character who plans to rape Ántonia. The hotel-keeping Mrs. Gardener in the novel was an actual Mrs. Holland, and so it goes.

It is no wonder that Willa Cather was pestered by literal-minded readers wanting to know where she got this and where she got that. The people in Red Cloud were continually playing detective games with her characters and incidents. It exasperated her, but she should have expected her dramas of memory to provoke this kind of response. Sometimes she was patient and discussed her sources with friends—sometimes she even answered letters from students—but usually her response was annoyance. Often she did not know where she got things, and after *My Ántonia* appeared, her father pointed out half a dozen different incidents that were based on things she had done or seen with him, all of which she thought she had invented. One such episode was the story within a story of the two crazy Russians and the wolves. She did admit writing Mrs. Miner into the novel as Mrs. Harling, but that was a special circumstance, as Mrs. Miner died while the novel was being written and the book was dedicated to her daughters Carrie and Irene. In all other instances, she maintained, her characters were composite figures, even Ántonia. When one is writing hard, she explained, one drives towards the main episodes, and the details take care of themselves. The detail must be spontaneous, unsought for by the writer.

The writing of the novel went on during the winter of 1916–1917 and into the spring. Willa Cather interrupted her work in June to visit Nebraska and to receive an honorary degree, her first, from her alma mater. She also visited her brother in Wyoming and then returned east. She apparently was ready to see Isabelle and her new husband, Jan Hambourg, a violinist from Toronto, and went up to Jaffrey, New Hampshire, where they were vacationing. That the meeting was somewhat strained can be inferred from a letter she wrote about six months later reporting that she finally had learned to like Jan Hambourg. As with most people, she added rather unflatteringly, he turned out to have many good qualities when one got to know him.

The Hambourgs moved on, and Willa Cather remained in Jaffrey through the summer and fall. She was immensely attracted to the place and nearly every year for the rest of her life returned for several weeks. She rented two small rooms on the top floor of the Shattuck Inn and went back to the same quarters on subsequent visits. Her rooms had sloping ceilings like her little upstairs bedroom in Red Cloud, and she liked listening to the rain on the roof directly overhead. Her windows looked out over woods and pastures filled with junipers, and off in the distance was Mount Monadnock. She put up a tent on a nearby farm called High Mowing, which two of her Pittsburgh friends had rented, and worked there as long as the weather was mild. Every morning after an early breakfast she crossed the Stony Brook Farm Road and cut through a hedge to the clearing where her tent was pitched. She carried her papers and pens with her but left her ink bottles, table, and camp chair in the tent. In the middle of the day she knocked off work, climbed a stone wall, and returned to the inn through the woods. There she wrote Book II, "The Hired Girls."

When she returned to New York in the fall, she had less than one third of the novel to finish, but she was unable to complete it until spring. There were constant interruptions, her illness, her maid's illness, the coming and going of icemen, scrubwomen, laundrymen, and the wartime fuel shortage that made it impossible for her to use her study. Yet she saw a great deal of her friends that winter. She had begun her Fridays at home, which became a Bank Street tradition, and on these occasions people she liked dropped in for tea. She also gave a good many dinner parties, and the war did not seem to touch her very deeply. When she was ill, Olive Fremstad sent her car every night, took her to her apartment, and gave her dinner. Mme. Fremstad was not very busy that winter, as there was no German opera during the war.

Few American novels are likely to be read longer than *My Ántonia*. In it theme, character, myth, and incident ride together comfortably on a clear, supple prose style. It is probably Willa Cather's greatest work. Everything went right—a splendid concept executed with perfect taste and mastery. Willa Cather combines the yea-saying vision of Whitman with a disciplined artistry learned from James, Flaubert, Sarah Orne Jewett, and others, and the novel goes considerably beyond either of its immediate predecessors. While Alexandra Bergson is the strong, intelligent tamer of the wild land, and Thea Kronborg, with the godlike name, is the successful climber of Olympus, Ántonia Shimerda is the mother of races. She is the most heroic figure of them all, both the Madonna of the Wheat Fields and the embodiment of the

American westering myth. The wonder of it all is that the novel, so rich in suggestiveness, is so artfully simple.

My Ántonia is a sunny novel. The laws of compensation seem suspended as Jim Burden visits Ántonia on her farm in the final book. Whereas Alexandra tames the land at the expense of personal tragedy and familial alienation and Thea Kronborg succeeds at the cost of many things most people hold dear, Ántonia ends her struggle richly rewarded. The suicide of her father, her hard life on the farm as a child and in town as a hired girl, the desertion by her fiancé, her bearing an illegitimate child—none of these things seems very important in the final chapter as Jim Burden drives to Hastings to take the train back to Black Hawk. Even a hardened reader finishes this novel choked up with emotion. How, one wonders, does Willa Cather manage to do it?

In *The Song of the Lark* Thea Kronborg's first teacher in Chicago, Andor Harsanyi, is asked, as he listens to her great triumph as Sieglinde in the final book, what is the secret of her success: " 'Her secret? It is every artist's secret'—he waved his hand—'passion. That is all. It is an open secret, and perfectly safe. Like heroism, it is inimitable in cheap materials.' " Passion too is Willa Cather's secret. One knows when he is in the presence of it, but the identification is somewhat intuitive, like Emily Dickinson recognizing poetry because it took the top of her head off. Although it is difficult to explain the passion, some of the elements contributing to it may be isolated. They lie in the subject, the author's attitude towards the material, and the execution of the project.

This novel is compounded of the things that, to use Sarah Orne Jewett's phrase, teased Willa Cather's mind for years and thus became a part of her. To this thorough assimilation of the material may be added the author's complete and abiding love for the people and the country, what she later called "the gift of sympathy." Perfect knowledge and boundless enthusiasm, however, would count for little if the artist had not mastered her instrument, and Willa Cather's technical skill after twenty-five years of steady practice enabled her to create a virtuoso performance. The organic form she worked out for *O Pioneers!* suited the materials used in *My Ántonia*, and she was willing to take nearly two years to write this medium-length novel.

The narrative method illustrates well the hazards and the achievement. The persona of Jim Burden, the narrator, is both a structural device and a point of view. Jim is a middle-aged lawyer from the East who can look at the subject both with familiarity and detachment. He retains many of his open middle-western boyish traits; he is childless and unhappily married to Ántonia's antithesis; and he has the experience of the world, which, as Willa Cather sees it, gives him the knowledge of the parish. He is in an ideal position to tell the story, and because he is not a professional writer he can indulge in naïveté that the professional would avoid. The chance for mawkish sentimentality with this method is great, but Willa Cather avoids sentimentality through her familiar use of contrasts. Good and evil are juxtaposed, and Jim Burden's golden memories are constantly interrupted by sterner realities. The idyl of Jim's boyhood is broken into by the killing of the rattlesnake, the suicide of Ántonia's father, the deviltries of Wick Cutter, the meanness of Ántonia's brother, and the horrible story of Pavel and Peter. While the cruel and ugly events keep the story from slipping into sentimentality, they do not tip the scales towards melodrama or tragedy because of the retrospective character of the narrative. The novel is a drama of memory in which sad recollections are placed in context with happy memories. The suicide of Ántonia's father is one of the tragedies of immigrant life, but out of death comes life and the book closes with a clear picture of Ántonia as "a rich mine of life, like the founders of early races."

The persona of Jim Burden also provides a suitable vehicle for the loosely episodic structure of the novel. To bridge the interval between the early books that take place on the farm and in town and the final episodes showing Ántonia as an adult, Willa Cather follows her narrator to college. She also is able to widen the perspective in this section by chronicling the success story of Lena Lingard, who learns dressmaking in Black Hawk and while Jim is at the University of Nebraska opens a shop in Lincoln. She is another type of second-generation immigrant who makes good in the New World. The Lincoln chapters also allow Willa Cather to use her own memories of college days and theater reviewing and to introduce one of the major themes of the novel. As Jim looks back on his boyhood, he reads in his Virgil: " . . . the best days are

WILLA CATHER

the first to flee. '*Optima dies . . . prima fugit.*' " This passage provides the appropriate note of elegy for a middle-aged lawyer reviewing his youth. It also strikes a note that sounds frequently in Willa Cather's fiction.

The westering theme successfully announced in *O Pioneers!* continues writ large in *My Ántonia.* In the scene by the river when Jim picnics with the hired girls just before leaving for college, Willa Cather creates one of her most vivid symbols. As the sun is going down over the prairie, Jim and the girls look across the high fields towards the horizon. There silhouetted against the setting sun is a great black object. Startled, they spring to their feet and strain their eyes toward it:

In a moment we realized what it was. On some upland farm, a plough had been left standing in the field. The sun was sinking just behind it. Magnified across the distance by the horizontal light, it stood out against the sun, was exactly contained within the circle of the disk; the handles, the tongue, the share—black against the molten red. There it was, heroic in size, a picture writing on the sun.

As metaphor for the Westward Movement, nothing could have been more appropriate.

Although the novel was not an immediate financial success, the critical reception was all that anyone could ask for. It came out a few weeks before the end of the First World War, inauspicious timing, and for the first three years sold poorly. Then the sales picked up, and for the next two decades the demand was regularly from four to six thousand copies a year without book clubs, reprint editions, dramatizations, or other sales stimuli. The reviewers were almost all enthusiastic. Mencken again led the chorus of praise and was warmly supported by Randolph Bourne, whom Willa Cather thought the best American critic. The reviewers were anticipated by Ferris Greenslet, who recognized immediately the book's quality. When it came into the Houghton Mifflin office, he experienced "the most thrilling shock of recognition of the real thing of any manuscript" he ever received.

The praise that pleased Willa Cather most came many years later from Justice Oliver Wendell Holmes, to whom Greenslet sent a copy in 1930. Holmes wrote that he had not had such a reading

sensation for a long time. The book had "unfailing charm, perhaps
not to be defined; a beautiful tenderness, a vivifying imagination
that transforms but does not distort or exaggerate—order, propor-
tion. It is a poem made from nature . . . that being read establishes
itself as true, and makes the reader love his country more." The
renewed sense of patriotism that *My Ántonia* gave the old judge,
who started his career as a Union officer in the Civil War, was an
unexpected and unplanned by-product.

Increased love of country, however, was an appropriate effect.
The book appeared about the time of the armistice ending the
First World War, and its earliest readers were simultaneously enjoying the novel and experiencing a sense of reinforced patriotism
and pride over America's successful participation in "the war to
end all wars." Willa Cather shared Ántonia's fierce attachment to
her new land and the values Americans had gone to France to
fight for. She had little to say about the war while it was going on,
but as soon as she finished reading proof for *My Ántonia,* she went
back to Red Cloud for a visit, and while she was there she read
the letters her young cousin G. P. Cather had written his mother
before he was killed at Cantigny in May. His letters made a great
impression on her, and before she left Nebraska in the fall she had
resolved to make him the subject of her next novel. This would be
a war novel, and increased love of country would be one of the
hoped-for results. She wrote Aunt Franc a tender letter of sympathy on Armistice Day, November eleventh, which she called the
first day of the great peace. For the first time since human society
existed, she exulted, the sun rose this morning upon a world in
which not one great monarchy or tyranny existed. Her heart
turned to her aunt, however, and she wished that G. P. could have
lived to see this day and to help in the reconstruction that must
follow. But she quoted from the last act of *Macbeth*, when they
bring word to Siward that his son has been killed in his first battle.
The old man says: "Why then, God's soldier be he!"

Willa Cather in writing a war novel was, in Henry James's
phrase, "flying in the face of presumptions." The hero would not
only be a man but also a soldier. The materials would be mostly
immediate ones, not subjects that had teased her mind for years.
The novel would have a purpose beyond the mere desire to tell a

story or to present a character as truthfully as possible. One would like to say that she succeeded, despite these obstacles, in writing another great novel; but she did not. *One of Ours*, which was thirty-nine months in the writing and more than four years between conception and publication, was a failure. She told Dorothy Canfield Fisher just after finishing the manuscript that she knew the story was doomed when she began it, and when she was reading proof she wrote that she had set herself an impossible task.

What was the inner compulsion that made her begin this novel in the fall of 1918? Was it a sudden awareness when she read her cousin's letters that she had made no overt contribution to the war effort? She had been so absorbed in writing *My Ántonia* that nothing else had impinged on her senses. Yet she felt deeply about the war, for she loved France and agonized over the havoc wrought by the conflict. And she certainly feared the loss of humanistic values in the holocaust. That she loved her country deeply is perfectly clear in *My Ántonia*, as Justice Holmes's reaction indicates. Whatever the impulse was, it was strong, and she began to work on the novel in New York in the fall of 1918.

After returning to 5 Bank Street, she invited Albert Donovan, a former Pittsburgh pupil who was stationed at an army post in New York, to bring soldiers to visit her. He came with three or four at a time, and they talked to her for hours. She worked throughout the winter of 1918–1919 and the next summer took her work-in-progress to Jaffrey, New Hampshire, and again wrote in the tent near the Shattuck Inn. Progress was painfully slow, however, and she worked on into the fall after the rains began. She almost got pneumonia writing out of doors in the wet weather and was ill for weeks, but there was one unexpected compensation. The local doctor who treated her had been a medical officer on a troopship during the war and loaned her his diary. But the book continued to go very slowly, and by the end of 1919 it was only about half-finished. She was struggling but had to go on. Meantime, as *My Ántonia* gained new readers, her critical reputation climbed steadily. Dorothy Canfield Fisher wrote William Allen White late that year: " . . . and don't I just agree with you that it is a wonderful book! That and *O Pioneers!* seem to me real honest-to-goodness master-pieces, such as the best in any literature can't beat."

CHAPTER 7

Dies Irae: 1920–1926

I

ONE DAY in the early spring of 1920 Willa Cather took the West
Side subway from Sheridan Square uptown to Forty-second Street.
On the nineteenth floor of the Candler Building she found a two-
room office occupied by young Alfred Knopf and his new publishing firm. She went in, introduced herself, discovered that he had
read *My Ántonia,* and they talked about books and publishing. She
had looked him up because she liked the appearance of his early
Borzoi books; they had more style than most books and seemed to
have been published by someone interested in bookmaking. The
interview went very well, and the two found themselves compati-
ble. Her hunch about Knopf's interest in bookmaking was correct,
for when she picked up some samples of blue binding-paper from
his desk, she found that he had been up to the Metropolitan Museum of Art to study Chinese blues. He was going to publish a
book of translations from Chinese poetry and wanted an appropriate color. At the end of the interview she asked him to be her
publisher.

Willa Cather had become increasingly dissatisfied with Houghton Mifflin. Ferris Greenslet was her long-time friend, but his
praises had not succeeded in convincing the company executives
that she was a valuable property. She had been very much annoyed throughout the printing of *The Song of the Lark.* It was
badly proofread, and while she admitted that she should have
been more careful, she also thought the publisher might have
backstopped her. The novel also was poorly designed, a dumpy
little volume with crowded pages; its format was not at all appropriate for a novel dealing seriously with the subject of art. Later

My Ántonia had come out with a drab, unattractive cover, and it seemed again as if she were just another author on the Houghton Mifflin list. The final exasperation was a printers' strike, which made her books unavailable, and what appeared to be massive indifference on the part of her publisher. Thus she went to Knopf with her proposition, and the result was twenty-seven years of complete satisfaction. Knopf gave her a great deal of personal attention, treated her like a valued friend, as indeed she was, promoted her books vigorously, and very soon provided her with a large income and financial security. She was able to indulge her interest in typography, binding, jacket design, and advertising copy as much as she wished. When she made suggestions, the advertising department carried them out, and when she felt like writing the jacket copy, the publisher was glad to use it.

Her chief reason for needing a new publisher was financial. By the spring of 1920 *My Ántonia* had been out a year and a half, and she had made, Edith Lewis remembers, only thirteen hundred dollars from it during the first twelve months. The second year's royalties would be a disastrous four hundred dollars. Meantime, she had been working on *One of Ours* since 1918, and getting along with it very slowly. She proposed to Knopf that he publish a collection of stories, four that never had been collected and four that originally had been published in *The Troll Garden* but now were long out of print. Knopf was willing to take her on these terms, though he really was interested in publishing her next novel, and brought out *Youth and the Bright Medusa* in the fall.

Under its inspired title this book returned to the subject that had preoccupied Willa Cather since the beginning of her career, the world of art and artists. She replaced the original metaphor of the trolls and the forest children with the myth of Medusa, the Gorgon maiden whose visage turned men to stone. Art remained for her the bright Medusa well into her middle years, and she did not stop writing about it until she completed her next-to-last novel, *Lucy Gayheart*, in 1935. The four stories reprinted from *The Troll Garden* were "Paul's Case," "A Wagner Matinee," "The Sculptor's Funeral," and "'A Death in the Desert'," arranged in that order in the second half of the collection. The four stories grouped together at the beginning were "Coming, Aphrodite!,"

186

"The Diamond Mine," "A Golden Slipper," and "Scandal." All of the newly collected stories deal with artists in relationship to the Philistine world, and the entire collection sounds an over-all note of death, defeat, frustration, and loss.

The only story that is at all sunny is the first one, "Coming, Aphrodite!" originally published in *Smart Set*. It is the tale that suggested the title, for it concerns two youthful artists whose lives briefly intersect. One is Don Hedger, painter, and the other Eden Bower, singer. Hedger paints for himself, and the world can take him or leave him; he is a Perseus who slays the Gorgon. Eden, who is Eve in her garden, Circe, and a golden Venus all in one, is on her way to Europe to study music. Her sense of destiny is just as sure as Hedger's, but for her, success is worship by the multitude. The two characters, who find themselves rooming side by side on Washington Square for one short summer, fall in love, and a brief, intense affair ensues. It ends when Eden's destiny arrives in the form of her Illinois millionaire businessman patron, who comes to take her to Europe. She is the willing plaything of the Philistine world. The story has an interesting ending that takes place eighteen years later. Eden, the glittering, befurred prima donna, returns to New York for an engagement. While passing Washington Square, she has her chauffeur stop so that she can look at the old rooming house. Then she visits a picture dealer to find out whatever happened to Hedger. He has become, she learns, a painter of great influence who commands enormous respect in the art world, though he is relatively unknown to the general public. Both Eden Bower and Don Hedger, it seems, have achieved the success they sought.

The second story, "The Diamond Mine," written soon after Willa Cather finished *The Song of the Lark*, suggests that she had material and ideas left over after completing the long novel. The protagonist of that tale is Cressida Garnet, a singer who might have been Thea Kronborg ten years after her triumphs at the Met. The story is a retrospective narrative of her life by a woman friend who bears somewhat the same relationship to her that Willa Cather did to Fremstad. Cressida Garnet went down on the *Titanic* worn out by the rapacity of her relatives, her singing coach, and her husbands. She was not a singer, like Thea Kronborg, to whom fortunate accidents happened. Her operatic career had been a great success, for there industry and determination counted and she had the gift of a fine voice. But in her private life she was the unluckiest of mortals. All those around her treated her like a diamond mine, a natural resource to be exploited shamelessly, and their greed knew no bounds.

The third and fourth stories, "A Gold Slipper" and "Scandal," also concern a prima donna exposed to the barbarians, but the singer is a different type, a Mary Garden rather than a Fremstad. Named Kitty Ayreshire (probably for Burns's native heath and Mary Garden's national origin), this singer is riding the crest of her fame. In "A Gold Slipper" she sings in Pittsburgh and after the concert finds herself in a Pullman car en route to New York with a bored coal merchant who had been dragged to hear her. What takes place in the story is mostly a witty dialogue between Kitty and this stolid Presbyterian Pittsburgher with his ready-made prejudices against art and artists. She bids him goodnight, promising to haunt him, and she succeeds. The second story is a rather slight tale, inferior in quality to the rest in the collection, that recounts a couple of episodes in Kitty's career. At the time of the narration, however, Kitty is ill with a lingering cold and in-flamed vocal cords that will not respond to treatment. The specter of the end of her singing career hangs over the tale, which concerns a nasty fraud perpetrated against her some years earlier. Needless to say, the fraud was carried out by one of the Philistines, an exploiter of artists.

Added to the somber shading of these stories is the distinctly ugly coloring of two of the characters. One is perplexed to find two thoroughly savage anti-Semitic portraits in Miletus Poppas in "The Diamond Mine" and Siegmund Stein in "Scandal." Anti-Semitism is not a charge that can be sustained against Willa Cather either from her novels or her letters; yet Poppas, Cressida Garnet's singing coach, is thoroughly disagreeable, and Stein is an ogre, a complete caricature of the social-climbing, garment-manufacturing, department-store-owning Jewish businessman. Poppas is a Svengali with a "thin lupine face," yellowish-green eyes "always gleaming with something like defeated fury," and in the final view of him, as he sits hunched up waiting for news of the *Titanic* disaster, "he looked as old as Jewry." Stein, who had come from Austria a beggar and worked his way up through the garment district, is "one of the most hideous men in New York." He has one of those "rigid, horse-like faces," "a long nose, flattened as if it had been tied down," cheeks "yellow as a Mongolian's," and puffy eyelids.

One must look in Willa Cather's private life for a possible explanation of these scurrilous characterizations. Both stories were written during the months immediately following the news that Isabelle McClung was going to marry Jan Hambourg. While she was unable to start a new novel because of the shock of the marriage, she did write "The Diamond Mine" and "Scandal" during the first half of 1916. Jan Hambourg, who spirited off the now affluent Isabelle, was of Russian-Jewish-English background. He played the violin and with his brother Boris, a cellist, and their father taught music in Toronto. Another brother was Mark, a pianist, whom Willa Cather had heard in her Pittsburgh days and had found too cold and intellectual. Willa Cather unconsciously may have taken out her resentment against Jan Hambourg by creating the obnoxious Svengali-like music coach Poppas. Stein in "Scandal" is too exaggerated to bear a resemblance to anyone and must be accounted an aberration. Willa Cather perhaps thought poorly of this story, because she waited three years to publish it.

After delivering her book manuscript to Knopf, she and Edith Lewis sailed for Europe. The last third of *One of Ours* takes place in France, and Willa Cather had to see the battlefields and get the feel of the country again before she could finish the novel. The voyage was magnificent, rough weather, which she always liked, and she wrote Viola Roseboro' that she always felt too good to be true at sea. They settled down for two months in Paris, living on the Quai Voltaire and seldom straying from the left bank of the Seine, except to visit the Louvre and occasionally the opera. Toward the end of their stay the Hambourgs arrived and took Willa Cather on a tour of the devastated areas of northeast France. She looked up her cousin's grave and brooded over the last chapters of her novel. In August she went south and wrote for six weeks in another tent, this time on the Mediterranean coast at Hyères. Then she continued on to Italy, visited friends who lived at Sorrento, and returned to the United States from Naples in November.

The winter of 1920–1921 was almost totally unproductive for her. The novel still was not finished and simply would not write itself. In March she was telling Dorothy Canfield Fisher about her problems and wishing the two of them could get together. She was sure Dorothy could give her some help. They did not see each other that year, however, though she did send her friend the French translation of *My Ántonia,* asking her to look it over to see if it would offend an intelligent French reader. In April she tried a desperate expedient and went to live with Isabelle and Jan Hambourg in Toronto for three or four months. The Hambourgs had been married for five years by this time, and Willa apparently now was getting on well with Jan. She must have thought that perhaps Isabelle could provide the protective atmosphere she needed for writing, as in the old days in Pittsburgh. She no sooner arrived, however, than Sinclair Lewis appeared for a lecture in Toronto and said such flattering things about her work that three reporters were at the Hambourgs' door the next morning. But Isabelle fought off the deluge of social opportunities, and Willa worked steadily on into July. When the novel was virtually finished, she went West for her first visit home in three years, and in Red Cloud she added some final touches before mailing the manuscript to Knopf. But the book was still more than a year away from publication.

The winter of 1921–1922 was just about as dismal as the preceding one. At the start she felt obliged to tinker with her manuscript again, and then from Christmas until spring she was sick on and off. For several weeks she hovered on the edge of another inflammation of the mastoid process, and then her doctors decided that her trouble was tonsillitis. So she had her tonsils out; but the operation was not simple, and she hemorrhaged and was very ill. As soon as she got out of the hospital, she went to a sanatorium at Wernersville, Pennsylvania, to recuperate, but after getting back to New York she had fresh anxiety over her mother's illness in Red Cloud. All the while she was hating herself for her physical weakness. By this time she was reading proof on *One of Ours* and realizing that her enormous effort was doomed to failure.

She had to console herself that it would be a moral victory. While she waited for the critics' reactions when the book came out in September, she accepted her only teaching assignment after leaving Allegheny High School and spent three weeks in July at the Breadloaf School at Middlebury, Vermont.

II

One of Ours is the story of Claude Wheeler, Nebraska farm boy whose nature is too sensitive and fine-grained to accept the coarse realities of farm life. His father is prosperous, good-natured, materialistic; his older brother a dessicated, money-grubbing farm-implement dealer. While his friends and younger brother grow up contentedly in the rural environment, Claude finds life hard to live. He suffers too much over little things and feels that somehow life ought to be splendid. The first half of the novel carries Claude through his sophomore year at a dismal little church college in Lincoln and two more years on the farm. He quits college when his father decides that he is needed at home, and goes to work on the farm. Then he falls in love with an impossible girl, a strong-willed religious fanatic and health-faddist, who turns out, after they are married, to be a frigid wife. At the time the United States enters the First World War, Claude never has done anything in his life that has given him any satisfaction. The last half of the novel chronicles Claude's life from his enlistment in the army until his death in the Argonne Forest offensive in October 1918. He goes to war as a release from the farm and his botched marriage, becomes a lieutenant of infantry, sails to France, and sees action briefly before he is killed. He finds fulfilment in his military career and dies "believing his own country better than it is, and France better than any country can ever be."

There are some fine things in *One of Ours,* both in characterization and in scene. All the elements that come vividly to life are made from materials that had teased the author's mind for years. Claude's patient, devoted, and understanding mother is authentic; so is old Mahailey, the family servant. These characters are based on women whom Willa Cather had known and loved for years, and they are three-dimensional figures like others in her best fiction. Then there are various scenes and actions that quicken before the reader's eye: Claude's visits to the Erlich home in Lincoln during his second year in college, the account of the great wheat harvest of 1914, and Claude's reactions when he first experiences French civilization. Willa Cather writes in her best vein when she is remembering her relationship with Mrs. Westermann and her sons from her student days at the University of Nebraska, and her emotional involvement with the harvesters on the Divide was a long-standing passion.

Some of the scenes in France are equally good. When Claude and his fellow officer David Gerhardt are billeted with Mme. Joubert and visit her on leave, when they go to see Mlle. Claire and her mother, and when Claude alone meets Mlle. de Courcy—these episodes are several levels above the surrounding pages. The reason is clear enough: Willa Cather's own response to France when she visited the country in 1902 is exactly Claude's. This part of the novel is a drama of memory. She was not the ignorant farmer that Claude is, but her long love affair with France raises these scenes to the level of art. The poignancy in these pages stems from Willa Cather's memory of her own relationship with Dorothy Canfield Fisher in 1902. Dorothy, like Lieutenant Gerhardt, then was thoroughly at home in France, fluent in the language, and Willa Cather both envied and admired her for this. She admitted writing this relationship into the novel, and was working on this part when she wrote that Dorothy was the only person who could help with the novel and wouldn't it be great if they could get together. But she managed without assistance. The emotion evoked rings true, and it does not matter here whether the character being exposed to France for the first time is a Nebraska farm boy or a Pittsburgh schoolmarm.

The basic difficulty with *One of Ours* is the entire subject. Willa Cather should not have tried to write a war novel, and the fact that the book succeeds at all is testimony to her craftsmanship and vast determination to bring it off. Nowhere is the book carelessly done, but seldom does it rise above the level of competent journeyman work. Most of the characters, settings, and incidents are worked up for the novel from immediate materials, a method that Willa Cather deplored and used badly; and the novel, also contrary to her critical dicta, is strangely overfurnished—about twice as long as *My Ántonia.* The farther she gets away from what she had experienced deeply, the less reality the book has. Her Nebraska material is authentic, and as long as the locale is Frankfort (Red Cloud) and the Divide, it carries conviction. But the account of the troopship crossing is no more distinguished than any professional writer might have managed. The scenes in France when they deal with activity behind the lines and concern mostly civilian life are excellent, but when the action moves into combat Willa Cather is hopelessly out of her element. She obviously knew the problems involved, and they undoubtedly account for the long delays in finishing the novel. Her soldier dialogue and army life are unbelievable and keep striking false notes, and her final battle scene in which Claude is killed is a stereotype. About this, Hemingway wrote Edmund Wilson: "Wasn't that last scene in the lines wonderful? Do you know where it came from? The battle scene in *Birth of a Nation.* I identified episode after episode, Catherized. Poor woman[,] she had to get her war experience somewhere." She avoided battle scenes as much as possible, however, and except for one patrol and one sniper action there is only the final battle scene, which is squeezed into thirteen pages.

Willa Cather described Claude Wheeler as an "inarticulate young man butting his way through the world." The idea for the characterization, as we have noted, came from reading the letters her young cousin wrote home during the war. She had not known this cousin very well, because he was much younger; but she always was interested in him, and when he went into the army she wrote Aunt Franc that she was proud of him. The image she got from the letters, however, surprised and appealed to her. The glimpse of a sensitive young man dissatisfied with the materialistic prosperity of Nebraska in 1917 and of his finding fulfillment in the war effort gave her the idea for the novel. That a young man could lose himself in a cause and die for an idea seemed to her remarkable and exciting. Then she later read letters written by a young concert violinist, David Hochstein, who also was killed in France in 1918. Though she had known Hochstein only slightly, he had made a great impression on her, and he too had volunteered for service and had lost himself in the cause. If two such dissimilar young men as G. P. Cather of Webster County, Nebraska, and David Hochstein of New York could find common cause in the war effort, certainly then this was a significant theme for fiction. Of course she was right in this conviction, and surely many young men who died early in combat never experienced the disillusionment that followed the great effort.

The hazards in carrying out this concept, however, were simply too great. Willa Cather told an interviewer in 1921 that she always had felt it presumptuous and silly for a woman to write about a male character but she had come to know Claude better than she knew herself. Thus she thought she could be Claude in her novel. She had not, of course, ever *really* thought it presumptuous and silly for her to adopt a male point of view, but when she had written *My Ántonia* from the viewpoint of Jim Burden, observer, her subject was a woman she had known since childhood. Claude Wheeler in some ways is Willa Cather, in his strong reactions to the ugly materialism of prosperous twentieth-century Nebraska and in his response to France, but this is not enough. As Sarah Orne Jewett had warned her many years before, a woman writer should not try in her fiction to be a man. Claude's wedding night, for example, when Enid locks him out of the stateroom on the Denver Express, seems beyond Willa Cather's capability to create. One does not experience Claude's reaction to this bitter sexual frustration; one is merely told about it. In other parts of the novel Claude is given no sex life, though Willa Cather is wise enough to let her other soldier characters fornicate on occasion. The David and Jonathan relationship between Claude and David Gerhardt, however, is convincingly portrayed, and Claude's relations with old Mahailey and his family, especially his mother, are authentic.

Willa Cather also told her interviewer that in this novel she had cut out all descriptive work—the thing that she did best—because her redheaded prairie boy does not see pictures. It was hard, she added, to change her method, but "we all have to pay a price for everything we accomplish and because I was willing to pay so much to write about this boy, I felt that I had a right to do so." This is a strange admission to come from a first-rate novelist, but it indicates pretty clearly that she knew the whole affair was a fiasco a year before the novel appeared. She continued to be defensive about the novel even after the important reviewers almost unanimously attacked it, and as late as 1925 she was saying that of all her books she liked *One of Ours* best.

The great irony of the entire enterprise was that the novel won her the Pulitzer Prize for 1922 and made her comparatively rich. Her royalties from Knopf for 1923 were nineteen thousand dollars, and the success of this novel stimulated the sales of her other books. Although Dorothy Canfield Fisher and a few others reviewed the novel favorably, Alfred Knopf was indulging in hyperbole when he wired her after reading it in manuscript: "Congratulations. It is masterly, a perfectly gorgeous novel, far ahead of anything you have ever yet done, and far ahead of anything I have read in a very long while. With it your position should be secure forever. I shall be proud to have my name associated with it." Knopf can be forgiven for his enthusiasm perhaps, as he was just beginning his relationship with Willa Cather.

Mencken, who had called *My Ántonia* "the finest thing of its sort ever done in America," came down hard on *One of Ours*. He liked the Nebraska part, but:

What spoils the story is simply that a year or so ago a young soldier named John Dos Passos printed a novel called *Three Soldiers*. Until *Three Soldiers* is forgotten and fancy achieves its inevitable victory over fact, no war story can be written in the United States without challenging comparison with it—and no story that is less meticulously true will stand up to it. At one blast it disposed of oceans of romance and blather. It changed the whole tone of American opinion about the war; it even challenged the recollections of actual veterans of the war.

Mencken characteristically exaggerates, but it is true the postwar disillusionment had set in by the time the novel appeared. E. E. Cummings's *The Enormous Room* appeared in the same year as *One of Ours;* so did Eliot's *The Waste Land* and Lewis's *Babbitt.* It made no difference that the epilogue to Willa Cather's novel indicates clearly that she did not believe the great crusade of the A.E.F. had made the world safe for democracy. It made no difference that the Nebraska chapters were vigorously critical of American materialism, the prodigal landhog, Nat Wheeler, and his son Bayliss. Claude thought of his older brother that "no battlefield or shattered country he had seen was as ugly as this world would be if men like his brother Bayliss controlled it altogether." The waste-land theme of the "lost generation" is rather prominent in this novel, but overriding all of this for contemporary reviewers was the "romance and blather." Willa Cather was hoist by the petard of her old fondness for romance.

Clues to the novel's conceptual limitations may be found in the literary allusions sprinkled throughout the book. Early in the story Claude is referred to by Mrs. Erlich's cousin as Claude Melnotte, the romantic hero of Bulwer Lytton's novel *Lady of Lyons.* In that implausible tale Claude Melnotte, after a fraudulent marriage, goes off to war in Napoleon's army and distinguishes himself, acquiring wealth and a colonelcy in the process. Elsewhere in *One of Ours,* Claude's mother whispers to him in her mind, "Rest, rest, perturbèd spirit," Hamlet's words to the ghost of his father, and in the war section of the novel Claude thinks of the death of the aviator friend he made on the troopship as like the death of Milton's rebel angels. The most interesting literary theme, however, is the *Parsifal* motif that Willa Cather buried in the novel. She originally had intended to entitle the last part of the novel "The Blameless Fool by Pity Enlightened," but instead she left the Claude-Parsifal characterization implicit rather than explicit and called the final section "Bidding the Eagles of the West Fly On," using a line from Vachel Lindsay's poem on William Jennings Bryan. The effect of this line out of context is to suggest jingoism and flag-waving patriotism, an unfortunate touch in 1922, although the line actually refers to the futile confrontation of populism against the eastern seats of power in 1896.

One of Ours marks a critical juncture in Willa Cather's life. When she wrote a prefatory note to the essays she collected in 1936 under the title *Not Under Forty,* she said flatly: "The world broke in two in 1922 or thereabouts." She still had ten very productive years ahead of her, but things were never the same for her after 1922. Beginning about this time a troubled note creeps into her fiction, and in *One of Ours* there is a querulous tone in her criticism of Nebraska. Although these thoughts are put into Claude's mind, they are more appropriate to their forty-nine-year-old author: "With prosperity came a kind of callousness; everybody wanted to destroy the old things they used to take pride in." They let their orchards die of neglect because it was easier to run into town to buy fruit than to grow it. In addition the people change. Claude can remember "when all the farmers in this community were friendly toward each other; now they were continually having lawsuits. Their sons were either stingy and grasping, or extravagant and lazy." This is Claude at the age of twenty-one mourning the good old pioneer days when he was a small child. Actually he was born about 1893, when times were dreadful. When Claude reflects that he knows something is wrong with him, the reader is tempted to view this as an autobiographical statement.

The hostile reception that *One of Ours* received was enough to sour any author, at least for awhile. The book had cost four years of effort, and she told a friend: "It took more out of me than any book I ever wrote." Added to the frustrations of this novel were the sieges of illness early in 1922, and again in the fall, and she could well have been going through the menopause at this time. She definitely was feeling alienated from the world of the twenties, a malaise that she shared with many other writers of that era, and she felt the need for faith.

There is a good deal of discussion of religion in *One of Ours.* Claude's mother thinks that the trouble with him is that he has not yet found his Saviour. He is a freethinker and skeptic throughout the novel, and he has no use for the narrow religious bigotry of his older brother or the fanaticism of his wife, whose real wish in life is to be a missionary in China. Willa Cather had outgrown the Baptist faith of her childhood, and Claude's gropings are clearly her own. She believed that faith was a gift and in the course of the novel grants that gift to Lieutenant Gerhardt shortly before he is killed in action. At the end of 1922 she went home at Thanksgiving to help her parents celebrate their golden wedding anniversary and remained until after the first of the year. Two days after Christmas she and her parents together joined the Episcopal Church. One of her problems at least was solved, and she remained an active member of the church for the rest of her life.

While she awaited the reviews of *One of Ours,* Willa Cather first visited Grand Manan Island, New Brunswick, at the mouth of the

Bay of Fundy. This was a happy event, for at last she found a place that suited her perfectly. She went back again two years later and then built Whale Cove Cottage, to which she returned summer after summer until the food shortages during the Second World War made life there too difficult. Only a few fishing villages marred the solitude of the heavily wooded island. Cliffs from two to four hundred feet high rimmed much of the island, and mail came only twice a week by steamer from St. John. Wild flowers grew in profusion, and clear streams rushed over the cliffs in spectacular waterfalls. Snowshoe hares nibbled at the grass around the cottage, and occasionally deer appeared at dusk or dawn. One could walk for miles along the cliffs without meeting a person, but there always was activity on the water, as small boats went back and forth setting out lines and visiting the herring weirs.

Willa Cather wrote Zoë Akins after moving into her new cottage that at last she had her own hut and her own five acres of woodland. The island was as green as Ireland and as cool as England. It was just right for sweaters, leather coats, and leggings even in mid-July. The place suited her more than any place in the world, though the living was very rough. Yet nothing was so hard to get in the world as silence, a piece of seashore that was wild and empty of humans, and wild forest. To have these things, she added, she could do without a bathtub. The rainy weather Willa Cather loved, and there was an abundance of firewood at hand. Above the living room was a large empty attic, furnished only with a table and chair, which she used for a study.

Grand Manan Island in 1922 must have been therapeutic. She wrote Dorothy Canfield Fisher about the first of September that she had written a long short story there, and Edith Lewis remembers that part of *A Lost Lady* also was written at this time. Since it was three years before she published another short story, it seems likely that the tale referred to was "Tom Outland's Story," which is the story-within-a-story in *The Professor's House*. This is Willa Cather at her best, as is the novel she was working on. When she got back to Bank Street at the end of September, she continued working on *A Lost Lady* and must have finished it before she went West two months later. It is a short novel—about fifty thousand words—and was serialized in the *Century* the following spring.

III

When *One of Ours* finally went to press, Willa Cather had been planning her next novel for about a year and was eager to get to work on it. While she had been visiting Isabelle Hambourg in Toronto and working on the war novel, she had received forwarded copies of the Red Cloud newspaper. In one issue was an account of the death in Spokane, Washington, of Lyra Anderson, who had been Mrs. Silas Garber, wife of former Governor Garber and once Red Cloud's great lady. The news shocked her, and the day being warm, she went to her room to rest. Within an hour the story was all in her mind as if she had read it somewhere. It was another of those inner explosions, such as she had experienced when she had met Fremstad or had seen Annie Pavelka and her children. The past came flooding back again and she remembered in vivid detail Mrs. Garber's voice and eyes and the house on the hill east of Red Cloud. Indeed, the cotton-wood grove around the Garber place was one of her most indelible memories. She once said that to work well she needed to be carefree, as if she were thirteen and going for a picnic in Garber's Grove. She had kept track of Mrs. Garber as long as the latter had lived in Red Cloud, and after visiting Nebraska in 1905 she had written that Mrs. Garber was as charming as ever though greatly aged and saddened by the governor's death.

In its setting and general outline the story was ready made. Former Governor Garber, one of the founders of Red Cloud, had married a beautiful, vivacious California woman much younger than he, and after his term as governor he had settled down in a large house on the outskirts of town. Mrs. Garber went to Colorado frequently for her health, and the Garbers entertained graciously. The old governor founded the Farmers' and Mer-chants' Bank in Red Cloud and lost most of his money when the bank failed. Later he had a stroke and spent his last days as a semi-invalid ministered to by his young wife. After his death she went back to California and eventually remarried. All of these details went into the novel with only minor modifications. Willa Cather's main addition to the plot was the creation of Frank Ellin-ger, the other man, and the result was a Nebraska version of *Madame Bovary*. One cannot push the analogy between Flaubert's novel and *A Lost Lady* very far, but Willa Cather must have been conscious of the similarity, for Flaubert was one of her masters, and she had admired his novel for a long time.

The technical problem of how to present this material gave her some trouble. She had just finished *One of Ours,* in which she had to get into the skin of Claude Wheeler, and she knew that the book was going to be a failure. Yet she wanted to present the story of Marian Forrester from the viewpoint of a young person in the town. She invented Niel Herbert, nephew of the town's lawyer and her own alter ego, and at first tried telling the story as a first-person narrative. But she discarded this effort, and it seems likely that her difficulties in being Claude Wheeler warned her away from trying to get inside of another male character so soon. If she had used a first-person method, however, the story would have been told in the same way she told *My Ántonia,* and for the same end—to create a woman whose image had teased her imagination. She might have done it with equal success. After trying a few chapters in both the first-person and third-person manners, she decided to use the latter. But most of the scenes introduce Niel Herbert playing a minor role so that the lost lady usually is presented through his eyes. This method actually gave Willa Cather more flexibility and enabled her to show the character both from the point of view of the omniscient author and through the eyes of other people in the town.

Willa Cather bounded back from the disaster of her war novel and in *A Lost Lady* produced one of her two or three best works. There is hardly a false note in it, and she was able to return to the thing she did best, create indelible pictures through her remarkable ability to conjure up the past. The figure of Marian Forrester is authentic, three-dimensional. The town of Sweet Water (Red Cloud) is as real here as Moonstone in *The Song of the Lark,* and the character of the old railroad-builder Daniel Forrester is as solid and believable as his stone bank building that still stands in Red Cloud. The entire story is told with admirable economy from the opening paragraph to the account of Mrs. Forrester's death about thirty-seven years later.

Willa Cather practiced her own critical principles in *A Lost Lady,* which is one of her best examples of the unfurnished novel. In "The Novel Démeublé" she quotes from an essay Mérimée wrote on Gogol: "The art of choosing from among the innumerable elements that nature offers us is, after all, much more difficult than observing them attentively and rendering them accurately." In another essay, "On the Art of Fiction," she wrote that almost the entire artistic process was one of simplification, "finding what conventions of form and what detail one can do without and yet preserve the spirit of the whole." The trick was to make the reader's consciousness supply the material suppressed and cut away. And she added: "Any first-rate novel or story must have in it the strength of a dozen fairly good stories that have been sacrificed to it. A good workman can't be a cheap workman; he can't be stingy about wasting material, and he cannot compromise."

All of these dicta are effectively illustrated in this novel. It opens with a five-page chapter of exposition setting the stage and supplying all the necessary background. The next chapter is a picnic in the cottonwood grove, in which Mrs. Forrester is seen through the eyes of twelve-year-old Niel. Then the novel skips seven years and is told in a series of sixteen chapters covering four years—from the time Niel is nineteen until he goes away from Sweet Water for good. No effort is made to supply a continuous narrative. Each chapter recounts a key episode: a gay dinner party at the Forresters before the bank failure; the winter sleigh ride to gather cedar boughs, in which Adolph Blum sees Marian and Frank Ellinger coming out of the woods together; Niel's arrival at the house when Captain Forrester is away, and his overhearing Ellinger's voice from Marian's bedroom; the bank failure; the Captain's stroke and Niel's departure for college. These chapters make up Part I, and all take place during the year Niel turns twenty; Part II then covers 1895–1896, when Niel stays home from college to take care of the Forresters. During this year the Captain dies, and Marian is seen gradually disintegrating under the blight of poverty and the demands of her invalid husband. In the last chapter, Niel leaves home for good, as Willa Cather did at the same time, and the rest of Mrs. Forrester's life is briefly narrated from secondhand sources.

The great thing in this novel is the portrait of Marian Forrester. Willa Cather employs her usual method of nostalgic evocation and contrast—Mrs. Forrester as she appears to the boy at twelve and nineteen, an untarnished goddess and aesthetic ideal, and Mrs. Forrester after Niel learns of her adultery and sees her brought down by misfortune. At the outset Niel and his friends picnic in the marsh below the Forrester mansion. Mrs. Forrester, who has been arranging roses, appears on the veranda and gives them permission to enter the property. At noon she takes them a batch of cookies. Later Niel falls out of a tree and is carried into the big house, where Mrs. Forrester puts him on her bed: "Niel opened his eyes and looked wonderingly about the big, half-darkened room, full of heavy, old-fashioned walnut furniture. He was lying on a white bed with ruffled pillow shams, and Mrs. Forrester was kneeling beside him, bathing his forehead with cologne." Later: "What soft fingers Mrs. Forrester had, and what a lovely lady she was! Inside the lace ruffle of her dress he saw her white throat rising and falling so quickly. . . . The little boy was thinking that he would probably never be in so nice a place again." Then follows a richly suggestive description of the room, the long green shutters on the windows, the filtered sunlight, the polished floor, the silver things on the dresser, and the marble-topped washstand.

The most poignant scene in the novel occurs when Niel is twenty, the June before he goes to M.I.T. to study architecture. He has been to the Forresters' house a good many times during the previous winter, for the times are hard and the Forresters are wintering at home instead of Colorado Springs as usual. Niel's worship of Mrs. Forrester continues, though the reader knows that she is not the creature Niel thinks she is. Frank Ellinger has been on the scene as a guest in the Forrester house, and one of Niel's friends, Adolph Blum, has seen Ellinger and Marian in one compromising moment. Captain Forrester and Niel's uncle have gone to Denver on business, and Niel is annoyed to find that Ellinger is registered at the hotel. He thinks it improper for him to visit Mrs. Forrester while the Captain is away, and anyway he never liked the fellow. He gets up early in the morning, walks out to the Forrester place, and on his way picks a bouquet of roses. He plans to place them outside the long floor-to-ceiling shutters of Mrs. Forrester's first-floor bedroom so that she will see them the minute she gets up. Just as he is about to put down his floral offering, he hears "from within a woman's soft laughter; impatient, indulgent, teasing, eager. Then another laugh, very different, a man's. And it was fat and lazy." Niel finds himself a moment later at the foot of the hill on the bridge, his face hot, his temples beating, his eyes filled with anger. He throws the flowers in a mudhole the cattle have trampled. "In that instant between stooping to the window-sill and rising, he had lost one of the most beautiful things in his life. . . . It was not a moral scruple she had outraged, but an aesthetic ideal."

This scene is handled with consummate skill: The reader, what-ever his age or background, experiences that moment of anguish. Subsequent scenes are also effective, and the portrayal of Marian Forrester through Niel's youthful consciousness in this book is one of the high points of the author's fiction. *A Lost Lady* is another drama of memory fashioned from materials that Willa Cather cared for greatly. The second half of the novel sketches the down-ward curve of Mrs. Forrester's fortunes and character and com-pletes the novel, but it is not inspired by youthful memories.

The ingredients of Part II are in good measure the author's ever-increasing disenchantment over the moral climate of the twenties. This is not at all a serene novel, though it is a polished work of art. The sharp criticism of American materialism that ap-pears in *One of Ours* is stepped up in *A Lost Lady*. There is very little polemical exposition attacking the money-grubbing of the era following the First-World War, but the subject is treated dramatically and is doubly effective. The time of the new material-ism has to be pushed back to the mid-nineties in order to fit into this book, but Willa Cather apparently did not worry about this theme being anachronistic. The theme appears in the opening chapter in the character of Ivy Peters, a thoroughly disagreeable figure, who at the age of eighteen already is a sadistic harbinger of the new materialism.

In the picnic scene, when the twelve-year-old boys are playing below the Forrester mansion, Peters appears to spoil the fun. He is a big boy with a.red, swollen face looking as though he had been stung by bees. His freckles are like rust spots, and his eyes are hard and unblinking, like a snake's or lizard's . "He was an ugly fellow, Ivy Peters, and he liked being ugly." Peters pulls out a sling-shot and stuns a woodpecker. When it comes to, he pulls out a sharp instrument and blinds the bird, then releases it, and it flies off bumping into trees. When it finally alights on a branch, Niel climbs the tree to get the bird to put it out of its misery. It is then that he falls out of the tree and breaks his arm. This scene is excruciatingly painful to the boys as well as to the reader.

When Ivy Peters appears again, he is a shyster lawyer who has managed to get his hooks into the Forresters. The old captain has lost his money in the bank closing, and his health from a stroke. Peters rents the marsh where the boys had played and which the captain had left untouched because he loved its wildness. He drains the land and plants it in wheat. He invests a little money for Mrs. Forrester in what she knows must be a crooked scheme, and eventually he takes over her business affairs from Niel's uncle, who has been the Forresters' lawyer for twenty years. The meek do not inherit the earth in Sweet Water; the cold, grasping, unscrupulous Ivy Peters takes over. Peters is the dominant figure in the disintegration and degradation of Mrs. Forrester in the second part of the novel, and under his evil influence she becomes another woman after the death of the old captain.

When Niel goes away from Sweet Water for good, he thinks that it was the sturdy pioneer captain who had been the reality, not Mrs. Forrester, although he always had thought it was she who had made that house so different from any other. As Niel leaves for the last time, he reflects: "The people, the very country itself, were changing so fast that there would be nothing to come back to. He had seen the end of an era, the sunset of the pioneer. He had come upon it when already its glory was nearly spent. . . . It was already gone, that age; nothing could ever bring it back." But he had caught the taste and smell of it. He had seen the vision of the pioneers in a kind of afterglow in their faces, and this would always be his. Willa Cather felt the same way. When the world had broken in two the year before, it had left her behind. She did not mind identifying with the past, but it was awkward having to live and draw sustenance from the present.

The critics were relieved when *A Lost Lady* followed *One of Ours.* No one ever had doubted Willa Cather's artistic integrity and her good intentions, and it was a happy day when she returned to characters and locales that were congenial. Edmund

Wilson, who had judged *One of Ours* a "pretty flat failure," pronounced *A Lost Lady* "a charming sketch performed with exceptional skill." Willa Cather, he added, is about the only writer who has been able to bring any real distinction to the life of the Middle West. Joseph Wood Krutch hailed the book as a nearly perfect novel. He thought it too short and slight to be called great, but he recognized that in *A Lost Lady* she had successfully achieved "that synthesis of qualities which alone can make a novel really fine." By this he meant that plot, setting, and character all were vivid and fresh and adroitly handled. In general the chorus of reviewers praised the novel and placed it qualitatively on the same level as *My Ántonia*.

Willa Cather by this time had become a popular as well as a critical success. This meant, of course, that she now could sell Hollywood the screen rights to her novels. Warner Brothers was first in line with a reported ten thousand dollars and carried off the rights to film *A Lost Lady*. Douglass Cather, who then lived in California, was invited to the Warner Brothers' Studio to meet Irene Rich and George Fawcett, who took the title roles, and when the movie had its premiere in Red Cloud in January 1925, all the local people thought the film portrayed the Garbers accurately. But Willa Cather did not like it and never again sold film rights to anything she wrote. She told Knopf that if she had wanted her books turned into plays, she would have written them as plays, and in her will she placed an absolute prohibition on the sale of any dramatic rights to her works. The only ripple that ever appeared on the surface of her long friendship with Zoë Akins occurred over a dramatization of *A Lost Lady*. Some young screenwriters that Zoë wanted to help turned the novel into a play script, and she sent it to Willa Cather hoping for permission to produce it. Willa was furious and wrote a long reply analyzing in great detail the fatuities of the script, which made Marian Forrester talk either like a corsetless old Methodist woman or a darling club woman and never like the character she had created.

About the time the first installment of *A Lost Lady* appeared in the *Century*, Willa Cather sailed for Europe for a six months' sojourn in France. Isabelle and Jan Hambourg had bought a place at Ville d'Avray near Paris and wanted her to come and stay with them. They hoped she would spend at least several months a year and fixed up a study for her, but she could not work there. She told an interviewer afterward: "I stayed for a time at Ville d'Avray, and loved the life there so much that I could hardly tear myself away; but I was so busy drinking in the beauty of the place that I could not work." Then she tried Paris, hoping to achieve a working state of mind, but again it proved impossible. "The Seine absorbed my thoughts. I could look at it for hours as it reflected every mood of the ever-changing skies, and the colorful life surging around me was utterly distracting as well." She decided that she would have to wait until she got back to her Bank Street apartment to write.

This explanation of her inability to write in France was issued to a magazine interviewer and hence for public consumption. The real reason she could not work that summer was ill health, specifically a stubborn neuritis in her right arm and shoulder. For most of the time she was abroad, she wrote Zoë Akins, the neuritis kept her idle. It made her very uncomfortable and at times discouraged. Finally in September she went south to Aix-les-Bains for hot mineral-bath treatments, and boiled her lame arm in the hot water daily for a month. She returned to Paris feeling a lot better. For a person who hated herself whenever she was sick, Willa Cather was going through a thoroughly distressing period. For two years in a row she had been beset by illnesses, and during the previous winter and spring she had been in and out of hospitals and sanatoria with three separate attacks of influenza. Then followed the neuritis.

Her one positive accomplishment of the summer was sitting for her portrait. The people of Omaha, wanting to honor their now-famous daughter, raised money to commission a portrait to hang in the public library. About the time that she was notified of her Pulitzer Prize, she also was asked to have her picture painted. She picked Leon Bakst, who lived in Paris, and sat for him both before and after her treatments at Aix-les-Bains. She enjoyed the sessions very much and found it exciting to be with Bakst in his beautiful studio; but she wrote her old friend Irene Miner Weisz that the Omaha people were not going to like the picture. It would not be a photographic likeness. The portrait was duly finished and now

hangs in the Omaha Public Library. Edith Lewis, no doubt reflecting Willa Cather's final judgment on it, thought the painting a flat
failure—a stiff, dark, heavy, lifeless unlikeness—everything that
Willa Cather was not. Certainly the painting is not flattering, but
Bakst was painting a middle-aged woman who was going through
a profound physical, emotional, and spiritual crisis. The portrait
bares the soul of Professor St. Peter, her next protagonist, a man
who has no will to live.

IV

The crisis that Willa Cather referred to when she said the world
broke in two in 1922 actually extended over a period of several
years. Her next novel, *The Professor's House,* which she began
after returning to New York in November 1923, reflects her personal malaise more clearly than anything else she ever wrote. In
a real sense the novel is a kind of spiritual autobiography, for her
protagonist Godfrey St. Peter, a middle-westerner exactly her age,
is a man whose world also has split. Ostensibly he is at the peak
of his career, as Willa Cather was, but he is intensely unhappy.
"You are not old enough for the pose you take," his wife tells him.
"Two years ago you were an impetuous young man. Now you save
yourself in everything. . . . Something has come over you." He
admits this, but he does not quite know what is wrong. "I seem to
be tremendously tired," he says, but adds, as the chapter ends,
"I'll get my second wind." Willa Cather did get her second wind
and wrote five more novels, including *Death Comes for the Archbishop,* which many critics think is her best, but for a writer who
believed with Michelet *"Le but n'est rien; le chemin c'est tout,"*
this was bound to be a difficult period.

The autobiographical parallels between Willa Cather and
Professor St. Peter are striking. He was born on a farm on the
shores of Lake Michigan, which has for him the same emotional
pull that the mountains of the Shenandoah Valley had for Willa
Cather. He had a strong-willed Protestant mother, a gentle father,
and a patriarchal grandfather. When he was eight, his parents
dragged him out to the wheatlands of central Kansas and "St.
Peter nearly died of it." As an adult, he went back to the region

of his childhood for his professional career. After he had been teaching a number of years, he conceived of his plan for a great historical work, *The Spanish Adventurers in North America*, and he devoted fifteen years of his life to completing it. "All the while that he was working so fiercely by night, he was earning his living during the day. . . . St. Peter had managed for years to live two lives. . . . But he had burned his candle at both ends to some purpose—he had got what he wanted." The first three volumes of his history made no stir at all. With the fourth volume (Willa Cather's fourth novel was *My Ántonia*) he began to attract attention; with the fifth and sixth he began to be well known; and with the last two volumes he achieved an international reputation. Then he won the Oxford Prize for History, which brought him five thousand pounds. Willa Cather's Pulitzer Prize was a modest sum, but her royalties from Knopf for the year before writing *The Professor's House* were close to the equivalent of five thousand pounds.

At this point the novel begins. St. Peter has allowed his wife to build a new house with his prize money so that they finally can move out of the cramped, dingy place they have rented for half a lifetime. St. Peter is reluctant to leave the old house, especially his attic study, which doubles as a sewing room. (One recalls here that *O Pioneers!* and *The Song of the Lark* were largely written in the attic study at the McClung house.) He insists on paying the rent on the old place and continuing to use his study. Not much happens in Book I, which occupies about three-fifths of the novel. The professor's wife, daughters, sons-in-law, and two of his colleagues are introduced; the background is sketched in. The professor and his wife have grown apart during the years of the great history project, and neither of his sons-in-law pleases him very much. One is a journalist, Scott McGregor, who writes good-cheer articles and feels like a prostitute doing them; the other is an aggressive Jewish engineer, Louie Marsellus, who has made a fortune promoting an invention of prime importance to the aviation industry. Kathleen, his younger daughter, is unchanged, but Rosamond, the elder, has been corrupted by Louie's money, and when St. Peter goes to Chicago to help her buy furniture for the Norwegian manor house she and Louie are building on the shore of Lake Michigan, he reports: "She was like Napoleon looting the Italian palaces."

Very early in the presentation of the family the name Tom Outland appears. Next to the professor, he is the most important character, though he has been dead nearly a decade at the time the novel takes place. Tom appeared out of the Southwest one day about 1906, twenty years old, with no family, self-educated, a rough diamond wanting to go to college. He had worked for the Sante Fe in New Mexico and punched cows on the open ranges of the territory. Tom became almost a member of the St. Peter family, and at the time the war broke out in Europe he was engaged to Rosamond. He also was the one student in St. Peter's career who had excited him: "In a lifetime of teaching, I've encountered just one remarkable mind," he tells his daughter. Tom and St. Peter developed a father-son relationship so close that his wife began to be jealous. For two summers Tom took the professor over the trails followed by the Spanish adventurers in the Southwest. Tom then stayed on at the university and became an instructor in physics, made an important discovery, and when the war came, enlisted and was killed. He willed his patent to Rosamond, whose husband Louie promoted it.

The second book is a seventy-page story-within-a-story, "Tom Outland's Story," the record of Tom's life before arriving at the professor's house nearly twenty years before. This is the tale inspired by Willa Cather's visit to Mesa Verde ten years earlier. It is an account of Tom's discovery of the cliff city high up under the rim of the Blue Mesa and of his explorations of the cliff-dwellings. Tom and another cowboy named Roddy Blake worked all summer among the ruins, excavating and cataloguing; then Tom went to Washington in the winter to announce his discovery to the director of the Smithsonian Institution. In Washington he met monumental indifference and after six frustrating months returned to New Mexico only to find that his partner meanwhile had sold all the artifacts to a German archeologist. Tom was desolate. He broke with his friend, hid himself in the cliff-dwellings for a time, then took his part of the proceeds of the sale and went to college.

The novel ends with a brief final book called "The Professor," which takes place in the late summer and early fall. The professor has stayed home while Louie and Rosamond have taken Mrs. St. Peter to Europe. Louie tried to get his father-in-law to go, but St. Peter begged off. As the fall term begins, the professor has no heart for his lectures. He feels a premonition of death and wants to be alone. His family is about to return from Europe, and he does not see how he can go on living with them. He lies down to take a nap in his attic study, and while he is sleeping, a storm comes up, the window blows shut, and his gas stove goes out. The old sewing woman, who has come to get the keys to the new house, arrives just in time to save him from asphyxiation. On his couch recovering, he realizes that his temporary unconsciousness has been beneficial. "He had let something go—and it was gone: something very precious, that he could not consciously have relinquished, probably." His family would not realize that he was no longer the same man, but he now could face the future with fortitude. Willa Cather too experienced something like a psychic annihilation at this period of her life.

While *The Professor's House* is Willa Cather's most interesting novel for the biographer, it is on the whole less successful artistically than her best work. The portrait of the professor is not entirely understandable without recourse to the author's own life, and the way Tom Outland runs away with the story results in what has seemed to many readers a flawed artistic entity. Many years later, in 1938, Willa Cather explained what she had tried to do in the novel when she inserted the long story-within-a-story into the novel. She wrote: "Just before I began the book I had seen, in Paris, an exhibition of old and modern Dutch paintings. In many of them the scene presented was a living-room warmly furnished, or a kitchen full of food and coppers. But in most of the interiors, whether drawing-room or kitchen, there was a square window, open, through which one saw the masts of ships, or a stretch of grey sea." She had wanted to open a window in the professor's house and let in the fresh air of the Blue Mesa. She also said that she had in mind an organizational pattern something like the sonata form in music. She is quite vague about this matter, but she probably meant no more than the use of a three-part form based on contrast. Her love of and interest in music did not include any formal knowledge of counterpoint, harmony, or musical structure. Her explanation of the organization in *The Professor's House,* however, comes long after the fact and may have been an afterthought. She already had inserted stories-within-stories in *My*

Ántonia and was familiar with the device from her reading of early French, Spanish, and English novels.

The real reason Tom Outland's story occupies such a large place in the novel lies in Willa Cather's own emotional involvement with the Southwest and the way in which the novel was written. Tom is her own dream self, and his adventure is high romance. It is also the story of youthful defeat. Willa Cather's emotions were fully engaged in telling this magical tale. The subject had teased her mind for ten years, and it provides striking contrast, in her usual manner, with the materialism that surrounds the professor in the rest of the novel. The story also had been written, at least in first draft, before she conceived the rest of the novel, and thus it was ready made to be inserted.

Although "Tom Outland's Story" gives the impression of rough carpentry where it joins the rest, the story, as E. K. Brown points out, is linked with the rest of the novel through the use of house symbolism. The professor clings to his old house where he has worked and written his great history. He does not feel at home in the pretentious new one his wife has built, and also dislikes intensely the misplaced Norwegian manor house, Outland, that Louie and Rosamond are building. In the Southwest, on the other hand, the Indian civilization that Tom discovered was perfectly adapted to its environment. The cliff-dwellings were simple, functional, open to the wind and sky. Yet the mesa Indians were not a primitive people; their houses showed a distinct feeling for design, and there was evidence on every hand that they had lived for something more than food and shelter. The cliff-dwellers in this story replace for Willa Cather the pioneers who generate the emotional charge in novels like *A Lost Lady* and *My Ántonia.*

Everything comes to money in the end, Rodney Blake tells Tom after selling the artifacts, and so it has in the world of Professor St. Peter. Tom Outland, that marvelous, idealistic youth, has left as his legacy the invention, and the invention, like King Midas, has turned everything to gold. For a moment, however, when Tom went back to the mesa alone after Rodney cleared out, he had a clear realization of the meaning of his experience. "The excitement of my first discovery was a very pale feeling compared to this one. For me the mesa was no longer an adventure, but a religious emotion." Willa Cather must have experienced similar emotions during those momentous hours in 1915 when she and Edith Lewis sat on the rock a thousand feet below the cliff city waiting to be rescued. The memory of that moment went into Tom Outland's diary:

The grey sagebrush and the blue-grey rock around me were already in shadow, but high above me the cañon walls were dyed flame-colour with the sunset, and the Cliff City lay in a gold haze against its dark cavern. In a few minutes it, too, was grey, and only the rim-rock at the top held the red light. When that was gone, I could still see the copper glow in the piñons along the edge of the top ledges. The arc of sky over the cañon was silvery blue, with its pale yellow moon, and presently stars shivered into it, like crystals dropped into perfectly clear water.

Willa Cather worked on *The Professor's House* from the fall of 1923 until the winter of 1924–1925. About the time she finished the manuscript, she showed part of it to Irene Weisz, her old friend from Red Cloud, whom she usually visited in Chicago en route to and from Nebraska. When Irene read the work-in-progress and approved, she was pleased. She was glad to know that her friend had got the really fierce feeling that lay behind the rather dry and impersonal manner of the telling. Later when she sold the serial rights for ten thousand dollars, she wrote Irene about it and a year later reported that the professor had bought her a mink coat, the first really valuable thing she ever had owned.

Willa Cather was getting used to being affluent and a celebrity, just as the professor would have become accustomed to it. She soon was able to joke about Dorothy Canfield Fisher's charge that she had written a middle-aged book, and told Dorothy that she was surprised at the book's favorable reception and large sale. During the months before and after the book's summer serialization in *Collier's*, she visited Red Cloud and the Southwest again and gave lectures at Bowdoin College, the University of Chicago, and in Cleveland. She had picked herself up following the crisis recorded in the novel and was keeping busy. By December she was back on Bank Street working like a steam engine and happy. Also during this period she found time and energy to collect the best stories of Sarah Orne Jewett and to write a preface. She also wrote introductions to a reissue of Gertrude Hall's *The Wagnerian Romances* and to Stephen Crane's *Wounds in the Rain,* the latter one of the volumes of Crane's collected works that Knopf brought out in 1926.

Willa Cather's next novel was *My Mortal Enemy,* published in the fall of 1926, but it was written more than a year earlier— before her day of wrath had completely passed. It is a novella actually, about eighteen thousand words, and another excellent example of the novel *démeublé.* But of all her works it has the most obscure provenance. Edith Lewis says almost nothing about it, and E. K. Brown only notes that the protagonist's prototype was a woman Willa Cather had "known well enough through connections in Lincoln, and who had died before the First World War." Only a couple of references to this story have turned up so far in her extant letters, and one only can conclude that she was reluctant to discuss the materials that went into this book. The reasons are clear enough: The novel is the bitterest piece of fiction she wrote. It apparently drained the last bit of gall from her system and cleared the way for the serene historical novels of her next half decade.

The novel is a study of Myra Henshawe, seen three different times—twice when she is forty-five and again ten years later. The story is a first-person narration by a young woman, one of the few female narrators in Willa Cather's fiction. The first view of Myra occurs when she and her husband Oswald return to their home town of Parthia for a visit with the narrator's aunt. (Willa Cather covers her tracks in this story by placing the town in southern Illinois.) Myra Driscoll was raised by a rich, savage Irish-Catholic great uncle, who cut her off without a cent when she eloped with the son of an Ulster Protestant. A few months after the visit to Parthia the narrator, Nellie Birdseye, and her aunt go to New York for the Christmas holidays and visit the Henshawes. He works for a railroad and they live comfortably, not affluently, in an apartment on Madison Square. The end of the visit coincides with a great quarrel between Myra and Oswald. Part II takes place ten years later, when Nellie is twenty-five and teaching in a college in San Francisco. She has a poor-paying job and has to live in a dingy, jerry-built apartment hotel. Her neighbors turn out to be the Henshawes, who have fallen on evil times and dropped out of her life completely. They are living in poverty, and Myra is dying of cancer. The story ends about five months later with Myra's death.

The novel is completely stripped of furniture except for the four chapters that take place in New York early in the century. There is no description at all of Parthia, which could have been placed in any midwestern state between Pennsylvania and Colorado; and the West Coast locale, which she never had visited, consists only of the apartment hotel and a "bare headland [somewhere around Point Lobos?], with only one twisted tree upon it, and the sea beneath." But she took pleasure in recalling the New York she remembered from her first visits, and the view of Madison Square on a snowy afternoon in winter is richly evocative. The square looks "like an open-air drawing-room" to Nellie Birdseye, as she stands there enchanted with the trees, shrubbery, fountain, buildings, and life going on about her. "It seemed . . . so neat, after the raggedness of our Western cities." In one of Willa Cather's few comments about this novel she wrote an old New York friend, Charlotte Stanfield, that she had taken pleasure in doing New York the way it was when she first knew it. She placed the time of the story at about 1904, but she used actual events in it that occurred several years earlier. The city in 1926 staggered her, but the novel showed it in another time and with other manners. This material has the nostalgic, elegiac tone that one finds in Willa Cather's best fiction.

Not only the external appearance of New York in 1900–1901 teased her mind, but also the interiors and the people. The Henshawes' apartment on the second floor of an old brownstone house on the north side of Madison Square charms Nellie Birdseye with its solidly built, high-ceilinged rooms, snug fireplaces, wide doors, and deep windows. The people who play small parts in the novel equally delight the young girl from the Middle West. One of Myra's friends is Helena Modjeska, with whom Willa Cather had lunched during her visit to New York in 1898. She comes to the Henshawes' New Year's Eve party with a Polish opera singer, and there are other attractive theater people on hand. On the last week end of the visit to New York Oswald takes Nellie to see Bernhardt and Coquelin play *Hamlet.*

The importance of this novel, however, lies in the sharp, bitter sketch of Myra Henshawe. There is a suggestion of Mrs. Garber and Marian Forrester in her sarcasm, which was "so quick, so fine at the point" that it was "like being touched by a metal so cold that one doesn't know whether one is burned or chilled." There also is a suggestion of Lillian St. Peter as she might have been without the small income she had inherited. As Godfrey St. Peter reflects on his life in the final section of *The Professor's House,* he notes that all the most important things in his life had been determined by chance. One of them was his wife's inheritance. "Lillian couldn't pinch and be shabby and do housework, as the wives of some of his colleagues did." Myra without money becomes a bitter, destructive, primitive character.

In the New York chapters where Myra and Oswald are seen living together, "as happy as most people," to quote Nellie's aunt, there are foreshadowings of the elemental character beneath the social veneer. Myra loves artistic people and cultivates them assiduously and extravagantly. She sends Modjeska a holly tree for Christmas, the most expensive thing in the florist's shop, to Oswald's distress. She also cultivates the rich and powerful in order to help Oswald in his business, but she hates this part of her circle. Her hate, however, is mostly the result of jealousy, and one day when she and Nellie are riding in a hansom cab, they pass a rich acquaintance in her private carriage. Nellie catches a glimpse of Myra's fierce longing for her own house and carriage. "It's very nasty, being poor," she tells Nellie. She is not poor, of course, but her desires far exceed Oswald's income.

In the second part of the novel, which takes place ten years later, Myra is a bitter old woman. Oswald, despite the fact she has destroyed him, ministers to her devotedly and ekes out a bare living working for the city traction company. Myra now openly admits that the mistake of her life was marrying for love and giving up her uncle's fortune. "I am a greedy, selfish, worldly woman," she tells Nellie; "I wanted success and a place in the world." Now she is left to die in a cheap apartment house where the neighbors upstairs tramp back and forth all day and drive her to distraction. When Nellie suggests that she is too hard on the faithful Oswald, she admits the charge, but she cannot help herself. "He's a sentimentalist, always was; he can look back on the best of these days when we were young and loved each other, and make himself believe it was all like that. It wasn't." And later she says, "Perhaps I can't forgive him for the harm I did him." Shortly before she dies, she murmurs in the presence of both her husband and Nellie: "Why must I die like this, alone with my mortal enemy?"

Before she dies, Myra returns to the Catholicism of her youth. Faith gives her the only solace she can find at the end of her unlucky life. When Nellie takes her driving one day along the headlands overlooking the Pacific, they watch the sun dropping into the ocean, and Myra says she would love to see that place at dawn: "That is always such a forgiving time. When that first cold, bright streak comes over the water, it's as if all our sins were pardoned; as if the sky leaned over the earth and kissed it and gave it absolution." A few hours before she dies, Myra summons her last strength, hires a cab, and goes again to the headland alone. She is found the next morning wrapped in a blanket, leaning against a tree facing out to sea. "There was every reason to believe she had lived to see the dawn."

This astringent portrayal of defeat and death marks the end of Willa Cather's own bitter years. It is her final comment on the destructive power of money and a society that worships the golden calf. What began mildly in *One of Ours,* like the rather superficial attacks on the "village virus" in Sinclair Lewis, stepped up in tempo with the savage portrait of Ivy Peters in *A Lost Lady,* and went on to annihilate psychologically Professor St. Peter, finally destroyed Myra Henshawe and her husband. There is more than a trace of Willa Cather in Myra, especially in her ability to hate. Willa Cather believed in creative hate, as she has Thea Kronborg say in *The Song of the Lark,* and she may have seen in Myra Henshawe a glimpse of what she might have come to if she had not had her art to sustain her. It was not long after this that Elizabeth Sergeant was astonished to have Willa Cather ask if she thought psychoanalysis might do her any good. Nothing came of this inquiry, however, but *My Mortal Enemy* seems to have provided a final catharsis. By the time the book was published, she had retreated into the past and was well along with *Death Comes for the Archibishop.*

"Past Is Prologue": 1927–1932

I

WILLA CATHER actually had been preparing to write *Death Comes for the Archbishop* since she first had visited the Southwest in 1912. The enchantment of Arizona and especially New Mexico had gotten into her blood stream, and though she had used this material from time to time, it seems in retrospect inevitable that one day there would be a novel about that area. The lure of the Southwest antedated her first visit, as one notes in "The Enchanted Bluff" (1909). Explaining this story, she had written Sarah Orne Jewett that in the West there was a Spanish influence, just as Miss Jewett had grown up in Maine with centuries of English tradition behind her. Spanish words enriched the English language, and even the cowboy saddle was made on the old Spanish model. There was something heady in the wind that blew up from Mexico, she said. One of the most memorable scenes in *My Ántonia* is the picnic by the river, in which Jim Burden tells the hired girls, Ántonia, Lena, and Tiny, about Coronado's search through the Midwest for the seven golden cities. "Charley Harling and I," Jim says, "had a strong belief that he had been along this very river," because a farmer in the country to the north "had turned up a metal stirrup of fine workmanship, and a sword with a Spanish inscription on the blade."

If chance had made her a professor of history like Godfrey St. Peter, Willa Cather would have been a success, and it is probable that her lifetime work would have been his topic, the Spanish adventurers in North America. Edith Lewis reports that she "had a great gift for imaginative historical reconstruction. . . . She could make the modern age almost disappear, fade away and become ghostlike, so completely was she able to invoke her vision of the past and recreate its reality." This is what she does in *Death Comes for the Archbishop*, though first the subject had to tease her mind for many years, and she had to make numerous trips to the Southwest. Specifically, she spent the summers of 1925 and 1926 there in order to look over the ground again and to rekindle her imagination. She always denied that she went West to gather material for stories, but she did admit that she derived inspiration from her travels.

The summer of 1925 was a memorable time. She did not go to New Mexico planning to write her book, but *The Professor's House* with its use of the Southwest had made her eager to revisit the area after an absence of ten years. She also had met D. H. and Frieda Lawrence in New York in the spring of 1924, when they had come to tea twice at her Bank Street apartment, and they were headed back to New Mexico. Lawrence had brought his wife back from England after their separation in Mexico earlier, and he was in a sunny mood. Willa Cather and the Lawrences promised each other to meet again in the Southwest. When she got to Santa Fe, Mabel Dodge Luhan invited her to visit Taos and offered her the same guest house the Lawrences had stayed in. She was there two weeks and during the visit took many auto trips about the country with Mabel's Indian husband, Tony. Edith Lewis, who accompanied her, remembers: "Tony would sit in the driver's seat, in his silver bracelets and purple blanket, often singing softly to himself; while we sat behind. He took us to some of the almost inaccessible Mexican villages hidden in the Cimmaron mountains." He did not talk much, but Willa Cather got a lot of information from him, and the character of Eusabio, the Navaho Indian in her novel, seems drawn from Tony. She also saw the Lawrences that summer, as they lived nearby on the ranch that Mabel Luhan had given them. Lawrence was living simply, baking his own bread and milking his own cow, and still in a state of euphoria; by the time Willa Cather returned to Taos the following year, he had returned to Europe and had not many years left to live.

The idea for *Death Comes for the Archbishop* came one summer night in Santa Fe. It was another of those inner explosions that she had experienced before. She had come across a book printed privately in Pueblo, Colorado, in 1908 by a priest named William Howlett: *The Life of the Right Reverend Joseph P. Macheboeuf.* She stayed up late reading the remarkable story of Father Macheboeuf, who had been vicar to Archbishop Lamy of New Mexico. By morning she had the plan of her book worked out. Here was a way of organizing the Southwest material that she loved into a full-length book. The time of the story would be the middle of the nineteenth century, a generation earlier than her stories of the Nebraska pioneers, but dealing with the same stage of development, the last phase of the pioneer era. She had pretty well exhausted her Nebraska material, at least for the present, but New Mexico was nearly a virgin topic.

The novel created a great deal of interest when it came out in 1927, and she received many letters asking about the book's sources, its provenance, and its historical accuracy. She wrote a letter to *Commonweal* to save answering the inquiries individually, and took the opportunity to acknowledge her indebtedness to Father Howlett's book, which she had not done anywhere in the novel. Her knowledge of the Southwest, she said, began during her first visit, when she encountered a Belgian priest, Father Haltermann, who lived in the parsonage behind the beautiful old church at Santa Cruz. He had a wonderful vegetable and flower garden and traveled about among his eighteen Indian missions in a spring wagon. He knew a great deal about the country and the Indians and was delighted to find someone interested in such matters. (Father Haltermann one recognizes as Father Duchene in "Tom Outland's Story.") She goes on to say: "The longer I stayed in the Southwest, the more I felt that the story of the Catholic Church in that country was the most interesting of all its stories. The old mission churches, even those which were abandoned and in ruins, had a moving reality about them." The hand-carved beams, the unconventional frescoes, the countless fanciful figures of saints seemed a "direct expression of some very real and lively human feeling." In the somber mountain churches the decorations were somber, the martyrdoms bloodier, and the grief of the Virgin more agonized. In the warm, mild valleys everything about the churches was gentler. Meantime, the bronze statue of Archbishop

Lamy, which stands under a locust tree before the Cathedral of Santa Fe, had attracted her attention and interest. She heard engaging stories about him from old Mexicans who remembered him, and the statue looked "well-bred and distinguished."

Willa Cather said in her letter that the writing of the book "took only a few months, because the book had all been lived many times before it was written." This is not really true. She worked on it during the fall of 1925 at Jaffrey, New Hampshire, and then again through the winter in New York. The next summer she went back to New Mexico to see some new places and check some details, and it was on this visit that she went to Ácoma and passed the Mesa Encantada, which had for so long captured her imagination. When she returned East in July 1926, she went to the Mac-Dowell Colony at Peterborough, New Hampshire, to write. It was her first and only stay there, for she did not much like the communal life of an artists' colony and soon retreated to the Shattuck Inn at Jaffrey. The book was finished in the fall of 1926 and serialized in the *Forum* beginning the following January.

She knew that she had accomplished something remarkable in this book. Knopf remembers that the only time Willa Cather ever asked him to increase her royalties was when she gave him the manuscript of the novel; but she only asked for an additional one per cent. She was convinced that the book would have a long and continuing sale and that Knopf's son years later would be paying royalties to her niece. She was right about the book's long life, and it continues to sell and to be read, but not more so than *My Ántonia.* She wrote E. K. Brown, her biographer, shortly before she died that she knew that *Death Comes for the Archbishop* was her best book.

Whether or not the book is a novel, however, seems to have bothered reviewers at the time the work appeared. Willa Cather preferred to call her story a narrative, and wrote Norman Foerster, who wanted to reprint a part of it, that it could easily be anthologized because it was scarcely a novel. She thought of the book as a narrative that moves along in a straight line on two white mules that do not hurry themselves very much. In her *Commonweal* letter she defines the novel as a "work of the imagination in which a writer tries to present the experiences and emotions of a group of people by the light of his own." Whatever it is, *Death Comes for the Archbishop* is a remarkably successful historical recreation of the missionary work of Fathers Lamy and Macheboeuf (Jean Marie Latour and Joseph Vaillant in the story). The main events of the novel are taken from Father Howlett's book and supplemented by Willa Cather's own experiences. The real as well as the fictitious events, however, are shaped by the author's creative imagination.

The novel begins with a prologue that takes place in Rome, in which a missionary bishop from America persuades a Spanish cardinal to use his influence to obtain the appointment of Jean Marie Latour to the new bishopric of New Mexico. The time of the prologue is 1848, just after the Mexican War and the annexation of the Southwest by the United States. Father Latour gets the appointment because, as the Spanish cardinal concedes, the French are the best missionaries: "They are the great organizers." Father Latour arrives in Santa Fe with his friend and fellow worker Joseph Vaillant, who comes as his vicar general. They both were seminarians together in their native Auvergne. The first book, "The Vicar Apostolic," deals with Father Latour's lonely journey from Santa Fe to Durango, Mexico, to obtain from the Mexican bishop the credentials that were not forwarded. The local priests in the New Mexico territory refuse to accept Father Latour's authority, and the fifteen-hundred-mile trek across trackless desert is a necessary prelude. The opening book sets the mood of the entire novel: the cheerful acceptance of the physical hardships and the joyful energy of the missionary labors. This mood is sustained throughout the book.

What plot there is concerns itself with the gradual organization of the vast diocese and the bringing under a central authority, after decades of neglect, all the parishes scattered over hundreds of miles of mountains and deserts. The book comes to an end in 1889 when the old archbishop dies in retirement long after his mission has been completed. At the end he looks back with the elegiac tone so characteristic of Willa Cather: "Yes, he had come with the buffalo, and he had lived to see railway trains running into Santa Fe. He had accomplished an historic period." The comment that the old Navaho Eusabio makes when he comes to see the old archbishop for the last time might have appeared in any one of several novels: "Men travel faster now, but I do not know if they go to better things." When the story closes, Father Vaillant also is dead, having ended his life as bishop of Denver. He left Bishop Latour when gold was discovered in Colorado and that area began filling up with people. In reality Father Macheboeuf outlived Father Lamy, but for artistic purposes Willa Cather reversed the order of their deaths.

The book is loosely episodic in a way reminiscent of earlier Cather novels, and it contains, also characteristically, stories-within-in-stories. Most of the chapters deal with the missionary work of the two priests between their arrival in 1851 and the building of the cathedral about ten years later; but the prelude takes place three years before, and Book IX begins at the time of the archbishop's death a generation afterwards. The chapters within the various books have a thematic arrangement, and the progression of books is generally chronological. Early in the novel Willa Cather relates the story of the Virgin of Guadaloupe, and toward the end tells one of the legends that grew up about the life of Father Junipero Serra in the California missions. These inserts are digressions but reinforce the tone of abiding faith and ecclesiastical energy.

The book also has plenty of variety and contrast. In Book II, "Missionary Journeys," for example, the sequence of chapters opens with an amusing account of how Father Vaillant separates Manuel Lujon from his prized white mules, Angelica and Contento, who then carry the missionaries through the rest of the novel. Immediately following this chapter is the story of the degenerate Yankee murderer Buck Scales and his abused Mexican wife, Magdalena, whom the priests meet on "The Lonely Road to Mora." Book IV, "Snake Root," is the chilling account of a night Bishop Latour and Jacinto, his Indian guide, spend in a cave used by the Indians to practice secretly their ancestral snake worship, and this tale is followed by the duel between the bishop and old Father Martinez of Taos in Book V. In this climactic battle the well-entrenched old reprobate Martinez is brought under the bishop's authority, the last hold-out of the old regime. The novel also provides an abundant contrast in character in the large gallery

222

of Indians, Mexicans, rich and poor, and even Yankees. The poor Mexican woman Saba is effectively contrasted with the rich Don Antonio Olivares and his coy wife, Doña Isabella. The pious native priest Padre Herrera is seen in juxtaposition with the high-living Father Gallegos of Albuquerque. And to contrast with Buck Scales, who is hanged for his crimes, is Kit Carson, one of the "good guys," who appears several times as an admirer and supporter of the bishop.

If Willa Cather's experience in the Southwest and Father Howlett's book provided the explosive force to create this novel, the visual arts gave her some ideas for organizing the material. She wrote in the *Commonweal* letter that she always had wanted to do something in the style of legend, "which is absolutely the reverse of dramatic treatment." She remembered the frescoes of the life of Saint Genevieve by Puvis de Chavannes and wanted to try something like that in prose. This series, which she had seen in Paris in 1902, treats the story of the patron saint of Paris with a simplicity not unlike Willa Cather's style *démeublé*. And like Cather, Puvis de Chavannes painted from memory rather than from nature. Thus the novel is somewhat analogous to painting, insofar as one can compare narrative, which is temporal, to an art form which is spatial. Further, Willa Cather said in her letter, she used Holbein's *Dance of Death* for her title. The specific work she refers to is a woodcut, in which death as a skeleton comes for an archbishop. It is one of a series in which Holbein's gay skeleton summons a host of mortals to their rewards. The whole series is instructive for a study of the novel, as are the Puvis de Chavannes frescoes. Death comes for a great many more people in the story than just the old Archbishop Latour—Indians, Mexicans, Yankees, as well as the French priests.

Although *Death Comes for the Archbishop* is disarmingly simple on a casual reading, there is a great deal of artistry concealed in the *démeublé* method. For example, no attempt is made to emphasize important events over trivial incidents, and in a dramatic composition such an arrangement of materials would be very unsuccessful. What Willa Cather was doing, however, was quite unconventional and quite deliberate. She explained in her *Commonweal* letter that she had gotten an idea from a literary

223

analogue, *The Golden Legend.* In this medieval manual of ecclesiastical lore, which contains many saints' lives, the martyrdom of the saints is dwelt upon no more than are the trivial incidents of their lives; "it is as though all human experiences, measured against one supreme spiritual experience, were of about the same importance." The essence of this kind of writing, she said, was to hold the note, not to use an incident for all there is in it. This she succeeds in doing in the novel, and it accounts for the way in which the major and minor events are treated with equal attention.

There are other literary analogues that she does not mention and which may have influenced the writing of the novel. One is the *Divine Comedy.* That she knew Dante's work is well known, but the parallels between the *Divine Comedy* and *Death Comes for the Archbishop* may be coincidental. Yet the nine books of the novel and the prologue are subdivided into thirty-three parts, as Dante's poem is divided into thirty-three cantos; and the first seven books treat the seven virtues and appropriate sins. Book VIII deals with fulfillment in the building of the cathedral, and the last book takes the archbishop to his just reward. Moreover, the prologue provides a frame for the story and prepares Father Latour for his journey through life and temptation to final salvation. This prologue is not found in Father Howlett's book but is Willa Cather's invention. The life journey towards salvation, however, is not Dante's exclusive property, and Father Latour's pilgrimage also invites comparison with the journey in another literary work that held an even greater place in Willa Cather's background than the *Divine Comedy*: Christian's journey in *Pilgrim's Progress.* But the more one examines this novel, the more echoes and reverberations and hidden art one finds in it.

One also finds here a recurring image that looks both backwards and forwards in Willa Cather's fiction. This is the symbol of the rock, which in "The Enchanted Bluff" represents youthful aspiration and in *The Professor's House* stands for harmony. Here it comes to mean faith. Book III, "The Mass at Ácoma," is a particularly vivid narrative sequence in which Bishop Latour and Jacinto visit the pueblo at Ácoma on the top of a barren mesa southwest of Albuquerque. This is a place the comfort-loving Father Gallegos never goes because it is too remote and too difficult to reach. As the bishop rides towards this outpost carrying the gospel, the country has the appearance of great antiquity and incompleteness, "as if, with all the materials for world-making assembled, the Creator has desisted, gone away and left everything on the point of being brought together. . . . The country was still waiting to be made into a landscape." Bishop Latour passes the Enchanted Mesa, which once had a village on it, and ponders the Indian instinct to build villages on the nearly inaccessible tops of the mesas. He knows that it was to obtain protection against marauding tribes of unfriendly neighbors, but his reflection continues: "The rock, when one came to think of it, was the utmost expression of human need. . . . Christ Himself had used that comparison for the disciple to whom He gave the keys of His Church." One can see here a foreshadowing of Willa Cather's next novel, *Shadows on the Rock*.

II

There is no doubt that the writing of *Death Comes for the Archbishop* was for Willa Cather something of a spiritual journey towards redemption. Although she had been confirmed in the Episcopal Church in 1922, the act of joining the church represented more a hope for faith than the consequence of a religious experience. This novel gave her the peace she had been seeking and the serenity to face her last two decades. There is a similarity, one might note, between Willa Cather writing this novel and T. S. Eliot writing *Ash Wednesday* at the end of the decade. These writers had nothing in common, but both responded to the wasteland of the twenties by finding support in Christianity. Willa Cather told Ida Tarbell after completing her novel that writing the book was the most unalloyed pleasure of her life and she missed her archbishop awfully. Working on him was like working with him, and her mood while writing the book was happy and serene.

It was fortunate that she had found a spiritual anchor for her life. She was fifty-four at the end of 1927 and at the apex of her career, a novelist internationally known, a commercial and critical success. But the vicissitudes of life were about to begin beating against her moorings. Within the next four years she lost both her father and mother. Already she had lost her Bank Street apartment, where she had lived happily for fifteen years.

The end of the Bank Street era was a hard blow. For most people, losing a house would not be a traumatic experience, but it was for Willa Cather. Her professor's reluctance, almost inability to move, was a strange prefiguring of her own life. In the summer of 1927 a new subway was being built through Greenwich Village, and a station was going in almost under 5 Bank Street. With the advent of the subway the house was scheduled to be torn down to make way for a new apartment house. There was no alternative to moving. In the same month that *Death Comes for the Archbishop* appeared, Willa Cather wrote Zoë Akins from Jaffrey, New Hampshire, where she and Miss Lewis had gone to recover from the ordeal of putting their furniture in storage. The experience was like having a funeral, she wrote, and she was going to lie around in the juniper pastures a few weeks before doing anything else. She did not even want to think about making plans. She temporized and moved into the Grosvenor Hotel at 35 Fifth Avenue while she decided where to go next. The temporary move to a hotel stretched into a sojourn of five years.

That summer she had gone West for a trip to Wyoming to see her brother, but she had to rush back to Red Cloud in August when her father had a heart attack. Her father recovered from the first seizure, and she returned East, canceling a planned trip to Europe and going instead to New Hampshire. Because of her father's illness she went back to Red Cloud for Christmas and stayed until late February, but she no sooner had returned to New York than her father had a fatal heart attack on March third. She reached Red Cloud the day after he died, about three in the morning. Friends met her and took her home. She went up to her father's room without waking anyone and found him lying on a couch in the bay window. She spent several unforgettable hours with him before anyone else in the house awoke. When the red dawn broke, it flushed his face with the rosy color which he always had, and he looked entirely himself and happy. It was a hard loss, for Charles Cather and his oldest daughter had been very close. All the kind, gentle fathers in Willa Cather's fiction have her

ther in them. Willa stayed on in Red Cloud at least a month after
he funeral, while her brother Douglass took her mother back to
southern California. She was reluctant to tear herself away from
he house where her father's presence still lingered.

The year 1928 was almost totally unproductive and discouraging for her. It began with her father's death and ended with her
mother's stroke. When she returned from Red Cloud in late April,
her chambermaid in the Grosvenor Hotel came down with a viru-
lent case of influenza; but before they took the maid off to the
hospital, she spread the virus. Willa Cather spent the rest of the
spring in bed or recuperating. She barely managed to summon
strength in June to accept an honorary degree from Columbia
University. Then she went to Grand Manan Island, where she had
her own cottage and plenty of quiet. She was too weak to travel
by way of Maine but took the train to Montreal and then pro-
ceeded by way of Quebec to St. John, where she caught the ferry
for Grand Manan. This was her first visit to Quebec, but it turned
out to be an eventful stopover. The rock of faith that looms up
large in *Death Comes for the Archbishop* loomed up still larger in
French-Catholic Quebec. She began to think about doing a novel
laid in seventeenth-century French Canada.

Shadows on the Rock, which had its genesis in this initial visit
to Quebec, was a long time in the writing, however. She went
back to Quebec for Thanksgiving that year and in December began working on the novel. Then came her mother's stroke and
paralysis, and for the next two years she had to watch her mother
dying slowly while she tried to finish her book. There were three
more visits to Quebec before she was satisfied that she had absorbed sufficiently the atmosphere of the Canadian locale and another return to France for inspiration. Finally *Shadows on the
Rock* was finished at the end of 1930 and published the following
year. But there also were three long, discouraging trips to southern
California before the novel was published.

Willa Cather spent the spring of 1929 in Long Beach, California, with her mother, then returned in June for another honorary degree, this time from Yale. She was in low spirits when she
wrote Mary Jewett in April. She was finding no time for anything
but the struggle with the grave material difficulties that confront

one in caring for a helpless sick person stricken away from home
If her mother only could have had her stroke in her own home an
among friends, and what Willa would not have given for a breat
of New England spring. She did not like southern California at al
though she admitted it was a good climate for invalids. To her
was like living on the stage. There was no reality about the plac
or the sunlight or the drifting, homeless people. After she went t
New Haven for commencement, she escaped to the cool, rain
climate of Grand Manan Island.

On her way to Grand Manan she again stopped off in Quebe
staying at the Château Frontenac, to soak up more atmosphere t
help her get on with the book. While she was at Whale Cov
Cottage in July and August, she managed to do a little work, an
then she spent her usual month at Jaffrey, New Hampshire. Sh
wrote Zona Gale, who had been importuning her to visit Portage
Wisconsin, that she might have to start off for California at an
time—certainly before Christmas. She would try to stop off on he
way West, but she never did. She returned to New York and ker
postponing her return to California. She obviously did not want t
go, and it was not until March that she actually went. By this tim
her mother was in a sanitarium in Pasadena at her expense and n
longer being cared for by members of the family in Long Beacl
On this second visit to California she stayed only about six week
before she ran off to France and was gone from May until Octo
ber.

The trip to France was therapeutic. After a great deal of sight
seeing and meeting people she went to Aix-les-Bains, where sh
had been in 1923, and put up at the Grand Hotel d'Aix. The tow
was a lovely, quiet place, she wrote Zoë Akins, as worldly as
capital and as simple as a village. The food was so good that sh
put on four pounds in the first couple of weeks. The hotel was a
old one built years before, but it had large rooms and a ver
comfortable atmosphere, and she liked it much better than th
smart new ones on the hills above the town. The Grand Hote
opened on a sloping little square that exhibited a bronze head c
Queen Victoria commemorating a visit she once had made to th
spa. The casino and opera house were just across the gardens.

While she was staying at the Grand Hotel, she had an amazin

dventure. Night after night she noticed in the dining room a
istinguished old French woman, well over eighty, who usually ate
lone. "The thing one especially noticed was her fine head, so well
et upon her shoulders and beautiful in shape, recalling some of
ne portrait busts of Roman ladies." In the mornings Willa Cather
lso saw the old lady come out of the hotel, get into her car, and
rive off with her chauffeur toward the mountains. She carried
aints and canvas and a camp stool with her, even though Aix was
aving one of its hottest Augusts in many years. Willa Cather,
hile reading French fluently, had little oral command of the lan-
uage and hesitated to speak to the old lady. One day, however,
ne Frenchwoman spoke to her in excellent English, and from this
eginning an acquaintanceship quickly developed.

Willa Cather has described this meeting vividly in "A Chance
1eeting," one of the essays in *Not Under Forty*. It was a great
xperience. At first she had no idea who the woman was, but
hen they began discussing writers and Willa Cather mentioned
urgenev, the Frenchwoman casually replied: "I knew him well at
ne time."

"I looked at her in astonishment. Yes, of course, it was possible.
he was very old."

The woman went on to say: "My mother died at my birth, and
was brought up in my uncle's house. He was more than father to
1e. My uncle also was a man of letters, Gustave Flaubert, you may
erhaps know. . . . "

Willa Cather knew immediately that this was the "Caro" of
'laubert's *Lettres à sa nièce Caroline*. "The room was absolutely
uiet, but there was nothing to say to this disclosure. It was like
eing suddenly brought up against a mountain of memories." The
ld lady, Mme. Franklin Grout, was astonished, of course, in her
urn to meet someone who not only knew her uncle's works but
new them intimately and was passionately fond of them. At their
ubsequent meetings they discussed at length various books of the
1aster, particularly *L'Éducation sentimentale* and Willa Cather's
vorite, the romantic *Salammbô*. Mme. Grout eventually discov-
red that her acquaintance was also a distinguished novelist, and
vited her to visit at Antibes. Willa said she had to return home
ecause of her mother's illness but would hope to return the fol-

229

lowing year. The visit never occurred, however, because Mm
Grout died the following February at the age of eighty-four.

In October Willa Cather sailed for home on the *Empress
France*, which traveled the northern route via the St. Lawren
River. She landed at Quebec and for several weeks looked at th
city again, then went to Jaffrey to work on her book. After retur
ing to the Grosvenor Hotel, she finished the novel, read part of th
proof, and departed again for California to see her mother for th
last time. Just before she finished the book, however, she inte
rupted her work to receive the gold medal of the Americ
Academy of Arts and Letters for *Death Comes for the Archbisho*
The death of her father and two years of anxiety over her mothe
illness had taken their toll. Hamlin Garland wrote in his diary aft
the ceremony: "Willa Cather was on the platform and I did n
recognize her, so changed was she. She is a plain, short, ungrac
ful, elderly woman. . . . I had remembered her in quite differe
guise. She spoke without force or grace, with awkward gestur
but she did a noble book."

When Willa Cather reached the sanitarium in Pasadena, sh
found her mother completely paralyzed on one side and almo
speechless, but her mind was perfectly clear. It was a ghast
experience to sit beside her day after day. She wrote Sara Tea
dale that the book had helped pull her through the long orde
and that Zoë Akins, who lived nearby, had been a great comfo
Just being with Zoë always made her happy. Willa Cather staye
in California until June, when she returned East to add still a
other honorary degree—from Princeton—to her collection. H
mother's long illness came to an end in August while she was
Grand Manan Island, and after the agony was over, she wro
Dorothy Canfield Fisher, whose own mother had died recentl
that they were now the older generation. It was painful reachir
this state, like dying twice.

After her mother's burial the Cather children planned a fami
reunion in Red Cloud. Willa arrived on December first alone
await the arrival of her brothers and sisters. Her mother's form
maid came from Colorado to keep house, and Willa prepared
spend her last Christmas in Nebraska. She also wanted a month
home with old friends as well as family. For two years her mot

er's jealousy had kept her from stopping off in Red Cloud on her way to California. She stayed in Red Cloud until after Christmas, and when she left to return to New York, it was for the last time.

III

The book that sustained Willa Cather during her mother's long illness appeared in the bookstores during the month her mother died. By the time she went back to Red Cloud for the last time, the book was climbing up the best-seller lists and enjoying the most immediate popular success she ever had. Even *Death Comes for the Archbishop*, which also was a best-seller, had not done as well. The reviewers as well as the public treated her kindly, though they generally agreed that the novel was less successful than its predecessor. John Chamberlain thought there was "little of the stuff of life that makes memorable fiction," and Carl Van Doren found it "dramatically thin" but "pictorially rich." Governor Wilbur Cross of Connecticut, formerly professor of English at Yale, wrote one of the most perceptive notices in the *Saturday Review of Literature*: "Purposely the sketches are slight and delicate like the pastels of Latour or Watteau. . . . It is all a delicate art, more difficult than the art of the traditional novel. Few have ever measurably succeeded. Miss Cather is among these few."

Cross's review brought a reply from the author, who wrote to thank him for the most understanding notice she had seen of her new book. He had seen what she was trying to do, and she elaborated on her aims. She had tried to state the mood and viewpoint in the book's title, for to her the rock of Quebec was both "a stronghold on which·many strange figures have for a little time cast a shadow in the sun" and "the curious endurance of a kind of culture." There was something different about Quebec, the persistence of another age down into the twentieth century, and this she had tried to put into a setting, "a series of pictures remembered rather than experienced." What interested her was the continuity of life in Quebec, "an orderly little French household that went on trying to live decently, just as ants begin to rebuild when you kick their house down." This sort of spirit in seventeenth-century Quebec interested her a great deal more than Indian raids or the wildlife in the forests. For readers who demand action and drama, she explained: " . . . once having taken your seat in the close air by the apothecary's fire, you can't explode into military glory, any more than you can pour champagne into a salad dressing." And she added that "a new society begins with the salad dressing more than with the destruction of Indian villages."

Although she struck out boldly in her letter to Governor Cross, Willa Cather was somewhat apologetic in letters to friends. She must have been astonished at the size of her royalties from *Shadows on the Rock*, because she admitted the book had no fire at all and almost no energy. She conceded that one simply had to like the book's quietness. It was all of a piece, but she knew the tone was good. To some people she feared the book would seem goody-goody, but the problem had been to keep the feeling of Quebec life all the year around. In music, she wrote Zoë Akins, one could have a stormy and passionate movement next to a reflective one, but one could not mix such things in writing. Yet she had done exactly that in *The Professor's House*, which she had called a novel in sonata form.

An historical novel laid in Quebec in the seventeenth century seems an unlikely product from the pen of Willa Cather. How does one reconcile this subject with the declaration that her heart never got across the Missouri River and that she only could write successfully about people or places she loved? And how does one reconcile this novel with her quotation from Sarah Orne Jewett that the "thing that teases the mind over and over for years . . . belongs to Literature"? The best resolution of these paradoxes comes also from her essay on Miss Jewett, in which she says that if a writer "achieves anything noble, anything enduring, it must be by giving himself absolutely to his material. And this gift of sympathy is his great gift." Willa Cather had the gift of sympathy, and it adds an extra dimension to her work. It is the secret ingredient in the formula. She wrote in an essay on Katherine Mansfield, a writer she much admired: "The qualities of a second-rate writer can easily be defined, but a first-rate writer can only be experienced. It is just the thing in him which escapes analysis that makes him first-rate." Willa Cather is one of the first-rate writers, and she succeeds fairly well, though not brilliantly, in this historical recreation.

The material, however, is not quite so alien as it appears at first glance. Even though she had been to Quebec only five times and never had lived there, a number of elements of the novel had been thoroughly assimilated. Her deep feeling for French culture was one of her oldest attachments and had been reinforced by her seven trips to Europe beginning in 1902. She had written as early as 1895 that "most things came from France, chefs and salads, gowns and bonnets, dolls and music boxes, plays and players, scientists and inventors, sculptors and painters, novelists and poets. . . . If it were to take a landslide into the channel some day there would not be much creative power of any sort left in the world." Her interest in the establishment of Catholicism in the New World went back to her early visits to the Southwest. Her knowledge of French housekeeping, which plays an important role in *Shadows on the Rock,* had been absorbed from her French maid, Josephine Bourda, over many years. (This she did not even realize until after she had finished the book.) Her acute rendering of the forests and rocky seascapes of Quebec was partly the result of her five summers spent among similar scenes at Grand Manan Island. Finally, the relationship between the apothecary Auclair and his twelve-year-old daughter Cécile derives from Willa Cather's memory of her father. His death a few months before she began working on the novel placed his image firmly in her mind as she created the main character.

While *Death Comes for the Archbishop* and *Shadows on the Rock* are both historical novels conceived of as a series of pictures, there is an important difference. The former has a linear progression in the organization of the material and is based on the journey motif; the latter is static, centered on the rock, which here symbolizes permanence and security. The novel takes place between October 1697 and November 1698, with a brief epilogue dated 1713. It makes no effort to tell a story, though there are numerous narrative vignettes inserted within the framework of the year in which the book is laid. The background material is sketched in at appropriate intervals, but the real story is one year in the life of the Québecois on their rock where nothing really changes. The novel is organized around the changing of the seasons and the rhythms of life in the colony, and it reminds one somewhat of the structural plan Thoreau used in *Walden.*

The novel is divided into six books, four of them dealing with characters and two with events. The central figure of the apothecary, Euclide Auclair, is introduced first in his combined shop and home built halfway between the upper and lower towns. He is forty-seven, a wise, gentle, timid soul who has come to the New World in the service of his patron, Count Frontenac. Auclair lives with his twelve-year-old daughter, Cécile, who has been keeping house for him since the death of his wife two years before. In the second book Cécile and Jacques, her six-year-old friend, are the central figures and are followed through various activities as fall turns to winter. Book III, "The Long Winter," is a group of narratives, mostly dealing with aspects of religion in French Canada: a profile of the proud young Bishop Saint-Vallier, who is contrasted through the novel with the humble old Bishop Laval; the story of Jeanne Le Ber, the recluse, and her miracle; an account of Father Hector's missionary work in the wilderness. Contrasted with these stories is the mournful tale of old Blinker, who left France to escape the horrors of his trade as a torturer in the king's prison at Rouen. The fourth book introduces an admirable young *coureur de bois*, Pierre Charron, who eventually marries Cécile, as one learns in the epilogue, and becomes the protector of the Auclairs after the death of the old count. As spring gives way to summer, the annual ships arrive from France, providing the subject matter for Book V, and the novel closes with the end of an era, the death of the count.

Shadows on the Rock contains a number of familiar Cather themes: the New World versus the Old, stability versus mutability, the virtues of friendship, and the perpetuation of tradition. The New World is free from the abuses of class society, the necessity to truckle to those in authority, the unjust operation of the laws. Old Blinker, who had been a torturer, and poor Bichet, who had been hanged in Paris for a petty theft on the evidence of a half-witted informer, illustrate the iniquity of Old World society as it affected the humble. Count Frontenac, one of the great figures of French colonial history, illustrates the evils of Europe and the *ancien régime* from the other end of the social spectrum. He never receives his due from Louis XIV and dies relatively poor because he was overly forthright and insufficiently obsequious. Just before his end the king even denies him his wish to return to France to die.

The theme of stability versus mutability is linked to the previous theme and chiefly carried by the central image of the rock. Here the temporal and spiritual metaphors merge, and in "The Long Winter" Willa Cather writes: "Quebec seemed shrunk to a mere group of shivering spires; the whole rock looked like one great white church, above the frozen river." At the end of the book when the new bishop, now an old man, returns from fifteen years of captivity in England and exile in France, he says to Auclair: "You have done well to remain here where nothing changes. Here with you I find everything the same." And the old apothecary thinks, as the book ends, that he was "indeed fortunate to spend his old age here where nothing changed; to watch his grandsons grow up in a country where the death of the King, the probable evils of a long regency, would never touch them."

Loyalty to friends was one of Willa Cather's most important traits, and in *Shadows on the Rock* all the characters are linked in interlocking relationships of amity. Auclair is loyal to his patron, the count, who in turn is devoted to his faithful apothecary; and the relationship is reciprocal despite the difference in social station. Auclair is loyal to the old derelict Blinker and to the memory of old Bichet. Cécile's great friend is little Jacques, whom she both mothers and plays with, and who is in turn unbelievably steadfast to father and daughter. Pierre Charron is both son and elder brother during most of the novel and beloved by both Auclairs. Old Bishop Laval's love for his flock is unstinting, and all the people in Quebec, except the proud young bishop, adore their old spiritual leader. And finally, binding the entire community together is the everlasting love of God, given and returned. Willa Cather said late in her life that nothing really matters but the people one loves, and she felt this increasingly as she approached her sixtieth year. But she admitted that if people realized this fact when young and spent their time sitting around loving one another, the beds would not get made and little of the world's work would get done.

The perpetuation of tradition, like friendship, became more and more important to Willa Cather as she grew older. In this novel the continuity of French culture is one of the enduring things like the rock on which the city is built. Some of the best things in the book pertain to this theme: Auclair's shop with all its orderly arrangement of herbs and medicines; the appointments of his living quarters with everything kept the same from year to year; the entire establishment an exact duplicate of his old shop and home in Paris on the Quai des Célestins; the old customs maintained; the traditions of French cookery carefully passed on from mother to daughter. Also the planting of the Church of Rome in North America is a key to the continuity of tradition and plays a very large role in the novel. Many of the characters are priests and nuns, and the life on the rock centers on the churches and religious observances. Willa Cather writes: "When an adventurer carries his gods with him into a remote and savage country, the colony he founds will, from the beginning, have graces, traditions, riches of the mind and spirit. Its history will shine with bright incidents, slight, perhaps, but precious, as in life itself, where the great matters are often as worthless as astronomical distances, and the trifles dear as the heart's blood."

Shadows on the Rock, while not one of Willa Cather's best novels, has many excellent scenes in it. Her ability to render landscape is superb, and her visits to Quebec at different times of the year resulted in some marvelous evocations of place. The novel opens with the apothecary standing on the top of Cap Diamant gazing down at the empty river after the supply ships have left on a day late in October. He looks down at the "scattered spires and slated roofs flashing in the rich, autumnal sunlight" and beyond to the great river "rolling north toward the purple line of the Laurentian Mountains" and across the river to the black pine forest that comes down to the water's edge. Later Quebec under the deep snows of the long winter is sketched memorably, especially when Cécile and Jacques go coasting on a December afternoon. They slide down the hill from the cathedral still bathed in sunlight "through constantly changing colour; deeper and deeper into violet, blue, purple, until at the bottom it was almost black." As they climb up again, they watch the "last flames of orange light burn off the high points of the rock." The slender spire of the Récollet Chapel, up by the Château, holds the "gleam longest of all." Winter gives way to spring reluctantly in that northern latitude, but finally the snows melt, the first swallow returns, and life begins to stir again. Summer brings the annual return of the supply ships, and on the day the ships are due the entire town turns out in holiday spirit. The great excitement of this event, the gaiety and carnival atmosphere, are vividly created, and the reader shares the deep emotional response of the people, who are for eight months of the year completely cut off from France.

The least satisfactory aspect of this novel is the characterization. Even though the apothecary is colored by Willa Cather's memory of her father, he never seems more than a two-dimensional figure. The relationship between father and daughter is warmly drawn, but Cécile has little reality. She is insufferably pious in town, and when she visits a farmer's family on the Île d'Orléans, she is intolerably priggish. Her friendship for little Jacques is touching, but the youngster, who actually was modeled after Willa Cather's nephew, is unbelievable. Although he is the offspring of a woman of the town, who neglects and mistreats him, he is as devout as Cécile and a sturdy refutation of all the probabilities of heredity and environment. The most interesting and effective characters are the historical figures, old Bishop Laval and old Count Frontenac. Willa Cather made good use of the historical sources for her novel, particularly Francis Parkman, whose view of the count she adopted; but Parkman's anti-Catholic bias sent her to other sources for her clerical character.

Although *Shadows on the Rock* appeared when Willa Cather was not yet sixty, it is an old woman's book and has a distinctly valetudinary flavor. Youthful striving is far behind the author of this novel. Here the emphasis is constantly on order, decorum, and resistance to change; and the central symbol of the novel, the rock, which stands for stability and permanence, also could stand for petrification and intransigence. Mme. Auclair once told her daughter: "Without order our lives would be disgusting, like those of the poor savages." And Cécile will grow to be a woman like her mother with the unattractive characteristics of the bourgeoisie as well as the virtues. She too will adhere blindly to tradition. Auclair, the apothecary, also resists change; but in the novel Willa Cather stacks the cards so that when he says, "I think the methods of the last century better than those of the present time," the statement in context makes him seem right. He is talking to the worldly bishop, who wants him to treat the old bishop with a medical nostrum that anyone in the twentieth century would know to be ridiculous.

During the time that seventeenth-century Quebec was her major preoccupation, Willa Cather also turned her attention to her own past. She wrote four of her best stories in this period, making use in three of them of her memories of her own family, her friends on the Divide, and Red Cloud. The three western stories, which are in her best vein, were collected in *Obscure Destinies* (1932), and the fourth, "Double Birthday," which has a Pittsburgh setting, appeared in *Forum* in 1929 and was never reprinted. Not since 1923, when *A Lost Lady* appeared, had she drawn her literary material from her Nebraska background. Her father's heart attack and subsequent death, her long visits in Red Cloud, and her mother's stroke and illness turned her mind back to her own past. The results were extraordinarily rich and effective—perhaps the last great fiction she wrote.

The first story in *Obscure Destinies* is "Neighbour Rosicky," a long story that stands as a sequel to *My Ántonia*. Although Annie Pavelka's husband sat for the portrait of the Bohemian farmer, Willa Cather's feelings about her father give the tale its power to involve the reader in an intense emotional experience. What she meant by the "gift of sympathy" is nowhere better illustrated than in "Neighbour Rosicky." She mixed her memories of her father into this character much more successfully than she was able to do in the portrayal of the apothecary Auclair. Anton Rosicky is shown in the last few months of his life, and the story is retrospective and elegiac. At the opening of the tale the doctor tells him that he has a bad heart and must no longer work in the fields or run the corn-sheller. He has five strong boys to take care of him and a devoted younger wife. The family, one recognizes, is Ántonia's family some ten years after Jim Burden left them prospering on their farm. The children that Jim saw running up out of the fruit cellar, "a veritable explosion of life out of the dark cave into sunlight," now are between twelve and twenty. Ántonia here is called Mary, an even more appropriate name for the Madonna of the Wheat Fields. The relationship between father and sons, husband and wife, is devoted and sympathetic, and the human equation in the Rosicky family always has taken precedence over the economic one. Rosicky, who would rather put color in his children's faces than sell his cream, has not prospered as have some of his neighbors, who are reminiscent of Nat Wheeler in *One of Ours;* but Rosicky owns his own land and has enjoyed life. The story has little plot, but what it has concerns Rosicky's successful efforts to draw his son's American wife Polly into the Bohemian family circle. The tale ends with Rosicky's fatal heart attack. The doctor, who also is an old friend, pronounces a benediction as he passes the country graveyard that adjoins Rosicky's land. The graveyard was merely a little patch of long grass that the winds stirred. There was nothing overhead but the sky, and "the many-coloured fields running on until they met the sky." Doctor Ed reflects: "Nothing could be more undeathlike than this place; nothing could be more right for a man who had helped to do the work of great cities and had always longed for the open country and had got to it at last. Rosicky's life seemed to him complete and beautiful."

"Old Mrs. Harris" is the story that draws on Grandma Boak and the Cather household at the time Willa went to college. She thought it the best one of the collection and wrote Zoë Akins that in it the right things came together in the right relation. Whether it is a better story than "Neighbour Rosicky" is a matter of individual preference, however; but she was right about the quality of the tale. Grandma Harris is a three-dimensional character, one of the most fully realized in all her fiction, and the ambience of the Cather home is highly evocative. The selfless old woman dies at the end of the tale, not wanting to be a burden to anyone, while her daughter and granddaughter are absorbed in their own problems. Victoria, the daughter, has taken to her bed after discovering that she is going to have another baby, and Vickie, the granddaughter, is annoyed that life at home is in a turmoil just when she must get ready to leave for college. Mrs. Harris slips out of the household, but Victoria and Vickie still have to "follow the long road that leads through things unguessed at and unforeseeable." When they are old they will come closer and closer to Grandma Harris and their lot will be like hers. They will regret that they heeded her so little and will say to themselves: "I was

WILLA CATHER

heartless, because I was young and strong and wanted things so much. But now I know." Willa Cather was in this mood when she wrote Irene Weisz from a train crossing Kansas in 1931 on her way to see her mother for the last time. She felt that she never had been a very thoughtful daughter and had taken her parents for granted. Her mind and heart were always full of her own all-absorbing passions. Soon after she returned East from this last visit to California, she wrote "Old Mrs. Harris."

The last story in *Obscure Destinies* is "Two Friends," which also drew on memories of Red Cloud. It was written during the months she was sitting with her mother in the sanitarium in Pasadena and thinking about her childhood in Nebraska. The story is another of her dramas of memory produced out of the effect the two friends had on her when she was between ten and thirteen. The tale, she explained to Carrie Sherwood, daughter of Mr. Dillon in the story, was not really a picture of her father and his friend but a picture of a memory. Her friends in Red Cloud were always too literal in trying to identify her characters and often complained that she did not get them right. She never could persuade people that stories were made out of emotions and not from the legs and arms and faces of one's friends.

"Double Birthday," never reprinted, probably was written about the same time as "Neighbour Rosicky." It is made out of Willa Cather's memories of Pittsburgh, which by this time had teased her mind long enough to be properly aged. It also revived her interest in singers, though the artistic career it describes is only a small part of the story, and it makes use of a character in Dr. Englehardt that probably owes a good deal to Willa Cather's old doctor-critic-bachelor friend Julius Tyndale of Lincoln. Other characters in the tale besides Dr. Englehardt are Albert, his nephew, Judge Hammersley, and the judge's widowed daughter, Margaret Parmenter. The last two characters are much as Judge McClung and Isabelle might have been, if the judge had lived on into the twenties and Isabelle had returned to Pittsburgh a widow.

The story opens with the judge meeting Albert, who lives with his old bachelor uncle, a retired throat specialist. The Judge strongly disapproves of Albert and his brothers, who ran through their patrimony, a manufacturing business left by their German

240

immigrant father. Albert at fifty-five, a clerk in the courthouse, does not feel sorry for himself. He enjoys life, plays the piano well, and lives quietly in a modest house in an unfashionable part of the city. He and his old uncle celebrate their birthdays on the same day, and the judge, who likes the old man, sends some champagne for the coming birthday party. Margaret Parmenter, who once knew Albert well, also brings the Englehardts her own gift of wine (these are Prohibition days) and is persuaded to stay for dinner. A fine nostalgic scene follows in which they all relive the past, and the reader learns of the great sorrow in the old doctor's life. He formerly specialized in treating singers, and one day discovered a Pittsburgh schoolgirl with a marvelous voice. He sent her to New York to study singing, but she died of cancer on the eve of what promised to be a brilliant career. The old doctor, now eighty, lives on with his memories of what might have been. The entire story is a highly successful remembrance of things past and should be exhumed from the dusty files of the now extinct *Forum*.

After *Obscure Destinies* was published, Willa Cather finally ended her five-year bivouac at the Grosvenor Hotel. The death of her mother put an end to her temporizing, and she finally had to make up her mind what to do next. She told Elizabeth Sergeant shortly after leaving Bank Street that she was undecided about her next residence because she thought she would like to live in the country, but Edith Lewis, who had a job in the city, wanted to go on living there. Willa Cather hated New York by this time, and her letters during the twenties complain bitterly about the increasingly ugly changes that were taking place in the city. As long as she was spending part of the year in California with her mother, she could postpone the decision.

In March 1932 she wrote Zoë Akins a very revealing letter. Zoë suddenly had gotten married in middle age, and Willa wrote a very warm letter of congratulations. She was sorry that she was not going to California again, for she would have liked to see Zoë in her new house with her husband. She had ever so many things she would like to talk over, particularly how the marriage had come about. She had only admiration for her friend, for Zoë was never afraid to take chances. She never was fussy about trifles, and she had a natural ability to enjoy life. Willa envied her. She had come, furthermore, to New York at the right time, left it at the right time, and bought a house at the right time. Willa went on to assert that if she had a little more courage she would quit New York and go to live in San Francisco.

But she did not have the courage to leave and stayed on in New York hating it. In November she finally found an apartment that she liked and signed a lease. Her new address would be 570 Park Avenue, and she moved in before Christmas. She was somewhat embarrassed to be living in an expensive Park Avenue apartment, but if one were going to stay in the city, it was a comfortable place to grow old in. When Elizabeth Sergeant, who was to become an ardent New Dealer, went to see her on Park Avenue, she was ushered into the lobby by a uniformed doorman. Other uniformed attendants seemed chiefly concerned with keeping unwanted people out. She wondered if Anton Rosicky or old Mrs. Harris even would be allowed to enter the building.

—————=⟫⟫⟫⟪Ⓠ⟪⟫⟫⟫⟫=—————

"The Rest Is Silence": 1933–1947

I

WILLA CATHER'S new apartment on Park Avenue was spacious, comfortable, and appropriate for an aging novelist in her affluent old age. She was close to Central Park, which she loved, and well protected from the growing vulgarities of the city and the distressing effects of the deepening Depression. She had picked her apartment mainly because it was quiet and secluded, and the fact that all the windows faced the blank wall of the Colony Club was to her a virtue. The walls and floors were thick, the roar of the avenue was far away, and no heels tramped back and forth over her head. Like Myra Henshawe in *My Mortal Enemy*, she never could stand having people walking about over her, and during her last years on Bank Street she had rented the apartment over hers to eliminate such noise. She bought new furniture for the new apartment, more formal than the old stuff she had used on Bank Street, but the George Sand engraving and the head of Keats went over the mantel as usual. Josephine Bourda, who had retired from service when Willa Cather went to the Grosvenor, now needed a job and came back to work for her.

Although the first birthday she celebrated on Park Avenue was only her sixtieth, she was already an old woman. Her health, which usually had been good, began to break down, and she narrowed her travels mainly to the annual treks to New Brunswick and New England. She wrote Zoë Akins about the time she moved to Park Avenue that life was rather a failure biologically. She added, however, that as one grew older something rather nice happened to the mind. A kind of golden light came as compensation for many losses. As her physical capabilities diminished, she wrote less and less, and during her last fourteen years she completed only two more novels and a few stories. She became increasingly crotchety about invasions of her privacy and made very few public appearances after this time. She became a bit paranoid in her efforts to prevent her works from being filmed, dramatized, anthologized, reprinted in cheap editions, or even read over the air.

She could not help doing a number of things for fame, however, and in 1933 she was persuaded to appear at a semipublic ceremony to accept the *Prix Femina Américain* for *Shadows on the Rock.* She insisted that there be no photographers, but when Edna St. Vincent Millay made the presentation, flash bulbs blazed and she froze into a statue. In the same year she consented to make a brief talk over NBC at a Princeton banquet in New York City. This was reciprocity for her great pleasure two years before when she had received the first honorary Princeton degree ever given to a woman. Charles Lindbergh and Robert Frost, two men she greatly admired, had been on the same commencement program, and she had been charmed to sit next to Lindbergh at a dinner on that occasion. After Princeton, however, only her old friend President William Allan Neilson of Smith College in 1933 managed to give her a final honorary degree. When Brown University later invited her two years in a row to accept another such honor, she first declined, then accepted, and finally had her doctor write that she was too ill to travel to Providence.

During her last fourteen years she lived mostly for her friends. She kept up her correspondence with old associates like Carrie Sherwood, even though she never went back to Red Cloud, and she entertained at tea other old friends like Elizabeth Sergeant, who lived in the New York area. One of her great joys in these years was her relationship with nephews and nieces, especially Mary Virginia Auld, who settled in New York after graduating from Wellesley. Mary Virginia, more like a daughter than a niece, visited her at Grand Manan Island in the summers, helped her shop, looked in on her when she was ill, and kept an eye on her generally. But the most enchanting relationship of all was her friendship with Yehudi Menuhin and his sisters.

Willa Cather met the Menuhin children in Paris in 1930 through Isabelle and Jan Hambourg, and she immediately was captivated

by them. Later when she was in southern California with her
mother, Yehudi was playing there and she got to know him well.
Back in New York she saw the Menuhins frequently during the
subsequent winters. They were the most gifted children she ever
had known, with a "wonderful aura of imaginative charm, pre-
cience, inspiration . . . also extremely lovable, affectionate, and
unspoiled." Her letters during the thirties are filled with admiring
comments about them. When Elizabeth Sergeant went to see Willa
Cather in her new apartment, she found an angelic photograph of
young Yehudi on a table in the living room and heard all about her
friend's rapturous admiration for his musical gifts. Yehudi was
then about sixteen and already a concert violinist of international
reputation. Willa Cather long had been interested in child prodigies, as well as musicians and singers, and she had written in the
Courier in 1895, apropos of Josef Hoffman, who had survived being a prodigy: "There have been certain great men, Mozart and
Paganini chief among them, who have been able to live down the
fact that they once were prodigies, but they had to be great indeed to do it." Yehudi, contrary to the children in her early story
"The Prodigies," also had been great enough to do it. When she
got to know him, she had to revise one of her long-held beliefs
that "art does not come at sixteen." With Yehudi it obviously had
come at least as early as his Carnegie Hall debut at the age of
twelve.

During the winter of 1934 when life seemed terribly com-
plicated and she was unable to work well, she wrote that the
Menuhin family was the bright spot of the winter. They lived
across the park, and the children were coming to her apartment
twice a week to read Shakespeare with her. She had voluntarily
returned to her former role as English teacher to broaden the
literary background of her musical prodigies. But her relationship
was not all literary with the Menuhins. She wrote Carrie Sherwood one February that she had been out in the park all morning
coasting with Yehudi and his sisters. She added that Yehudi stored
his sled with her every winter. They passed spring as well as
winter mornings in the park, and on another occasion she break-
fasted with Yehudi and then spent several hours in the park with
him the day before he sailed for Europe for a summer concert

tour. His whole nature, she wrote, is as beautiful as his face and his talent. Edith Lewis remembers the Menuhin family's winter visits to New York "as a sort of continuous festival, full of concerts and gay parties; orange trees and great baskets of flowers for Willa Cather arriving in the midst of snow-storms; birthday luncheons with Russian caviare and champagne; excursions to the opera . . . long walks around the reservoir in Central Park."

Willa Cather's loyalty to her friends often took the form of private benefactions. She hated the whole concept of the welfare state and disapproved of the Roosevelt Administration, but when her old Nebraska friends were burned out by the drought, she sent an unending stream of checks westward. Old neighbors like the Lambrechts received regular gifts of food, clothes, and money and Annie Pavelka was never overlooked. On one occasion Annie's check went to pay taxes, and on another it bought a washing machine. Many times Willa Cather sent checks to her farmer friends to buy seed during the terrible dry years. Three times at least she saved the farms of her friends by paying the interest on their loans. Nothing, she said, ever gave her more pleasure than helping these people buy the land they had worked since she was ten years old. She wrote Zoë Akins one blistering summer that she felt wicked to be at green and flowery Grand Manan Island and wearing sweaters when so many sad and bitter things were happening to her old friends in Nebraska. She could send them canned fruit and vegetables and checks, but she could not bring back to life their dead trees and ruined pastures. Five terrible years of drought had ruined their farms and their health, and worrying about them had taken all the energy out of her. She also had to worry about her former boss, S. S. McClure, who in his mid-seventies was another Depression victim. The old man had been one of her first dinner guests in the new Park Avenue apartment, and she had spent a very pleasant evening with him in March reminiscing about the old days on the magazine. She must have been startled in the fall to receive a letter from Ida Tarbell asking for a contribution for McClure's support. Miss Tarbell wrote that the old editor was destitute and that she and John Phillips were undertaking to raise enough money to give him an income of one hundred dollars a month, which was to be paid to him by the bank with the donors to remain anonymous. Willa Cather responded promptly and thereafter sent an annual contribution to the fund. Her affection for McClure was undimmed, and in her last public appearance, in 1944, when the National Institute of Arts and Letters awarded her a gold medal, McClure also was on the platform to be honored for his services to journalism and literature. When she met him on the stage, she spontaneously threw her arms around him and hugged him publicly. It was a thoroughly uncharacteristic gesture but indicative of her great affection for the old editor.

Shortly after Willa Cather moved into her new apartment, Dorothy Canfield Fisher was asked by the New York *Herald Tribune* to write a retrospective essay on her old friend's work. Willa said she would rather have Dorothy write it than anyone else and she hoped the legend could be put to rest that she was a pale creature who had sacrificed herself to art. She actually had led a life of indulgence, she said, though she acknowledged the struggles of youth; but then the purpose of youth is struggle. And she never had shut herself off from people she cared for, only the crowd. She was apprehensive about this article, however, and after Dorothy sent a copy of the essay, she apparently fired off a hasty telgram asking her to abandon the project. Later she calmed down and wrote her friend rationally. Articles about herself, she said, made her self-conscious. As soon as she began thinking of herself in the past—in Red Cloud, Colorado, New Mexico—the scenes were spoiled. She had been a jumble of sensations, not a person, and had been running from herself all her life.

Mrs. Fisher wrote in her article: "I offer you a hypothesis about Willa Cather's work: that the one real subject of all her books is the effect a new country—our new country—has on people transplanted to it from the old traditions of a stable, complex civilization." Willa Cather summarized this thesis in one word, "escape," and agreed that this theme ran through all her work, but the summary seemed strange because she never had thought of doing things consistently. Each book had seemed totally new. Yet she often had had the feeling of escape while traveling by train through miles of empty countryside with the sky stretching endlessly ahead and the wind blowing. This was her happiest feeling,

247

one that she had experienced since childhood, a feeling that still made her homesick. If she had stopped to count up, she would have discovered that her novels and stories are full of scenes laid on trains, or in the case of Bishop Latour and his vicar, on mule-back. In 1933, however, this sensation could only be remembered, no longer experienced. She must have realized this with a sort of terror when she first read Mrs. Fisher's article, for she had awakened the next day feeling that life was over, there was no further use in going on, and she might as well lay her ashes beside those of the real pioneers. She felt old and decrepit in her luxuriously upholstered cocoon on Park Avenue.

II

Despite diminished vitality and feeling that life was really over, Willa Cather found that the habits of a lifetime kept her working. Her final visit to Red Cloud at the end of 1931 must have given her an idea for a new novel, for she began work on *Lucy Gayheart* after getting well settled in her new apartment. The new novel was to take place partly in Red Cloud and partly in Chicago and to deal with pianists, a singer, and villagers. It would invite comparison with *The Song of the Lark* but actually would be quite different. The chief character would be a silly young girl to whom unfortunate things happened—exactly the antithesis of Thea Kronborg. Perhaps she was too old to create this sort of unsympathetic heroine, because she began the new novel without the holiday mood that her writing usually induced. She had not yet recovered from the strain of the preceding years, and as Edith Lewis reports, she often wrote "very tired" or "deadly tired" in the line-a-day diary she began keeping about this time. Nevertheless, she worked on *Lucy Gayheart* during the spring, summer, and fall, carrying the manuscript with her to Grand Manan Island, Jaffrey, New Hampshire, and back to Park Avenue.

During the winter some of the misfortunes that she gave her ill-starred heroine overtook her. She tore the big tendon of her left wrist in February and for three months had to have her hand strapped to a thin board day and night. She was not left-handed, but the accident kept her from working until April and put such a strain on her right hand that she could not even write letters. She had to stay in New York until the middle of July to finish the novel before she could leave for New Brunswick and a vacation. But the book did not appear until August 1935, after she had published it serially in the *Woman's Home Companion.* She wished she did not have to serialize the book, but because of the hard times she wanted the extra income to help her friends in Nebraska and to recoup her own losses from gilt-edged bonds that had not withstood the onslaughts of the Depression.

The rather trivial accident to her hand was for Willa Cather a traumatic experience. Since her Virginia childhood when a half-witted boy had threatened to cut off her hand, she had had a horror of mutilation. "But lop away so much as a finger, and you have wounded the creature beyond reparation," she wrote in her early story "The Profile." In "The Bohemian Girl" Eric tears his hand on a corn-sheller, and "Behind the Singer Tower," a story based on a celebrated New York hotel fire, an opera tenor jumps from the burning building, throws out his hand, and it is "snapped off at the wrist as cleanly as if it had been taken off by a cutlass." In *Shadows on the Rock* one of the French missionaries is tormented by the Iroquois, who, after inviting him to a feast, fish a human hand out of the pot. In her unfinished and unpublished last novel, which was laid in medieval Avignon, one of the main characters was hung up by the thumbs for theft and mutilated for life. There are other instances of this sort of thing in Willa Cather's fiction, and in reality her remaining years were plagued by a smashed hand in 1938 and another injury to the tendon of her right wrist while she was writing *Sapphira and the Slave Girl* in 1940.

Lucy Gayheart is a rather conventional novel told in the third person and containing a great deal more plot than Willa Cather usually allowed herself. Where *Shadows on the Rock* was intended to be read slowly around a winter fire, she said, *Lucy Gayheart* was meant to be read at a gallop. Except for the opening pages, Book I, more than half of the novel, takes place in Chicago, where Lucy is a piano teacher and student of Paul Auerbach. Lucy meets Clement Sebastian, American-born baritone, who engages her to be his rehearsal accompanist. Lucy falls in love with Sebastian, whose uncongenial wife stays in France while he fulfills concert engagements in America. The baritone is captivated by Lucy's youth, vitality, and adoration and tells her he loves her. Then he goes off to Europe on a summer concert tour, planning to see Lucy again in the fall, and while vacationing at Lake Como is drowned. In Book II Lucy returns to Haverford, Nebraska, and from September until Christmas silently drags her broken heart about the prairie village. By the first of the year (1902), however, she is ready to face life again, writes Auerbach to ask for her old job in his studio, and plans to return to Chicago in March to resume her musical career. Later in the winter she goes skating on the river, not knowing it has changed course since she left home, skates into the main channel where the ice is thin, breaks through, and is drowned. Book III, which takes place twenty-five years later, is narrated from the point of view of Harry Gordon, Lucy's old lover, who has carried the torch for her ever since her death. He had gone to Chicago to propose to her just at the time she was falling in love with Sebastian. She had dismissed him, and in pique he had married a woman he did not love. After Lucy's return from Chicago he had stubbornly refused to be friendly to her because of injured vanity even though she had needed him and had tried desperately to reach out to him.

This story had its genesis in the memory of a Red Cloud girl named Sadie Becker, who had been the accompanist of a popular local singer, had been disappointed in love, and had gone off to study music. When Harry Gordon as a middle-aged banker remembers the "girl he had seen in the skating-rink, gliding about to the music in her red jersey," it is Willa Cather recalling Lucy Gayheart's prototype. Several years after writing the novel, Willa Cather wrote her old friend Carrie Sherwood wanting to know if Sadie Becker actually had golden-brown eyes. The picture of her was perfectly clear when she was writing the book, but since then she had been having doubts. She could hear Sadie's contralto laugh, however, just as clearly as when she was twelve years old.

There is also the suggestion of Lucy Gayheart's character in a story written during the *McClure's* period, "The Joy of Nelly Deane." This tale, which Willa Cather never reprinted, depicts a gay, talented, vibrant young woman who charms all the matrons of the village, as Lucy does during her adolescent years. She also has a beautiful untrained voice and loves to go skating. She even breaks through the ice on a couple of her madcap adventures and is disappointed in love. Her tragedy, however, is entirely different from Lucy's. After being jilted by a traveling salesman, she marries a dour merchant, settles down to the dull existence of the small town, and dies in childbirth. The story is told retrospectively by a friend who returns years later to the prairie village, and in narrative form it invites comparison with the last book of *Lucy Gayheart*.

Willa Cather knew that *Lucy Gayheart* was not up to her usual standard and admitted as much to close associates. She was pleased that her musical friends like Myra Hess and the Hambourgs thought highly of the novel, and she no doubt was gratified that the book quickly climbed to the top of the best-seller list and stayed there for weeks. But she probably was not surprised that a good many reviewers ranked the novel low among her productions. Stephen Vincent Benét in the New York *Herald Tribune* thought it was one of her rare failures, William Troy in the *Nation* called it a grave disappointment, and even J. Donald Adams in *The New York Times* had reservations. An anonymous reviewer for the *Christian Science Monitor* wrote: "One does not get the impression that the hand of the potter shook, but only that it grew weary, and rounded off its work in haste." There was no faulting Willa Cather's narrative skill or her competent prose; the difficulty lay elsewhere.

When the manuscript was nearly completed she wrote Zoë Akins that she had lost patience with her silly young heroine. This is a surprising statement to come from a novelist who knew that she only wrote well when she dealt with characters she loved and admired. Lucy's story does not grip the reader the way Thea Kronborg's and Marian Forrester's do, and the best explanation is that the author could not kindle an emotional response because she did not feel it herself. Sadie Becker was only an acquaintance, not an old friend, and the performance is one of the head rather than of the heart. The only scene in the entire book that is full of passion is Lucy's desperate plea to her sister Pauline not to cut down the old apple orchard to make an onion patch. This is Willa

Cather herself pleading, and the emotional intensity is white-hot. Elsewhere the novel throws off sparks but emits little heat.

The love affair between Lucy and Sebastian is quite unconvincing. Of course, it is the infatuation of a foolish girl for a middle-aged man, and the reader knows it can only bring grief; but Willa Cather never makes one feel the girl's predicament. She disapproves of the silly infatuation just as much as any older reader would. The result is that Lucy's story never rises above a sort of symbolic tale of youthful frustration and defeat, and Lucy never comes alive. Where Thea Kronborg is a flesh-and-blood character, Lucy Gayheart is a pallid, disembodied spirit. Lucy does not have the talent of Thea, and her story is not the successful struggle of a great artist, but the difference in character should not have made the difference between unreality and reality, sentimentality and sentiment.

There are a good many places in this novel, unfortunately, where the sentiment spills over into sentimentality. When Sebastian, for example, invites Lucy to tea in his apartment shortly after she has blurted out to him the secret of her love, he says: "Don't be frightened, Lucy. I am not going to make love to you. Though it's true I love you." Then he sits down on the arm of her chair, and she shrinks away. "Why do you crouch away from me like that?" he asks, and then adds: "And your little hands are so cold." This speech sounds appropriate enough coming from Rudolfo when he and Mimi hunt for her key in the dark, but it needs Puccini's music to make it go.

The novel has a basic integrity, however, in its development toward the accidental drowning at the end of Book II. Lucy trails her bleeding heart about Haverford only from September until Christmas. At the time she dies, she has recovered from her romance and is determined to return to Chicago and to get on with her career. Although some of the town busybodies hint that her death was suicide, Willa Cather makes it quite clear that Lucy was not the type. Her brutal rebuff by Harry Gordon just before she dies adds pathos to the story but has nothing to do with her drowning. The incident was probably invented to provide motivation for the last book, in which Harry is seen living out a lifetime of regret. This coda to the story, which shows Harry at the end hanging onto the old Gayheart place as a souvenir and preserving the sidewalk with Lucy's bare footprints in the cement, is surely a false note.

There are a great many things about the novel, however, that are very good Willa Cather. Nothing from her pen ever was clumsily constructed or slovenly written, and *Lucy Gayheart* has structure, disciplined prose, well-rendered landscape, and a gallery of well-drawn minor characters. Willa Cather's second-best work is still first-rate by the standards of most novelists. The opening scene on the river evokes her youthful memories of skating on the Republican River, one of Willa Cather's favorite pastimes. The picture of Lucy and Harry flashing over the ice arm in arm is a memorable creation. As they sit down to rest and have a drink: "The round red sun was falling like a heavy weight; it touched the horizon line and sent quivering fans of red and gold over the wide country. For a moment Lucy and Harry Gordon were sitting in a stream of blinding light; it burned on their skates and on the flask and the metal cup. Their faces became so brilliant that they looked at each other and laughed." This is an appropriate opening for a story that ends a year later with a procession of wagons crawling back to town from the river through the winter night carrying Lucy's body.

Scenes in Haverford, which is Red Cloud, even though located on the Platte River, also are effectively rendered: Lucy as a child skipping gaily through town, old Mrs. Ramsay sitting in her window watching Lucy and everyone else go by, the Gayheart house on the edge of town, and others. Minor characters like sister Pauline, Mrs. Ramsay, giddy little Fairy Blair, and Harry's cashier at the bank, Milton Chase, are authentic bit players. Old Jacob Gayheart, the gentle German watchmaker and flute-playing father, is especially good, and the relationship between Lucy and her father has the tenderness of Auclair's relationship with Cécile and Willa Cather's memories of her father. It is interesting to note that in both *Shadows on the Rock* and *Lucy Gayheart* the father is a widower.

After finishing *Lucy Gayheart*, it was three years before she was able to begin another novel. She devoted most of 1935 to Isabelle Hambourg, who came to the United States in March to consult

American doctors for a malady that proved to be incurable. She spent most of April and part of May visiting Isabelle daily in a New York hospital while Jan Hambourg was off on a concert tour to make some money. When Jan went to Chicago to teach a summer course and Isabelle insisted on joining her husband there, Willa Cather went with her friend. In August the Hambourgs returned to Europe, and Willa followed them a few days later. She rested up at Cortina d'Ampezzo in the Dolomites of northern Italy and later in Venice, then paid a visit to the Hambourgs in France. When she returned to the United States, she knew that she probably would not see Isabelle again. Isabelle, she had written Zoë Akins in April, was the sweetest and most appreciative invalid and one of the noblest creatures in the world. To look out for her was one of the deepest satisfactions of her life. Isabelle died in Sorrento three years later.

During the next year Willa Cather managed to produce a book for Knopf's fall list, *Not Under Forty*, her only collection of essays; but all the pieces except the one on Thomas Mann had been published previously. The essays on Mrs. Fields ("148 Charles Street"), Sarah Orne Jewett, and Katherine Mansfield were revised and expanded from their earlier forms, and the collection includes also the account of meeting Mme. Franklin Grout and the well-known essay "The Novel Démeublé." It is a good book, except for the title, and that she changed to *Literary Encounters* in her collected works. Her one-paragraph prefatory note, which contains the oft-quoted sentence about the world breaking in two in 1922, has in its brevity a rather chip-on-the-shoulder air reflecting her mood of the hour. She places herself squarely with the people over forty, for whom the book was issued. Thomas Mann, she admits, belongs to the "forward-goers," but he also goes back a long way and it is his backwardness that interests her. "It is for the backward, and by one of their number, that these sketches were written," she concludes somewhat truculently.

Her mood of the mid-thirties is further underscored by the new material she added to her essay on Sarah Orne Jewett. A taste for Miss Jewett's work, she writes, "must always remain a special taste" because "she wrote for a limited audience." This defensive attitude no doubt reflects her feeling about her own work, as some of the younger critics in the ideological thirties were beginning to attack her books. It is easy to see, she notes, why some of the younger generation have turned away from artists like Miss Jewett [and Willa Cather]: "Imagine a young man, or woman, born in New York City, educated at a New York university, violently inoculated with Freud, hurried into journalism, knowing no more about New England country people . . . than he has caught from motor trips . . . [W]hat is there for him in *The Country of the Pointed Firs*?" This is the voice of an elderly midwesterner nurtured in rural America and growing old in the sprawling megalopolis of the urban East with its hordes of unassimilated Jews, Italians, and Negroes.

She had other comments to make about the issues that were troubling writers and critics of the thirties. When the editor of *Commonweal* asked her to comment on art as escape, she unloaded both barrels in a long letter to the magazine. When was art ever anything but an escape? she began. The arts of primitive man did not come into existence as a means of increasing the game supply or of promoting tribal security. "They sprang from an unaccountable predilection of the one unaccountable thing in man"— that is, the desire to create. The condition every art requires, she went on, is "not so much freedom from restriction, as freedom from adulteration and from the intrusions of foreign matter." And she concludes the paragraph: "Economics and art are strangers." This was her answer to critics like Granville Hicks, who had accused her of falling into "supine romanticism because of a refusal to examine life as it is." She had no use for writers who enlisted their creativity in the cause of reform, but her position on these matters had not changed. She had consistently opposed mixing propaganda with literature since her days on *McClure's*, when muckraking was riding high. Yet she clearly found herself on the other side of the generation gap of the thirties, as she admits in her prefatory note to *Not Under Forty*.

Life was not all bleak in the mid-thirties, however, for she rekindled her old interest in music. During the years she camped out at the Grosvenor Hotel she heard very little music, but after meeting the Menuhins and moving into her Park Avenue apartment she began attending concerts. Opera, her former love, gave way

---

to instrumental music, both symphony concerts and chamber ensembles. The Knopfs gave her an expensive phonograph, and Yehudi Menuhin sent her all his recordings. She got great comfort from the late Beethoven quartets and enjoyed playing her records with friends like Ethel Litchfield, who had come to New York to live after her husband's death. Through her she met Joseph Lhevinne and never missed one of his concerts. Myra Hess, whom she met at the Knopfs', became a friend, and Harold Samuels, who played Bach beautifully, sometimes came to tea.

Although the creative fires were burning low at this time, she did write one long story in 1936. This is "The Old Beauty," a nostalgic tale laid in Aix-les-Bains in that fateful (for her) year 1922, the year before she had been there for the baths. The story is not vintage Cather, and when Gertrude Lane, editor of the *Woman's Home Companion* was offered the story, she said she would print it though she did not like it very well. Willa Cather then asked her to return the manuscript and never published the story anywhere. It finally appeared in print posthumously in *The Old Beauty and Others* with two additional stories written shortly before she died.

Willa Cather, according to Miss Lewis, thought highly of "The Old Beauty," but few readers today are likely to think it confronts time and change very serenely. The nostalgia it evokes is not for a heroic age of pioneers but the world of society and the affairs of men in the 1890's. The story is told in a series of flashbacks largely from the point of view of an American businessman, aged fifty-five, who encounters the old beauty at Aix during the last summer of her life. As a young man, he had known her as Lady Longstreet when she was in her prime. As he thinks about her, he reflects: "Plain women . . . when they grow old are—simply plain women. . . . But a beautiful woman may become a ruin." This is the case with the once-dazzling Gabrielle Longstreet. The ruin is symbolic, as the reader discovers during the course of the tale, for Gabrielle's world also lies in ruins, and she lives with her memories and travels with the pictures of her now-deceased friends. While she is still a *grande dame*, she has no sympathy for or understanding of the younger generation—only a sort of disinterested disgust. Cherry Beamish, her companion, who was once a music hall comedienne, also has grown old, but she has kept in touch with youth through her many nephews and nieces. She too is nostalgic for the good old days, and her attitude more generally reflects Willa Cather's views than that of Gabrielle, who is an extreme case. There is no doubt that Willa Cather accomplished what she set out to do in this story—create a mood and evoke an era long past. The trouble with the story, which Gertrude Lane no doubt felt, is that no one really cares very much—except Gabrielle —about the world she has lost.

During most of 1937 Willa Cather devoted her attention to preparing a complete edition of her works. Maxwell Perkins of Scribner's proposed the project to Knopf, who did not publish subscription editions, and offered liberal terms; but Houghton Mifflin, which held the rights to the first four novels, wanted to bring out the edition. Knopf worked out the details with Houghton Mifflin, told Willa Cather he wanted her to do it, and she reluctantly consented. Bruce Rogers was commissioned to design the books, and the collected works came out both in a library edition and in a handsome limited edition of 970 autographed and numbered copies. This set was issued in twelve volumes in 1937–1938 and increased to thirteen with the addition of *Sapphira and the Slave Girl* in 1941.

Willa Cather should have been greatly pleased with the project, but she wrote Zoë Akins a rather querulous letter in November. Nothing disturbed her more, she said, than to work with Houghton Mifflin, and now she was back in their net because Knopf said she had to do it. The whole affair had given her a hell of a spring and summer and now was breaking into her winter. She had started a new book and God and man were conspiring to keep her from working on it. All she wanted was to be left alone to write. Then she added that the movies were after *My Ántonia* and she was in terror that Houghton Mifflin would sell her out. They could have, but they did not.

The chance to issue a complete edition of her works, despite her disclaimers, gave her an opportunity to manage the canon of her writings. She made *O Pioneers!* Volume I and moved *Alexander's Bridge* to III, where it was combined with *April Twilights*. She was able to drop additional poems that she no longer cared for, and she was able to present *The Song of the Lark* with the cuts she had already made for the 1932 reissue. *My Ántonia* also appeared with a revised introduction written in 1926, and she was able to make further changes in "A Wagner Matinee," "The Sculptor's Funeral," "Paul's Case," and to drop " 'A Death in the Desert' " entirely. She also dropped the epigraph by Christina Rossetti from *Youth and the Bright Medusa*, in which these stories appeared, and she eliminated the prickly prefatory note to *Not Under Forty* when she changed it to *Literary Encounters.*

Although she started *Sapphira and the Slave Girl* in the fall of 1937, she did not finish the novel until three years later. Life, death, and nature conspired against her. Her beloved brother Douglass from California visited her on her birthday in December, and they had a happy time together. She stuffed the turkey, because her French maid could not do it for Douglass the way Grandma Boak used to, and the two relived the days of their youth in Red Cloud. The following June without warning Douglass died of a heart attack, and Willa was too crushed to go to the funeral. Four months later word came from Jan Hambourg that Isabelle had died in Sorrento. Although this death was not unexpected, the sense of loss was no easier to bear. Now of the people in her life closest to her only her brother Roscoe was left. She went to Jaffrey, New Hampshire, that fall hardly knowing how she could go on living, and found there that the great hurricane of September had wrecked the woods for miles around. In mid-November she was still in a comatose state and unable to feel anything. The following year the Second World War broke out, and when France fell to Hitler's armies, she wrote in her line-a-day diary: "There seems to be no future at all for people of my generation."

III

She worked doggedly at her new novel during all these catastrophes as though her only salvation lay in continuing the work in progress. She stayed on in New York well into July during both 1938 and 1939 in order to work on the book. She finally finished the novel at Grand Manan Island in September 1940, and Knopf hurriedly got the book out in time for the Christmas trade in December. Knowing the circumstances under which *Sapphira and the Slave Girl* was written, one would not expect the work to rank high among Willa Cather's productions, but this is not the case. The novel is austerely written, a cool performance, and lacks the passion of her best works; but it is the output of a disciplined intelligence. Somehow she summoned hidden reserves and produced one last novel of undeniable excellence.

Sapphira and the Slave Girl, except for the epilogue described in Chapter 1, takes place in 1856 in the Shenandoah Valley of Willa Cather's early childhood. Sapphira Dodderidge Colbert is an imperious old woman, semi-invalid, who originally came from Loudoun County on the Potomac. She has inexplicably married Henry Colbert, a miller, and taken her husband and twenty slaves to live at Back Creek on property that she has inherited. Her widowed daughter Rachel Blake lives nearby with her children, and the story opens with a breakfast-table scene between Sapphira and Henry. The marriage has been one of form mostly, with Sapphira managing the farm efficiently and Henry running the mill. He spends his time in the millhouse, and each goes his own way. At the breakfast table the reader learns that Sapphira wants to sell her housemaid Nancy, a very attractive, bright mulatto girl who is the by-blow of an itinerant portrait-painter and old Till, the housekeeper. Henry will not hear of such a sale. He is very fond of Nancy, who besides being a lady's maid also acts as housekeeper for him at the mill. Sapphira is jealous of the girl— apparently with some reason.

From this situation develops an increasingly tense relationship between husband and wife with Nancy as the pawn. Sapphira, since she cannot sell the girl without Henry's approval, sets about to get rid of her in some other way. She invites Henry's handsome, wastrel nephew to visit and plans to give him every opportunity either to seduce or to rape Nancy. Martin Colbert comes and pursues Nancy as expected, but he is circumvented one way or another until finally Mrs. Blake plans a midnight escape and takes the girl to free soil where she makes her way to Canada via the Underground Railroad. The one thing that Sapphira never counted on was that her own daughter, even though she had Yankee ideas, would steal a slave with the connivance of her own husband. Henry, to be sure, is too much of a southerner to aid his daughter openly, but he puts money in his coat, which he leaves hanging near an open window on the night the escape is planned.

As we have noted, the story of *Sapphira and the Slave Girl* was ready made. When Willa Cather sent Viola Roseboro' an advance copy of the novel, she wrote that the story was so largely made up of family and neighborhood stories that she scarcely knew where her own contribution to it began. Willa Cather's great-grandparents, Jacob and Ruhamah Seibert, supplied the prototypes for Henry and Sapphira Colbert; Mrs. Blake, of course, was Grandmother Boak; and Till and Nancy appear in the novel without name change. The setting at Willow Shade, called the Mill House in the novel, the old mill on Back Creek, and the countryside all come from the author's memories of Virginia. They were refreshed by a visit to the area that Willa Cather and Edith Lewis made in the spring of 1938, but the novel was planned and begun before this return took place.

Readers often wonder why Willa Cather waited until the end of her career before she made use of Virginia as a setting for a novel, or conversely why she ever turned to her early memories at all since she had not used them in mid-career. She said on several occasions that the years from eight to fifteen are the years when a writer gathers his thematic material, and she was only nine when the family left Back Creek. Yet the story was all there in her mind fifty-nine years after Nancy came home, and she had gone back to Virginia to visit her Aunt Gore and to see the places of her childhood almost as soon as she left Red Cloud to work in Pittsburgh. Her family kept up with relatives and old friends in Virginia and subscribed to the Winchester newspaper. The answer must lie in her reaction to Virginia and the South when she went back again in 1913 just after she had discovered Nebraska as her great subject and had published *O Pioneers!*

On the occasion of her return she wrote Elizabeth Sergeant that she no longer cared at all about the holy and sacred peculiarities of the people she had known when she was little. She was eager to get away from the romantic southern attitude. The people she really loved as a child were all dead, and the southern male she found cowed and housebroken and good for nothing but to carry wraps and dance. When she moved from Winchester to the Valley Home Inn at Gore, she liked the area better. The mountains were still beautiful, and the weather was rainy. Since she liked nothing better than tramping about the mountains in wet weather, the trip was not a total loss.

There is an interesting foreshadowing of Willa Cather's lack of sympathy for the South, however, even in her early childhood. She told Edith Lewis that she always had felt something smothering in the polite social conventions of southern society and that if one fell in with all the sentimental attitudes and euphemisms one lost touch with reality. Once an old judge had come to Willow Shade to visit. He stroked her curls and talked to her in the playful platitudes that southern convention prescribed for little girls. She recalled shocking her southern mother by exclaiming to the startled judge: "I'se a dang'ous nigger, I is!" But there was nothing of the social rebel in Willa Cather; only a desire for honesty and forthrightness.

By 1937 New York had grown hateful to her, she no longer was going back to Nebraska, and she had not seen the Southwest for a decade. She loved the Northeast but already had used French Canada as a locale and probably felt timid about competing with Sarah Orne Jewett in a New England setting. By a process of elimination only Virginia was left out of her usable past and present. But she also seems to have felt at this time that the South represented a bastion of tradition in a changing world. When Viola Roseboro' praised the novel, Willa Cather was delighted because she had hoped her friend, who also was a southerner in origin, would find the book true to that civilization which was, in Miss Roseboro's term, so "pleasantly surfaced." She also revealed that writing the book had eased the hurt of bitter sorrow, because when the present was painful, it was a help to turn back to those early memories. When she revisited Virginia in the spring of 1938, Miss Lewis remembers, "it was as memorable an experience, as intense and thrilling in its way, as those journeys into New Mexico, when she was writing the *Archbishop*." She found wild azaleas growing on the gravelly banks of the road up Timber Ridge and the dogwood blooming in the still leafless woods. The countryside and her old home were much changed, but she looked through and beyond them into the past.

The quality of *Sapphira and the Slave Girl* does not rest on any one of the elements of setting, character, or plot. All three are blended together in a successful compound and mutually reinforce each other. The delight that Willa Cather felt in visiting the Shenandoah Valley again is obvious in the skillful rendering of place. The house, the mill, the road up Timber Ridge, the woods, the wheat field, the wild flowers, the village of Back Creek—all these things spring to life under the author's sensuous prose. Miss Lewis reports that the original draft of the novel contained two or three times as much as was finally kept, and surely most of the excised material was setting.

The novel also contains good characterization, particularly in Sapphira, the cool, crafty antiheroine. Her relationship with her daughter, husband, and slaves rings true. She was capable of having Nancy debauched in order to get rid of her, but she also knew how to manage her slaves and felt a sense of *noblesse oblige*. She treats Tansy Dave, a half-witted field hand who keeps running away, with singular indulgence, and she has real affection for Till and Till's mother, Old Jezebel, an African-born slave who dies at the age of ninety-five. She takes part in celebrations and likes to see her people happy. "On Christmas morning she sat in the long hall and had all the men on the place come in to get their Christmas drink. She served each man a strong toddy in one of the big glass tumblers that had been her father's. When Tap, the mill boy, smacked his lips and said: 'Miss Sapphy, if my mammy's titty had a-tasted like that, I never would a-got weaned,' she laughed as if she had never heard the old joke before."

The plot of *Sapphira and the Slave Girl* could easily have become melodrama, but the key is kept low, and the action never runs away with the development of character and situation. Yet the conflicts in the story and the escape, no matter how much they are held under control, are dramatic. The story develops in a leisurely fashion, typical of Willa Cather, but without digressions. The narrative insertions are all flashbacks to fill in the background of various characters. The narrative method is third-person, which Willa Cather always believed proper for a story of action, and gives her a chance to move in and out of the consciousnesses of the main characters, the miller, Sapphira, and Rachel Blake. The deliberate pacing provides an opportunity to create a vivid impression of life on the Colbert place, and interludes such as Book III, which deals with Jezebel's death, or Book IV, which shows Mrs. Blake traveling about ministering to the sick, contribute effectively to the book's verisimilitude.

A novel laid in the South five years before the Civil War cannot help dealing with the issue of slavery. Willa Cather, however, keeps polemics out of her fiction by design and is primarily interested in creating a picture of western Virginia as it must have been in 1856. She had the racial attitudes one would expect in an elderly midwesterner in the thirties, that is to say, a theoretical belief in complete equality and a practical acquaintance with Negroes only as servants or laborers. Her sympathies in the novel are clearly with Mrs. Blake, with Nancy's desire to escape, and with the miller's dilemma. The miller, who lives uncomfortably with slavery, worries that Nancy may be going to a worse life in a northern city than she is escaping from. She will have "to make her own way in this world where nobody is altogether free. . . . Sapphira's darkies were better cared for, better fed and better clothed, than the poor whites in the mountains. Yet what ragged, shag-haired, squirrel-shooting mountain man would change places with Sampson, his trusted head miller?"

Publication day for *Sapphira and the Slave Girl* was December seventh, Willa Cather's sixty-seventh birthday. The strain of finishing the book had caused severe inflammation of the tendon of her right thumb, and when the book appeared she was wearing her arm in a sling and her hand bandaged to a splint. The reviews were mostly flattering; in fact, she thought the novel had a better press than any of her previous books. Morton Zabel in the *Nation*, for example, ranked the novel as one of her five best, and Henry Canby in the *Saturday Review of Literature* wrote a notice that she found so sound and discerning that she sent copies to friends. By the time the reviews were appearing, however, she was in the French Hospital in New York and under the care of an orthopedic surgeon. After spending the Christmas holidays and part of January in the hospital, she went back to her apartment with her hand

in a specially designed steel and leather brace. She had to wear
the brace for eight months, and since she found it impossible to
dictate anything more than letters, she could do no creative writing that year.

Despite her physical affliction the summer of 1941 was a joyful
time. She went to California to visit her brother Roscoe, who had
been ill in the spring. She was determined to see him one more
time and undertook her last long journey to do it. Edith Lewis
went with her because she had to have a companion and could not
even dress herself, but the trip was a great success. They took the
Santa Fe from Chicago and once again traveled across New Mexico and Arizona, the country she loved best. It was June, and the
acacias were in bloom. There had been plenty of rain the preceding winter, and the land was green and inviting. Willa Cather
knew that she was seeing for the last time the land she had written about in *Death Comes for the Archbishop*. In California her
destination was San Francisco, where she stayed at the Fairmont
Hotel for a month. Her brother and his wife came down from
Colusa to join her, and they had a completely satisfying reunion.
When she returned East, she went by way of Vancouver and the
Canadian Rockies, but the return trip was exhausting and far less
pleasant than the journey out. Canada already was in the war, and
the movement of military personnel and matériel was disrupting
civilian life. She and Miss Lewis had to cross the continent in a
Pullman car that had been returned to service after twenty years
of retirement.

Willa Cather's great happiness in seeing her brother again is
clearly revealed in "The Best Years," one of the stories collected
posthumously in *The Old Beauty and Others*. Although she waited
four years before writing the tale, it was inspired by the happy
month she and Roscoe spent together in San Francisco. The story
is a poignant evocation of the Cather family home when Willa and
her brothers were growing up and sharing that long, dormitory-
like attic that was their world. The central figure is a sixteen-year-
old girl, Lesley Ferguesson, who has gotten a job as a rural
schoolteacher to help out her family. Most of the story depicts a
week end she spends at home with her four brothers, all of whom
she adores and misses dreadfully when she is boarding out in the

country during the school term. She is especially close to the old-est boy, Hector, who in action is practical and executive but in mind is a dreamer. This seems a good likeness of Willa Cather's brother Roscoe. After the idyllic week end and a short Christmas Eve section showing Hector on his rounds as telegraph messenger boy, the story moves to Lincoln later in the winter. Miss Evange-line Knightly, the county superintendent and friend of Lesley Ferguesson, is caught there while a great blizzard paralyzes the country. When the trains begin running again and Miss Knightly can return to MacAlpin (Red Cloud), she learns that Lesley caught pneumonia in her lonely schoolhouse and died during the storm. In an epilogue twenty years later the former superintendent goes back to visit and finds that all the boys turned out well and they cherish the memory of their devoted sister. It is a beautiful little story with the genuine Cather tone of elegy and exquisite regret.

Willa Cather finished this tale shortly before she received a telegram saying that Roscoe had died. She then was vacationing at Northeast Harbor, Maine, where she went when wartime short-ages made it impossible to return to Grand Manan Island. His death, she said, broke the last spring in her and she no longer cared about writing. Even though she was well along with another novel, her story laid in medieval Avignon, she no longer had the heart or energy to put her manuscript into final shape for Knopf to publish. Douglass's death in 1938 had been a crushing blow, but she had quarreled twice with Douglass. Between Roscoe and her there never had been the slightest cloud, and never a fort-night went by that they did not write each other. His death sev-ered the last close link with her past.

Between her visit to see Roscoe in California and his death four years later Willa Cather lived in quiet seclusion. The year 1942 was a hard one, for she had to have a gall-bladder operation in July, and she did not fully recover her health after that. She never looked or acted like an invalid, however, and with old friends her conversation never lost its animation and vivacity. She read and thought a lot during the last years, and though she had to wear her brace off and on for the rest of her life, she wrote a great many letters by dictation. Her correspondence burgeoned in these years, particularly after she was persuaded to let her books be published in armed forces editions. She began getting letters from servicemen from all over the world, and she did her bit for the war effort by answering as many as possible. It was difficult for an old woman to keep house during the war, but she did not complain very much. She and Miss Lewis got their own breakfasts and then wandered about the Godforsaken city looking for decent places to have dinner.

Willa Cather did not talk about the war very often, but in letters to old friends she revealed her intense concern. The war touched her closely because husbands of nieces were in the services and all the younger members of her family had their lives disrupted in one way or another. She wrote Viola Roseboro' in February 1944 that she had been thinking a great deal lately about the death of the world they had known and had thought would last forever. Why should the beautiful old cities that were a thousand years in the making have to come tumbling down in their brief lifetime? Why did they have to live to see countries sponged off the map as they used to erase them from the schoolroom blackboard? She had heard Sir James Jeans say once in a lecture: "Next to man's longing for personal immortality, he longs to feel that his world is immortal and will go on indefinitely as he has known it." Yet in all the countless years this little moment was the witness to everything laid waste.

No one was doing what he wanted to do, was intended to do, or had prepared to do. She had received letters from two young Amherst College professors written from the mud of Guadalcanal. Her dearest young niece knew only that her husband was on an aircraft carrier "somewhere in the Pacific." She felt bitter because so many of the boys from Red Cloud had been shunted out to the terrible islands of the Pacific. To be killed may be uncomfortable, she wrote, but to lie in slime and to be eaten up by bugs is a punishment no boy deserves. She was feeling strongly the outrageousness of fate. In another letter of this period she asked Alexander Woollcott why this little planet was not left empty of life like the rest of the solar system.

She also was feeling outraged that science and technology had brought man to the abyss. She concluded her letter to Miss Roseboro' by accusing the world's smart scientists of bringing about this fate, and one cannot help being reminded of her persona Professor St. Peter lecturing his students on science versus art and religion. He did not think much of science as a phase of human development. Art and religion, which came to the same thing in the end, he asserted, had given man the only happiness he ever had known. At the conclusion of his lecture St. Peter ironically says to a student: "You might tell me next week, Miller, what you think science has done for us, besides making us very comfortable."

This mood of anger and despair permeates the next-to-last story Willa Cather completed, "Before Breakfast," written in the same year as the above letter and also included in *The Old Beauty and Others.* This is a bleak tale laid on Grand Manan Island, in which an aging businessman, Henry Grenfell, senior partner of a brokerage house, reflects on life and death in his cabin and in a before-breakfast walk along the cliffs. His island cabin, which tallies exactly with Willa Cather's cottage, lies in a small clearing between a spruce wood and the sea about fifty yards back from a red sandstone cliff that drops two hundred feet to a narrow beach. Grenfell is out of sorts with the world. He comes to the island each year to get away from his family and his business. His wife is a terribly efficient person, his sons have turned out well, one of them being a distinguished physicist, but they are cold as ice. The father is the only humanist of the bunch, despite the fact he has fought his way up in business, and one of the books he brings with him is *Henry IV, Part I.* Normally he loves getting back to the rocky, wooded island, but the night before he had ridden across the Bay of Fundy on a ferry with a geologist who had annoyed him greatly by giving him the geologic history of the island. The scientist had taken all the romance out of his hideaway and put him in a foul mood. He gets up early and is about to insert his eye drops, but he does not squeeze the bulb. He looks out toward the eastern horizon as dawn is beginning to break. There is a red streak on the water, a fleecy rose cloud in the sky, and Venus shining in the brightening sky. "Merciless perfection, ageless sovereignty. . . . Poor Grenfell and his eye-drops!" He is overwhelmed by human frailty in the face of nature. "Why patch up? What was the use . . . of anything?"

When he goes for his walk before breakfast, he sees someone down on the shingle beach. It is a girl, the daughter of the geologist he had met. She is preparing for a morning dip. He is appalled at the thought of anyone trying to swim in that cold water, but he is powerless to stop her. She opens her robe, shivers, closes it, and then steps out of it. He sees she is wearing a pink bathing suit. "If a clam stood upright and graciously opened its shell, it would look like that," Grenfell thinks. She plunges in, struggles to a rock offshore, rests a moment there, and then weaves her way back. He thinks she is crazy to pull such a stunt. It is surely foolhardy, but her triumphant emergence from the sea somehow changes his mood. He returns to his cabin hungry and ready to face the world. Life will go on. That girl on the beach, like the first creatures that crawled out of the primèval seas, will endure. Willa Cather would have applauded William Faulkner's Nobel Prize speech in 1950, in which he said that not only would man endure but that he would prevail. Grenfell also thinks as he walks back to his cabin: "Plucky youth is more bracing than enduring age."

From the death of Roscoe until Willa Cather's own death "the rest is silence," to quote one of her favorite lines from *Hamlet*. She was only seventy-two, but her health was steadily deteriorating. She did no more writing and did not revise the unfinished novel about Avignon. During the last eighteen months of her life she was calmly waiting for the end. She was never bedridden, and she continued to see friends. She wrote Zoë Akins early in 1945 that she had gotten a good deal of what she had wanted out of life. Above all, she had escaped the things she violently did not want, such as too much money, noisy publicity, the bother of meeting lots of people. She was reasonably satisfied with her career, and her last letters do not suggest in any way that she felt unfulfilled. She had worked hard, and she knew that her accomplishments were significant.

In May 1946 she wrote that she had been in disgrace with herself all winter and that there had been no spring. She had influenza in February, and it lasted until April. She spent a month at Atlantic City but got no good from it. She could not pull up from the deaths of her brothers, who had shared so much of her life with her, and her oldest and dearest friend Isabelle. The one bright spot of the ugly winter was the presence of Yehudi Menu-hin, and he was again on hand the next winter, which was her last. During the final months it was the little things she lived for: the pleasure of flowers, letters from old friends, visits of nieces, and Menuhin's records. Edith Lewis remembers that she also "turned almost entirely to Shakespeare and Chaucer that last winter; as if in their company she found her greatest content, best preferred to confront the future."

During her last spring she began to pull herself up. She attended a concert in which Menuhin and his sister played together, but that was the last time she went out. In March Yehudi and his wife and son, and Hephzibah and her husband and two boys, came to see her for the last time. They were about to sail for England for a concert tour, but once again for a few hours her apartment was full of the gaiety of the children and the charm of Menuhin and his sister. Twelve days before she died she was beginning to make summer plans and was talking about another trip West. She also was thinking about doing some writing once more. A week before the end she wrote Dorothy Canfield Fisher wanting to know what she remembered about their visit to Housman.

On April twenty-fourth she stayed in bed all morning and had her lunch brought to her. "She was never more herself than on the last morning," Miss Lewis writes. "Her spirit was as high, her grasp of reality as firm as always. And she had kept that warmth of heart, that youthful, fiery generosity which life so often burns out." After lunch she went to sleep and awoke in mid-afternoon complaining of a headache. Death came for her about four P.M.—one quick cerebral hemorrhage. She was buried four days later at Jaffrey, New Hampshire, on the hillside spot that she had selected.

BIBLIOGRAPHY

As a convenience for the reader I have listed below in chronological order Willa Cather's works and the book-length studies devoted to her life and art. Scattered throughout my notes are other bibliographical items, but there is no need for me to duplicate a long, comprehensive, and up-to-date bibliographical essay by Bernice Slote in Jackson R. Bryer, ed., *Fifteen Modern American Authors* (Durham, N. C., 1969), pp. 23–63. This essay is particularly useful in evaluating and winnowing the large amount of critical material that has appeared in the past fifty years.

Willa Cather's Works

April Twilights (1903), *The Troll Garden* (1905), *Alexander's Bridge* (1912), *O Pioneers!* (1913), *The Song of the Lark* (1915), *My Ántonia* (1918), *Youth and the Bright Medusa* (1920), *One of Ours* (1922), *April Twilights and Other Poems* (1923), *A Lost Lady* (1923), *The Professor's House* (1925), *My Mortal Enemy* (1926), *Death Comes for the Archbishop* (1927), *Shadows on the Rock* (1931), *Obscure Destinies* (1932), *Lucy Gayheart* (1935), *Not Under Forty* (1936), *The Novels and Stories of Willa Cather* (1937–1941), *Sapphira and the Slave Girl* (1940).

BIBLIOGRAPHY AND NOTES

Some Important Posthumous Editions

The Qld Beauty and Others (1948); *Willa Cather on Writing* (1949); James Shively, ed., *Writings from Willa Cather's Campus Years* (1950); *Willa Cather in Europe,* Introduction and Notes by George N. Kates (1956); Bernice Slote, ed., *April Twilights (1903),* With Introduction (1962, 1968); [Virginia Faulkner, ed.], *Collected Short Fiction, 1892-1912,* Introduction by Mildred R. Bennett (1965); Bernice Slote, ed., *The Kingdom of Art: Willa Cather's First Principles and Critical Statements* (1967); William M. Curtin, ed., *The World and the Parish: Willa Cather's Articles and Reviews, 1893-1902* (1970).

Books About Willa Cather

René Rapin, *Willa Cather* (1930); Yvonne Handy, *L'Oeuvre de Willa Cather* (1940); Mildred Bennett, *The World of Willa Cather* (1951); David Daiches, *Willa Cather: A Critical Introduction* (1951); E. K. Brown, *Willa Cather: A Critical Biography* (1953); Edith Lewis, *Willa Cather Living* (1953); Elizabeth Sergeant, *Willa Cather: A Memoir* (1953); John H. Randall III, *The Landscape and the Looking Glass: Willa Cather's Search for Value* (1960); Dorothy Van Ghent, *Willa Cather* (University of Minnesota Pamphlet, 1964); James Schroeter, ed., *Willa Cather and Her Critics* (1967); Richard Giannone, *Music in Willa Cather's Fiction*(1968).

NOTES

Explanation of Notes

WC	Willa Cather	SOJ	Sarah Orne Jewett
CMS	Carrie Miner Sherwood	SSM	S. S. McClure
CSF	*Collected Short Fiction*	*WC&HC*	*Willa Cather and Her Critics*
DCF	Dorothy Canfield Fisher		
EL	Edith Lewis	WCPM	Willa Cather Pioneer Memorial at Red Cloud
ES	Elizabeth Sergeant		
KA	*Kingdom of Art*	*W&P*	*The World and the Parish*
IMW	Irene Miner Weisz	ZA	Zoë Akins

I have made no note of my source if it comes from one of WC's published works and the context of the quotation or reference makes the source clear. Wherever possible I have quoted from the 1937–1941 edition of the *Novels and Stories*. In the case of other works that have been reprinted, I have given either the original or the most available source. When my text makes clear the approximate date and identifies the correspondent of a letter I have paraphrased or extracted data from, I usually have not repeated this information in my notes. All letters to CMS are at WCPM (unless otherwise indicated), to DCF at the University of Vermont, to ES at the University of Virginia, to IMW at the Newberry Library, to SSM at the University of Indiana, and to ZA at the Huntington Library in San Marino, California (unless otherwise indicated). When I refer to Bennett, Brown, Lewis, and Sergeant, I mean their books on WC as listed above.

Chapter 1: Virginia and Nebraska

I. Both Bennett and Lewis discuss the Cather family origin, though they differ in details. There seems little doubt that the name comes from the Welsh *cadair*, which means chair or cradle, and is similar to the Gaelic *cathair*, which means seat, throne, or fortified city. Other details of the Cather family history come from Bennett, Brown, and Lewis. Material on WC's Virginia childhood, not from her own works, is from the same sources plus WC to Mrs. Ackroyd, May 16, December 27, 1941 (University of Virginia); and WC to Miss Masterton, March 15, 1943 (WCPM). The chronology in *Sapphira* has Nancy returning in 1881, when the author-narrator is "something over five." Because WC customarily gave her birthdate as 1876 and pretended to be younger than she was, I have assumed that the incident probably occurred when she really was five, *i.e.* in 1879. "The Elopement of Allen Poole" appears in the appendix to *KA* and the second edition of CSF.

II. My description of Nebraska comes largely from WC's essay in *Nation* (September 5, 1923). The 1913 interview (Philadelphia *Record*) is reprinted *KA*; the 1921 interview, Omaha *Bee*, October 29. Also used here: interviews from Lincoln *Star*, October 24,

1915, reprinted in *KA*; and by Latrobe Carroll, *Bookman*, Vol. LIII (May 1921). WC's early life in Nebraska comes from Bennett, Lewis, Brown, and her own writings. WC's relationship to Annie, the Lambrechts, and other neighbors is documented in letters at WCPM. The letter to Witter Bynner (June 7, 1905) is at Harvard.

III. The history and description of Red Cloud are from Bennett and my own observations. The reminiscence of Miss King: WC to E. J. Overing, Jr., Red Cloud *Chief*, May 27, 1909; also see Bennett, pp. 256–257. The letter to Mrs. Goudy (May 3, 1908) is at WCPM. WC's books and reading: see *KA*, pp. 39–40; Lewis, p. 14; several letters to Cyril Clemens (WCPM); *W&P* (*Home Monthly*, January 1897); the inscription to Pyle is in *Colophon*, Vol. I (1939). Identification of Dillon and Trueman: WC to CMS, January 27, 1934. WC's relationship with Mrs. Miner: WC to CMS, October 17, 1929 (University of Virginia). For WC's relationship to music: Giannone's book has good and full discussion of the topic. WC's memory of the opera house: Omaha *World Herald*, October 27, 1929; reprinted by Mildred Bennett in *Nebraska History*, Vol. XLIX (Winter 1968). Brown reprints, pp. 44–46, about five hundred words of WC's graduation oration.

Chapter 2: The Lincoln Years

I. My information on Lincoln and the University of Nebraska comes from Slote, "Writer in Nebraska," *KA*, pp. 3 ff. The same source, plus Bennett and Lewis, supplies details about WC's college career. William Westermann's memory of WC comes from Brown. The letters to Mrs. Goudy, quoted by EL, apparently have been destroyed. Both the Carlyle and Shakespeare essays are reprinted in the appendix to *KA*. WC's memory of the essay and Charles Gere was written to W. O. Jones and published in the *Nebraska State Journal*, July 24, 1927. All of the early stories discussed in this and subsequent chapters are reprinted in *CSF*. Letters to the Gere family, chiefly to Mariel, are at the Nebraska Historical Society. Beerbohm Tree is quoted in *W&P* (*Journal*, April 14, 1895). Brown deals with Professor Sherman much more

extensively than I do. *Writings from WC's Campus Years* prints
letters about WC from classmates and contemporaries at the University of Nebraska, some of which are quite unflattering. Further
light on the WC-Pound relationship will be available in 1974,
when a group of letters from WC to Louise Pound at the Duke
University Library are opened for use. Three letters of 1911–1912
to Miss Pound (University of Virginia) show that something of the
old friendship was restored. The relationship with DCF is documented by eighty letters at the University of Vermont. The
Courier's complaint: *KA*, p. 14.

II. The quotations from WC's newspaper columns come either
from *KA* or *W&P* and may be located through the indexes. Comments on WC as drama critic are in "Writer in Nebraska." "A
critic's first instincts": *W&P* (*Journal*, October 21, 1894). The
Chautauqua experience: See Bernice Slote, *Prairie Schooner*, Vol.
XLIII (Spring 1969). The Taft letter is at the Chicago Historical
Society. "When I Knew Stephen Crane" and "The Personal Side
of William Jennings Bryan" are reprinted in *W&P*. The Poe essay
is in *KA*; also the quotations from the *Nebraska Editor* and the
Beatrice *Weekly Express*. The letter dated "Siberia" and others of
this period are to Mariel Gere.

Chapter 3: Pittsburgh

A good bit of attention has been given to WC's Pittsburgh years.
Besides the information in Lewis and Brown, there are: Elizabeth
Moorhead, *These Too Were Here: Louise Homer and WC* (1950);
DCF, "Novelist Recalls Christmas in Blue-and-Gold Pittsburgh,"
Chicago *Tribune*, December 21, 1947; George Seibel, "WC from
'April Twilights' to April Midnight," *Musical Forecast*, June 1947;
and "Miss WC from Nebraska," *New Colophon*, Vol. II (September
1949); John P. Hinz, "WC in Pittsburgh," *New Colophon*, Vol. III
(1950); Phyllis M. Hutchinson, "Reminiscences of WC as a
Teacher," *Bulletin of the New York Public Library*, Vol. LX (June
1956); Mildred R. Bennett, "WC in Pittsburgh," *Prairie Schooner*,
Vol. XXXIII (March 1959); Kathleen D. Byrne, "WC's Pittsburgh
Years, 1896–1906," *Western Pennsylvania Historical Magazine*,
Vol. LI (January 1968). In addition I have used WC's letters to

Mariel Gere and various writings from these years reprinted in *W&P*. WC's opinion of Howells is found both in *W&P* and *KA*. It is interesting to note that Howells, who was so perspicacious in discovering younger writers like Crane or in recognizing the importance of Emily Dickinson, never had anything to say about WC. The Ruskin essay is in both *KA* and *W&P*.

II. Sale of the *Home Monthly*: WC to Helen Seibel, July 23, 1897. On WC's love life: The fact of the snake ring comes from the notes to *W&P*, the proposals from letters to Mariel Gere, remarks on *The Mill on the Floss* from *W&P*. Comments on marriage are scattered through Bennett, *KA*, *W&P*, and letters. One might argue that Thea Kronborg marries happily, but her marriage is barely alluded to in the epilogue and takes place sometime after the real ending of the novel. Other data concerning Pittsburgh friends: WC to Marie Willard, May 6, 1941 (University of Virginia); WC's article on Nevin (in *W&P*). Earlier accounts place the meeting with Isabelle in 1901, but WC to DCF, October 10, 1899, shows this to be in error. WC to Jones, September 29, 1900 (University of Virginia). Besides Hutchinson's memoir of WC as teacher, there is Foerster's memory quoted by Brown. The letter to WC's home room is in Byrne's essay.

Chapter 4: Literary Debut

I. The *Journal* letters have been reprinted in *WC in Europe* and more accurately in *W&P*. Brown's account of the visit to Housman needs revising, as he accepted the *Journal* letter as fact. See William White, "A Note on Scholarship: WC on A. E. Housman," *Victorian Newsletter*, No. 13 (1958). I have supplemented Brown's account with two letters to Viola Roseboro', June 14, 1903, and undated (Harvard). Also see WC's letters to Cyril Clemens (WCPM) and Carl Weber (Colby College). Ford's version is in *Return to Yesterday* (1932).

II. Miss Slote's "WC and Her First Book" in the revised edition of *April Twilights* (1968) is the definitive study of WC's poetry. Add to this WC to Will Jones, January 2, 1903 (University of Virginia). WC made substantive changes in "Prairie Dawn" in her collected works, and I have quoted the original version. The account in Sergeant of trying to get a copy of poems is freely adapted from WC to ES, June 2, 1912. The WC-ES relationship is documented by sixty-six letters at the University of Virginia. These are used very freely in ES's memoir, and I have gone to the originals, though I cite the memoir unless there is an important disparity. WC's review of the anthology of younger poets is in *W&P*. WC's letters to Miss Guiney are at Holy Cross College; WC to Sara Teasdale, May 10, 1931 (Wellesley).

III. The key letter to Will Jones about SSM, May 7, 1903 (University of Virginia), has not been used before. "The world is weary": *W&P* (*Courier*, August 10, 1901). *KA* reprints part of *The Roman and the Teuton*. Reinhart's funeral is reported in *W&P*. Knopf has allowed "The Sculptor's Funeral" to be reprinted since WC's death. DCF's review of *Youth: Yale Review*, Vol. X (1921). Jones on "A Wagner Matinee": Bennett, p. 254. WC's reply: March 6, 1904 (University of Virginia). WC to Viola Roseboro' is undated; I have only seen a copy in the Seibel Papers. WC on "Paul's Case": WC to John Phillipson, March 15, 1943 (WCPM).

Chapter 5: *McClure's Magazine*

I. One general source for this chapter, besides the files of *McClure's Magazine*, is Peter Lyon's very competent *Success Story: The Life and Times of SSM* (1963). All the letters to and from SSM are at Indiana University. SSM's letter to Phillips and Bynner's memory are quoted by Lyon. The account of the Twain dinner is from *The New York Times*. Ellery Sedgwick's memory: *The Happy Profession* (1948), pp. 142–143. I also have used EL's chapter on the *McClure's* period.

II. The best accounts of WC's relationships with Mrs. Fields and SOJ are in *Not Under Forty*. The two surviving letters to Mrs. Fields are at Harvard, as are all the SOJ letters. See also WC to Howe, November 11, 1931 (Harvard). SOJ's letters to WC are in Annie Fields, ed., *The Letters of SOJ* (1911). For the WC-EL relationship, see chiefly Lewis's memoir. ES's comment on EL is in her memoir. WC's introduction to *The Secrets of the Schlüsselberg: McClure's*, Vol. XXXIV (December 1909). WC to Mrs. G. P. Cather (Aunt Franc): January 5, 1911. WC's letters to Norman

Foerster are at University of Nebraska. The account of ES's meeting with WC is well told in her memoir. The ZA relationship is documented by ninety-three letters at the Huntington Library and eleven at the University of Virginia.

III. There is evidence that WC completed an unpublished novel as early as 1905. See Bernice Slote, "WC as a Regional Writer," *Kansas Quarterly* (Winter 1970), which quotes an item from the *Journal* reporting completion of a novel laid in Pittsburgh. It was said to be promised for publication in the fall of 1905. What happened to it is a mystery. Anyone interested in WC and myth criticism will find many suggestions in Miss Slote's excellent essay, "The Kingdom of Art," *KA*, pp. 85 ff. WC's 1931 view of her first novel is in *WC on Writing*. WC to Aunt Franc: February 23, 1913. Curtis Brady on SSM's troubles is quoted from Lyon. Before the SSM Papers and the ES letters were available, it was never clear just when WC left the magazine, but the chronology worked out here is based on these collections.

Chapter 6: Triumphant Years

I. The 1932 introduction is in both the currently in-print Houghton Mifflin edition of the novel and in the *Novels and Stories*. WC was writing ES often at the time of this western trip; her letters contain much more information than ES's memoir uses. The quotation from Balzac: "In the desert, you see, there is everything and there is nothing: God, without men." Her mind washed and ironed: WC to SSM, June 12, 1912. L. V. Jacks, "The Classics and WC," *Prairie Schooner*, Vol. XXXV (December 1961), suggests the Marie-Emil story has an analogue in the Pyramus and Thisbe story. The "inner explosion" is described by Sergeant. There is much about the writing of *O Pioneers!* in WC's letters to ES. See also "My First Novels" in *WC on Writing*. On shining for the home folks: WC to ZA, October 31, 1912 (University of Virginia). Inscription in presentation copy to CMS is reproduced in Bennett. I've silently corrected the line from Schubert's "Der Wanderer," in which *geliebtes* is printed as *geliebtest* in all editions. Though WC studied German in college, her knowledge of the language was not very great; WC to DCF, January 3 [N.Y.], speaks of translating Heine's "The Three Holy Kings," although she could not have conjugated a German verb. The quotation from Michelet occurs several times in WC's work, but see at least "Old Mrs. Harris." Greenslet's opinion is quoted from Brown. Dell's review was in the Chicago *Evening Post*, July 25, 1913.

II. The Bank Street apartment is described in Lewis. Josephine is often referred to in letters to various correspondents. SSM's autobiography: see WC to SSM, April 22, June 9, June 12, 1912; WC to Jones, May 29, 1914 (University of Virginia). The letter from Daniels is quoted from Lyon. The Fremstad interview is reported by EL and in WC to ES, April 20, April 28, 1913. WC's relationship with Fremstad is scattered through her letters to ES; also details of the pinprick and the writing of the novel. The 1921 interview: Omaha *World-Herald*, November 27. The review of Bennett is in "Plays of Real Life," *McClure's*, Vol. XL (March 1913). Giannone has a good discussion of the *Lark*. The Dumas quotation recurs several times, but see *Lark*, p. 177, and "The Novel Démeublé" in *Not Under Forty* or *WC on Writing*. Mencken's review is in *WC&HC*. Fremstad's reaction: WC to ES, December 7, 1915; and Lewis.

III. Proposed trip to Germany: WC to ES, July 28, 1915; Grant Overton, *The Women Who Make Our Novels* (1918). Most of the trip to Mesa Verde comes from Lewis. Isabelle's marriage: WC to DCF, March 15, 1916; WC to ES, August 3, 1916; and Sergeant. The letter to Mary Jewett is at Harvard. WC on *School of Femininity*: WC to CMS, June 28, 1939. 1921 interview: Lincoln *Star*, November 6. On 1914 harvest: WC to ES, August 10. The con. cept of *My Ántonia* is described in Sergeant. Heinemann's rejection of the *Lark* is recalled in "My First Novels." On point of view: WC to Jones, May 20, 1919 (University of Virginia). Bennett is good on the relation of fact to fiction in novel. On sources: WC to CMS, January 27, 1934; WC to IMW, January 6, 1945. About Mrs. Miner: WC to CMS, October 29, 1917 (University of Virginia). On Jan Hambourg: WC to CMS, March 13, 1918. On writing at Jaffrey: see Lewis, Sergeant, and WC to Lieutenant Blaine, December 20, 1940 (WCPM). Mencken's review is in *WC&HC*. Bourne reviewed the novel for the *Dial*, December 14, 1918. Holmes's comments are quoted by Sergeant. For the genesis of *One of Ours*, see

Bennett and Lewis. For a discussion of it as a war novel, see Stanley Cooperman, *World War I and the American Novel* (1967), pp. 129–137. DCF's opinion is in letter to White, November 28, 1919 (Library of Congress).

Chapter 7: *Dies Irae*

I. I have used WC's own memoir of Knopf, which is reprinted in Lewis, pp. 108–115. Knopf recounts his relationship with WC in *Bulletin of the New York Public Library*, Vol. LXVIII (November 1964), and *Proceedings of the Massachusetts Historical Society*, Vol. LXXIV (1961). Complaints about Houghton Mifflin: various references in letters to ES (1915–1920); also Brown. The earnings from *My Ántonia* are reported by EL and confirmed by Houghton Mifflin. The identification of Mary Garden as a model for Kitty Ayreshire is suggested by a reference in the story to an opera written for her by the "veteran French composer who adored her," which would seem to be *Pelleas and Melisande* by Debussy. Leon Edel in *Literary Biography* and James Schroeter in *WC&HC* both suggest that Louie Marsellus in *The Professor's House* is a portrait of Jan Hambourg. The account of WC's 1920 trip to France in Lewis and Brown needs correction: See WC to Mrs. Stanfield, June 12, 1921 (University of Virginia); the same letter reports Sinclair Lewis's visit to Toronto. While WC was writing *One of Ours*, she wrote DCF often. 1921–1922 illnesses: WC to Mrs. Stanfield, June 10, 1922 (University of Virginia). The Breadloaf plans come from several letters at Middlebury College.

II. Hemingway's opinion is in Edmund Wilson's *Shores of Light*. "Inarticulate young man": interview in *Journal*, April 25, 1925. WC to Aunt Franc: September 9, 1917. Hochstein was the subject of a long interview in the New York *Herald*, December 24, 1922 (reprinted by Sergeant). The 1921 interview: Omaha *World Herald*, November 27. Mencken's review is in *WC&HC*. Knopf's wire was printed in the *Journal*, September 25, 1921. The *Parsifal* theme: WC to Mr. Johns, November 17, 1922 (University of Virginia). "It took a lot more out of me": quoted by Bennett. On joining the church: See Bennett and Brown. Lewis describes Grand Manan, but there are other accounts scattered through WC's letters to ZA.

III. Genesis of *A Lost Lady*: WC to IMW, January 6, 1945. WC reported visiting Mrs. Garber in 1905 to Mariel Gere (Nebraska Historical Society). WC discussed writing novel in *Journal* interview, April 25, 1925. Also see Lewis. The views of Wilson and Krutch are in *WC&HC*. Bennett describes the movie premiere in Red Cloud. A copy of WC's will is at Nebraska Historical Society. On dramatization: WC to ZA, April 19, 1937. "I stayed for a time": interview in *Century*,Vol. CX (July 1925). See Lewis and Brown for details of the portrait; alsoWC to IMW, August 11, 1923. It is used as frontispiece in *WC&HC*.

IV. Roddy Blake probably was suggested by Tooker, whom WC met on the 1912 trip to Arizona. There is a little of Douglass Cather in Tom Outland. WC's account of writing *The Professor* is in *WC on Writing*. See also Giannone. Grant Overton reports the early version of "Tom Outland's Story." Edel's psychoanalysis of WC through this novel in his *Literary Biography* is extremely interesting. The fur coat: WC to IMW, January 11, 1926. WC was writing IMW frequently at this period. The prefaces to SOJ, Gertrude Hall, and Stephen Crane are reprinted in *WC on Writing*. WC to Mrs. Stanfield, October 16, 1926 (University of Virginia).

Chapter 8: "Past Is Prologue"

I. On the West: WC to SOJ, October 24, 1908 (Harvard). WC's "great gift": Lewis, pp. 119–120. Going West for inspiration: interview in Lincoln *Star*, November 6, 1921. Meeting the Lawrences: reported by Lewis but with wrong dates. WC wrote CMS about Tony, April 29, 1945. Lewis describes the visit to Taos. The genesis of the *Archbishop* is discussed by Sergeant and Bennett. The *Commonweal* letter is in *WC on Writing*. Sergeant describes WC at the MacDowell Colony. For Knopf's memory, see note for Chap. 7. *Archbishop* as best book: WC to E. K. Brown, *c.* 1946 (copy at Newberry). WC to Foerster, May 22, 1933 (University of Nebraska). The relationship of the novel to Puvis de Chavannes, Holbein, and Dante is discussed by D. H. Stewart, "WC's Mortal Comedy," *Queen's Quarterly*, Vol. LXXIII (Summer 1966).

II. Charles Cather's death: WC to ZA, June 7, 1941. Having influenza: WC to Mary Jewett, May 30, 1928 (Harvard). Genesis of

Shadows: See Lewis, pp. 151 ff. WC's letters to Zona Gale are at the Wisconsin Historical Society. Visit to Aix-les-Bains: WC to ZA, August 22, 1930 (University of Virginia). Garland's report: Donald Pizer, ed., *Hamlin Garland's Diaries* (1968), p. 117. WC to Sara Teasdale, May 10, 1931 (Wellesley). On plans for reunion: WC to ZA, December 18, 1931.

III. Reviews of *Shadows*: Chamberlain in *The New York Times*, August 2, 1931; Van Doren in New York *Herald Tribune*, August 2, 1931; Cross on August 22, 1931; WC's letter to Cross is in *WC on Writing*. WC said her heart never got across the Missouri River to CMS, September 1, 1922. The essay on Mansfield is in *WC on Writing* and *Not Under Forty*. On *Shadows*: WC to ZA, December 18, 1931. "Most things come from France": *W&P* (*Journal*, January 27, 1895). WC on French cooking: see *Century* interview (Vol. CX, July 1925) and WC to ZA, December 31, 1933. WC on friendship: WC to IMW, October 22, 1945. Both Brown and Lewis discuss use of sources for *Shadows*. For identification of Rosicky, see Bennett. WC to ZA, September 16, 1932. WC to IMW, March 12, 1931. On "Two Friends": WC to CMS, January 27, 1934. Sergeant has good account of WC's Park Avenue apartment.

Chapter 9: "The Rest Is Silence"

I. Josephine's return: WC to ZA, December 31, 1933. Life as biological failure: WC to ZA, November 21, 1932. On privacy and protecting her works, there are many references scattered through letters to all her close friends. On *Prix Femina*, see *The New York Times*, February 4, 1933; and Sergeant. There is a Ms. of WC's NBC talk, at Princeton. The Princeton commencement: WC to CMS [n.d.] Letters about the proferred Brown degree are in Brown University Library. There are many references to Mary Virginia Auld in WC's letters of this period. The same is true of the Menuhins, but Lewis also is good on this relationship. On prodigies: *W&P* (October 26, 1895). There are many letters at WCPM documenting WC's private benefactions; also see WC to ZA [n.d.]; WC to DCF, January 11, 1933; several undated letters to Ida Tarbell (Allegheny College). DCF's article was in the New York *Herald Tribune*, May 28, 1933, and the Omaha *World*, June

2, 1933; four letters from WC to DCF deal with this article; the only one dated is June 22, 1933.

II. WC's attitude while writing *Lucy*: WC to ZA, January 2, August 26, 1934. Lewis discusses the wrist injuries; also there are many references in letters to ZA, CMS; see also WC to Zona Gale, May 23, 1934 (Wisconsin Historical Society); WC to A. Woollcott, March 17, 1941 (Harvard). WC's horror of mutilation is discussed in Mrs. Bennett's introduction to *CSF*. Identification of Lucy: WC to CMS, June 28, 1939. See also Bennett. Reviews of *Lucy*: Benét, August 4, 1935; Troy, August 14, 1935; Adams, August 4, 1935; *Christian Science Monitor*, July 31, 1935. Isabelle's illness: WC to IMW, July 13, 1935; WC to ZA, April 19, 1935; also see Lewis. Isabelle's death: WC to IMW, October 14, 1938; WC to ZA, May 20, 1946. Hick's criticism is in *WC&HC*. The letter on escapism in *WC on Writing*. WC's musical tastes in the thirties: See Lewis, Brown, and various letters. Lane's opinion of "The Old Beauty" is from Lewis. On collected works: WC to ZA, November 8, 1937 [?]; see also Lewis. Douglass's visit and death: WC to CMS, June 28, 1939; WC to ZA, November 13, 1938. Quotations from WC's line-a-day diary are from Lewis.

III. Provenance of *Sapphira*: WC to Viola Roseboro', November 9, 1940 (University of Virginia). Trip back to Virginia in 1913: See several letters to ES. The episode of shocking the judge is in Lewis. The visit to Roscoe and his death: WC to CMS, May 16, 1941; WC to ZA, September 14, 1941; WC to IMW, October, 22, 1945. Operation and last days: Lewis and several letters to ZA. Remarks on Second World War: WC to V. Roseboro', February 12, 1944 (University of Virginia); WC to A. Woollcott, December 14 [?], 1943 (Harvard). "No spring": WC to ZA, May 20, 1946. The Menuhins' last visit is recounted by Lewis. Death: See Lewis, Brown, and *The New York Times* obituary, April 25, 1947.